PAN AMERICAN

KUWAIT

U.S. AIR FORCE

WESTERN

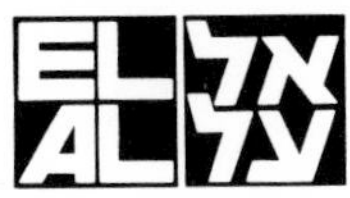

EL AL

AIR INDIA

AIR MADAGASCAR

GATX-BOOTHE

ICELANDAIR

MEXICANA

CHINA AIR

ANSETT-ANA

IRAN AIR

KLM

ALLEGHENY

IRISH

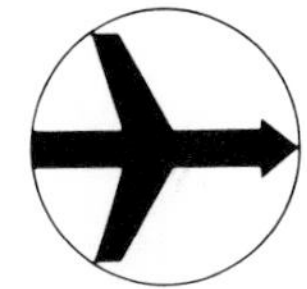
SWISSAIR

AIR ASIA

UNITED

FLYING TIGER

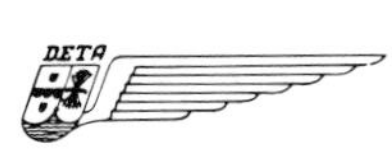

DETA

WORLD

BWIA

AIR FRANCE

AIRLIFT

FAUCETT

FRONTIER

BOAC

IBERIA

ARGENTINAS

ALASKA

WARDAIR

VASP

QANTAS

AVIANCA

UNITED ARAB

NAC-NEW ZEALAND

FAA

SCANDINAVIAN

PIEDMONT

AIR CANADA

MIDDLE EAST

747 - Story Of The Boeing SUPER JET

DEDICATED TO:

My wife, Mary Sue, whose patience, understanding and support made writing this book possible

And TO:

The men and women of The Boeing Company, Pratt & Whitney Aircraft, and the scheduled airlines of the world who made possible the wings of the 747 and gave us The Spacious Age.

747

Story Of The Boeing

SUPER JET

by Douglas J. Ingells

Foreword by Stuart G. Tipton,

President of the Air Transport Association of America

Aero Publishers, Inc.

329 Aviation Road

Fallbrook, California 92028

Library of Congress Catalog Card Number

78-135055

Cloth ISBN -0-8168-8700-4
Paper ISBN -0-8168-8704-7

Printed and Published in the United States by Aero Publishers, Inc.

FOREWORD

NEW YEAR'S DAY, 1914, marked an important milestone in the history of transportation. On that date, the world's first regularly scheduled air passenger service was started over a 22-mile route between Tampa and St. Petersburg, Florida. The plane was a small Benoist flying boat capable of carrying a pilot and one passenger. Tony Jannus, a famous cross-country flyer, was the pilot, and the first passenger was A. C. Pheil, Mayor of St. Petersburg. Some 6,000 persons gathered for the inaugural ceremonies, and for a brief unwitting glimpse into the future of commercial air transportation.

The operation of the airline lasted only a few weeks, after which the service had to be discontinued because of financial losses. But, certainly, we can point with pride to the pioneering effort that launched the wings of commercial air transport, a position of leadership the United States has maintained for more than half a century in the progressive development of a world-wide scheduled air transportation system.

U.S. scheduled air transportation, as measured by the aircraft in airline fleets, has been undergoing a continuous revolution during its 56 years of service. The latest stage in this revolution is symbolized by the Boeing 747, which initiated in January of 1970 what has been referred to as the "spacious age".

Ten scheduled carriers, U.S. and foreign, were operating 53 B-747's at the end of July of this year. At that time, the service performance of those aircraft was well ahead of the pace set by the original Boeing 707's when they were placed in service at the end of 1958. In their seven months of service, the 747's carried more than 1.1 million passengers, whereas it took the 707's one year to reach the million mark. An idea of the future passenger impact of the 747 is suggested by the fact that U.S. scheduled airlines, alone, will be flying about 130 of these aircraft by the end of 1972.

Because of its size, the 747 has introduced a whole new environment for the air traveler. Moreover, its design and configuration have permitted the use of highly sophisticated automatic flight controls and navigational aids. These devices promise to greatly enhance the safety of air transportation, while at the same time increasing the productivity which will help to maintain fare levels and provide better service.

The 747 will be followed in 1971 by other wide-bodied jets – the Douglas DC-10 and the Lockheed L-1011. At a time when more and more people are traveling by air and when shippers are using the facilities of air freight to an increasing degree, the advent of the family of wide-bodied jets offers hopeful solutions to the problems of growth and to the problems attendant upon growth - air traffic control congestion.

The story of how the 747 came into being is an excellent example of the cooperation between airlines and manufacturers over the years. As partners in progress, the Boeing Company, Pratt & Whitney Aircraft, who designed and developed the 747's engines, and the scheduled airlines of the world had the vision and courage to bring such a plane into existence.

This book tells the story of this cooperative effort from concept to creation. But it is far more than just the story of a single aircraft. It is also a narrative history of The Boeing Company and the many contributions Boeing has made to the development of modern aircraft and the air transport system which these aircraft have helped to make possible.

Stuart G. Tipton,
President of the Air Transport Association of America

PREFACE

August 8, 1970
Ludington, Michigan

THIS is a saga of the sky that is far more than the story of a great aircraft, even though it is the largest commercial jetliner ever built, the Boeing 747, "Superjet." The story begins, really, at a time when the flying machine was a skeleton thing of cloth and wire and sticks and glue; more than 56 years ago, when William Edward Boeing, a Seattle businessman, ventured aloft in one of these frail winged machines, and decided to go into the aircraft manufacturing business. From this point in time, it is a narrative of *evolution* and *revolution* in the design, development and utilization of a whole family of Boeing-built aircraft, and the role of The Boeing Company in helping to build today's world-wide system of scheduled air transportation.

This theme developed because, the author believes that, more than any other aircraft manufacturer, Bill Boeing, went one step beyond: His "vision" was not just to build safe airplanes which today make up more than half the fleets of the commercial airlines of the world, but in the establishment of Boeing Air Transport in the late '20s, he put the company's product to work pioneering a highly successful airline operation destined to one day become United Air Lines, largest U.S. scheduled airline.

For this reason, the author, has attempted to trace the history of Boeing's contribution to commercial aviation, culminating with the design and development of the 747 "Superjet", the advent of "The Spacious Age" which the big plane brought with it, and the promise of "The Supersonic Age" on the high horizon.

Where necessary, he has included stories of The Boeing Company's role in producing military pursuit planes and bombers. The latter including the famous "Flying Fortresses", (B-17s) of World War II, the B-29 which dropped the A-bomb on Hiroshima, and the eight engined B-52 "Stratofortresses" that are daily flying missions in Viet Nam skies. Although strictly military aircraft, each of these planes contributed technical "know-how" that helped make possible the wings of the 747, the plane of the seventies, further advancing the state of the art.

It is with great pride, that I can say, I have ridden as a passenger in every commercial airliner built by Boeing from the Model-247 of the early 30s to the wide-bodies 747, the plane with the "spiral staircase and all the room in the world."

I beg the reader's pardon for bits of nostalgia.

Beyond this, the pride swells, when I recall the first time my wife, Mary Sue, and I, on a visit to the Boeing Everett facility in 1968, saw six of the huge 747s moving down the assembly lines, both knowing full well that The Boeing Company had risked a billion dollars, private capital, to bring about such an incredible achievement. It was then, I decided to write this book as a tribute to such vision and courage.

Douglas J. Ingells

ACKNOWLEDGEMENTS

The author wishes to extend grateful thanks to all of those who helped him in gathering the material and pictures during the preparation of this book. Space does not permit naming all those who gave of their time and experience in personal interviews, in helping to document facts and dates, and in compiling the many photographs, and who took time to read the galleys. They were wonderful to work with, and without them this book would have been nigh impossible to put together.

Most especially, he wishes to thank the gang in Public Relations at The Boeing Company, Pratt & Whitney Aircraft and Pan American World Airways for their patience and splendid cooperation.

There are, of course, many individuals whom I would like to list by name, but fearful of leaving someone out, I have chosen to trust that their names which appear in the story itself, will show my deepest gratitude.

D. J. Ingells

PHOTO CREDITS

The Boeing Company, Pan American World Airways, Trans World Airlines, Pratt & Whitney Aircraft, United Aircraft Corporation, Japan Air Lines, The National Smithsonian Institution (Air Museum), United States Air Force, Douglas Aircraft Company, Lockheed Aircraft Corporation, Air Transport Association, McDonnel/Douglas Aircraft Corporation, Conductron Division, The Link Group, Singer General Precision, Inc., The Henry Ford Museum, and The Air Transport Association of America. All photographs appearing in this book were supplied by these companies and organizations.

Table Of Contents

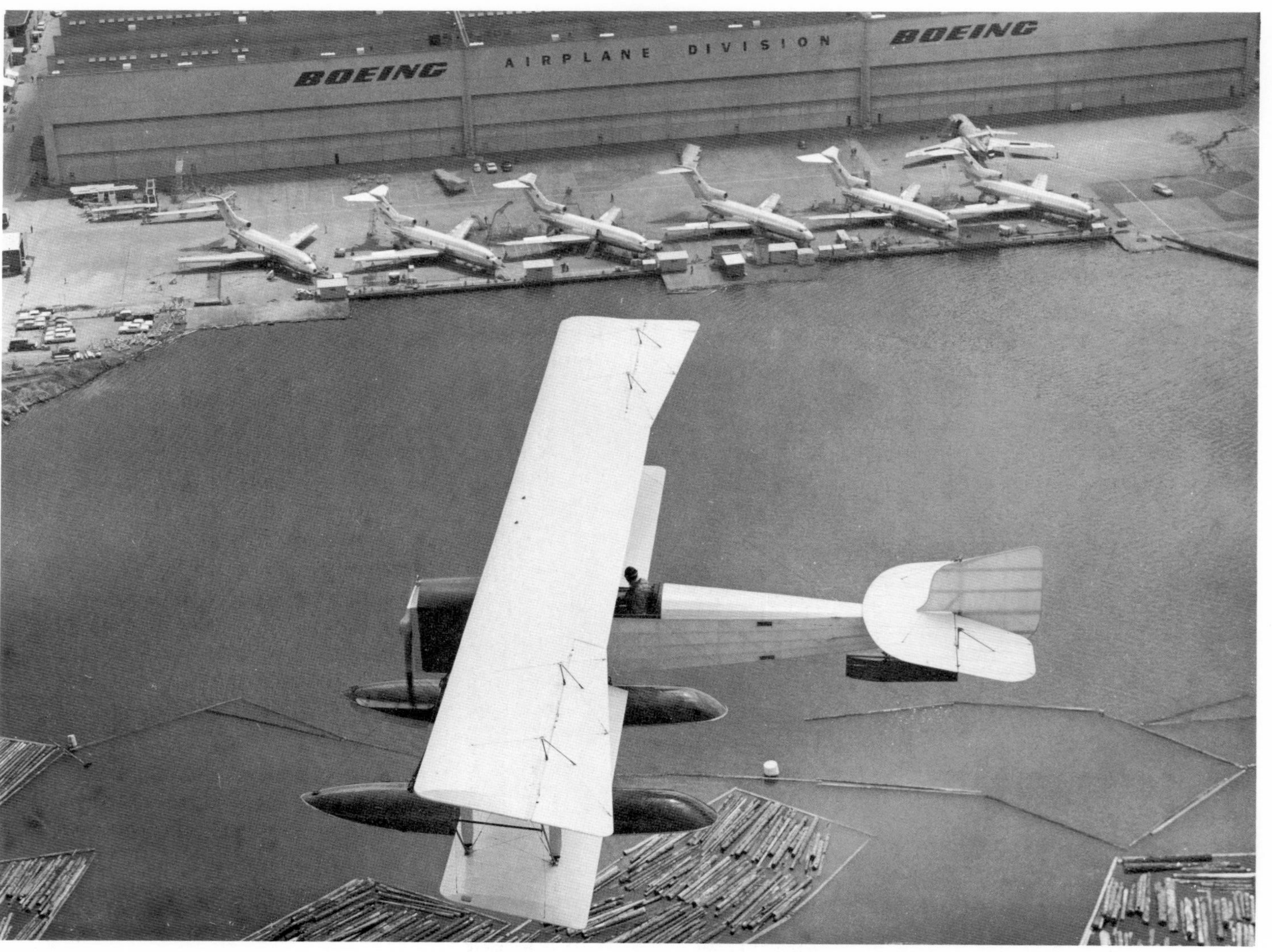

A replica of the "B&W", first Boeing-built aircraft, vintage 1916, flies over the Renton, Washington manufacturing facility, Boeing Airplane Division in salute to newest member of Boeing family of jetliners, the popular 727 on ramp below. Occasion marked 50th Boeing Anniversary, July, 1966. About the same time decision was made to build the 747.

CHAPTER ONE

Wings Above The Duwamish

FLAGS were flying from almost every business establishment and many homes. Old Glory, proudly unfurled, flapped in the slight breeze that was blowing. The strains of martial music filled the air, and a colorful parade moved through the downtown streets of Seattle, Washington. Later, thousands of picnickers lined the banks of the Duwamish River and along the shorelines of Lake Washington and Lake Union. In traditional style the city was celebrating Independence Day. It was July 4, 1914.

A special event had been arranged as part of the program. There was a barnstorming aviator named Terah Maroney with his Curtiss pusher-type biplane who had been hired to put on an aerial exhibition. The aeroplane was new in these parts of the country, and the holiday crowd was anxious to see man and machine perform. There was a local flyer, Herb Munter, and his home-built flying machine, but Maroney's machine was different.

It was a strange-looking contraption. The wings were of wooden rib and spar contruction covered with muslin. The fuselage was a skeleton frame supporting a vertical rudder and horizontal stabilizer. The thing was held together with baling wire, nails and glue. There was a water-cooled engine with a bulky radiator hung between the wings on a strut arrangement; the engine drove a two-bladed wooden propeller whose arc barely missed the trailing edge of the wings. All of this rested on a single, sled-like float for an undercarriage.

Maroney called his machine a "hydroplane". He explained that it was designed to take-off and land on the water.

The plane was parked at a special ramp along the shores of Lake Washington. Curious observers milled around the machine, waiting for the pilot to do something. Shortly after noon, Maroney climbed aboard and started the engine. The plane moved slowly out toward the center of the lake. Then, there was a loud roar, and the crowd saw the machine skipping over the water, and soar like a giant bird into the sky.

For the next few minutes the on-lookers were awed by the machine's capabilities and the skill of its operator as he put the craft through a series of thrilling maneuvers. There was a loud cheer and clapping applause when Maroney made a graceful landing and taxied back to the ramp.

There, when the engine had stopped, he stood on the nose of the float and proudly announced that he was, "ready to take up passengers for sight-seeing trips over the city."

A young man, about 33, stepped forward. He was tall and scholarly-looking, wearing thin-rimmed glasses, and dressed in sporty clothes. Many of the people gathered around the plane recognized him. His name was William Edward Boeing.

Bill Boeing was born in Detroit, Michigan on October 1, 1881. He was the son of a German-born immigrant father who had amassed a fortune during Michigan's great lumber boom and from mining interests in the Mesabi Range. His father died when

William Edward Boeing, founder of The Boeing Airplane Company. He not only built planes, but he pioneered air transportation.

Bill was eight years old, and the youth was raised by his Viennese mother who was very strict. The boy attended private schools in this country and in Switzerland.

When his mother remarried, young Boeing struck out for himself. He was worth a small fortune in his own right, an inheritance his father had left him. To further his education, he entered Yale University and studied engineering at the Sheffield Scientific School. He was graduated in the class of '04, about the same time that Wilbur and Orville Wright were making numerous flights with their heavier-than-air flying machine from Huffman Prairie in their hometown of Dayton, Ohio.

In his science classes at Sheffield, Boeing had read of the exploits of the Wright Brothers. But many years later, he admitted in an interview he never dreamed the Wrights' invention of the aeroplane would influence his life in the manner it did. "At the time," he confessed, "I never gave it a thought."

Indeed, he had made up his mind to pursue an unrelated career. The year before his graduation he had visited the northwest region, invested considerable sums in vast timber reserves, and decided to follow in his father's footsteps and learn the lumber business. In this field and from other interests during the next decade he made his own fortune. In the summer of 1914 he was regarded as one of the most successful and conservative businessmen in the Pacific Northwest.

Perhaps, for this reason there were some lifted eyebrows among those in the group gathered around Maroney's machine when Bill Boeing stepped forward to take a ride. Those who recognized him also knew that his hobby was ships and sailing. He owned a yacht which was anchored not far from Maroney's hydroplane. He was shy, very much an introvert, and it wasn't like him to take chances. Flying was considered pretty risky at this stage of the game. What they didn't know was that Bill Boeing had been waiting four years for this opportunity.

In 1910 on a business trip to Los Angeles he had attended, as a spectator, the first International Air Meet held at the old Dominguez Ranch just south of the city. The great Glenn Curtiss, the famous French aviator, Monsieur Paulhan, and many other "early birdmen" were there with their magnificant flying machines. He thrilled as he watched them perform, fascinated by this new sport of wings. He had even tried to get one of the fliers present to take him up for a ride, but it never happened.

Now, on this beautiful Fourth of July with the blue sky above and the sun shining brightly, he had the chance with Maroney. Full of excitement and anticipation he climbed aboard the plane, and took his place with its pilot in a side-by-side seating arrangement on the leading edge of the lower wing.

Maroney handed him a helmet and a pair of goggles. "You'll need these in the airstream," the pilot admonished.

Then, Maroney's mechanic gave the propeller a yank through, and the engine started with a roar like that of a farm tractor. The mechanic pushed the machine away from the ramp, and it slipped into the water like a small marine craft being launched down the ways.

The pilot gunned the engine several times letting it warm up until it was running smoothly, its pusher propeller fanning the air and causing ripples on the lake's surface. The machine shook and trembled. It rocked slightly as Maroney taxied it out into the lake.

The next instant there was a throaty roar, and the plane was racing through the water like a speedboat. Spray hit Boeing in the face, and he hung on for dear life. The stinging spray stopped. There was only the rushing air. He sensed they were airborne. The lake dropped away.

Higher and higher they climbed. The noise was deafening, but the sensation of flying was exhilarating.

The plane levelled off at about 1500 feet altitude and Boeing relaxed, taking in a bird's-eye view of the surroundings he dearly loved. Seattle, its buildings and streets and people seemed like a Lilliputian world below. The big Navy shipyards slipped beneath the wings, and the ships, themselves, anchored in the waters of Puget Sound appeared as small models in a pond. The earth was a patchwork quilt with its farms and orchards of varying colors and contours. He saw his own timber re-

The first Boeing 747 Super jet in airline colors, Pan American World Airways', "Clipper Young America", makes its maiden flight.

serves, pine, hemlock, fir, and spruce trees reaching up to try and touch the wings. And far in the distance he could see the peaks of the Olympic Range.

Flight was a panoramic ecstasy.

And what a land of giants was spread out below; There were the snow-capped mountains, the towering timber, the roaring rivers and the glistening waters of the Sound. Boeing could see them all from his winged platform.

What he could not see, because it was far in the future, was a giant winged thing, biggest of the world's commercial jetliners, the 747 *Super jet,* that one day would soar majestically through these same skies. The name BOEING proudly lettered on its sleek, smooth, glistening skin.

For Bill Boeing the flight with Maroney was just the beginning. It was over much too soon. The roar of the little plane's engine lessened, and the machine started to descend. Swooping down like a mechanical gull, it settled with a splash, skipping over the lake's surface to a stop. Maroney taxied it slowly back to the ramp.

Boeing climbed out of the seat.

"Wonderful! Just wonderful!" he exclaimed, shaking hands with Maroney. "We must do it again."

"It sure beats yachting all to pieces," he added.

Another passenger climbed board, Conrad Westervelt, a young naval engineering officer stationed in Seattle and a friend of Bill Boeing's. They had met at the University Club, played cards together, and spent long week-ends on Boeing's yacht which Westervelt had helped design.

The plane took off again, and Boeing watched as Maroney repeated the same aerial tour for Westervelt. When he came down Westervelt, like Boeing had done, expressed exhuberant enthusiasm about his first flight experience.

For the next few hours, they talked of nothing else except the state of the art of aerostation. Both agreed that these new vehicles of the air could no longer be ignored. The science of aeronautics was the coming thing, a new dimension for transportation, opening up new vistas of trade and commerce. The discussion lasted until the last Roman candle blossomed in the night sky to end the fireworks.

Independence Day, 1914, set Boeing free. His flight with Maroney unshackled his earthly ties. It made him decide to accept the challenge of the sky.

II

MARONEY with his aeroplane hung around for a while, and both Boeing and Westervelt made several more flights. When Maroney left, they went over to Harbor Island where Herb Munter, the local flyer, kept his self-built flying machine, and they talked to Munter about flying. The flights with Maroney and the talks with Munter stimulated their interest more and more. They began to collect and read all the published data they could get their hands on about the science of aeronautics, such as it was in those days, and about the progressive development of flying machines.

Boeing had the "bug" bad. Perhaps, it was because he liked to hunt and fish, and everytime he took a flight with Maroney, it occurred to him, that the airplane was the ideal transportation to get into isolated regions where fish and game must be plentiful. Especially, a seaplane like Maroney's would be just the thing. And he had read about a fellow named Glenn Martin down in Los Angeles who was building pontoon-equipped biplanes for sale. The Martin, according to the aeronautical publications, was a good airplane, priced at only $10,000. Boeing decided to learn to fly and buy one.

Probably the first home-built flying machine seen around the Seattle area was this pusher-type built by Herb Munter, whom Bill Boeing later hired as test pilot. The tricycle landing gear was unique for its period. Ailerons are seen in Boeing-Westervelt "B&W" design.

Thus, we find him in the summer of 1915 at Griffith Park in Los Angeles, Glenn Martin's base, taking flight lessons from Floyd Smith, Martin's instructor. Smith remembered Boeing in later years as a determined, cautious student, who wanted to know everything about the machine he was learning to fly. When he felt confident and qualified, Boeing returned to Seattle. The Martin he bought was being shipped. He forgot about the yacht.

Bill Boeing, Westervelt and Munter, then decided to form the Aero Club of Seattle. The Martin and the Munter buzzing over the city generated a lot of interest. Several other businessmen with sporting blood wanted to fly. The club membership grew like Topsy. Seattle was air-minded.

Then, one day Munter was flying the Martin with a passenger and something went wrong. The plane dived into the lake. Luckily, nobody was injured. But the Mar-

Glenn L. Martin seaplane which was considered to be one of the best designs flying in 1915-16. Boeing bought one, but never liked the single-float idea which led him to go to twin pontoons on "B&W". Note the four-bladed propeller.

tin needed repairs.

Boeing called Glenn Martin long distance.

"How soon can you get me some new parts?"

"It'll take about six months," was the answer.

"Hell, I can build me a plane in that time," Boeing said and hung up.

That night at the University Club he put the proposition to Westervelt. "How about it, Westy," he asked, "do you think we could build a plane as good as the Martin or Munter's?"

Westervelt, seeing the glint in Boeing's eyes, replied — "Let's try it and see."

Before the evening was over, they had agreed to build a flying machine of their own design. They even had a name for it.

They called it, the "B&W" for Boeing and Westervelt.

The design and construction of the new plane was a challenge. As might be expected of men of their backgrounds they approached the problem methodically and scientifically. Westervelt took it upon himself to write to friends in the Navy Department who were aviation oriented. Glenn Curtiss with his seaplanes had stirred up considerable interest among Navy personnel suggesting that planes be used as "eyes for the Fleet."

The Navy contacts put Westervelt in touch with Jerome "Jerry" Hunsaker, a young aerodynamist at the Massachusetts Institute of Technology. Just about everybody agreed Hunsaker was far ahead of his time in know-how. M.I.T. was regarded as the "cradle of flight research." Hunsaker came through with some valuable suggestions. The "B&W" design progressed on paper.

Meanwhile, Boeing was busy in another direction. To house the Martin, he had built a small hangar and launching ramp on the shores of Lake Union. He also owned the Heath Shipyard, where he had built his yacht, a small frame building located on the Duwamish River in the mud flats almost in the center of downtown Seattle. The loft he turned into a design and drafting room, and he hired a small group of draftsmen and engineers from nearby University of Washington. Downstairs, work started on the fabrication of parts for the "B&W", Ed Heath building the pontoons, a small force of women to do the necessary sewing for the fabric covering on wings and fuselage. The plane was slowly taking shape. They would haul the pieces to the Lake Union hangar

It was here in the loft of the Ed Heath Shipyard building on the shores of Duwamish that Boeing set up first engineering and drafting room. This picture was taken in 1917 when draftsmen were working on plans for Navy modified Model-C trainers.

While the doughboys were "Over There" fighting World War One, women at home played important role in aircraft industry as we can see here. The scene is second story of Heath Shipyard Building, and women are "covering" wings of Boeing-built Model-C trainers.

for final assembly.

Actually, they had decided to build two planes, one for sale in case they might go into the aircraft manufacturing business, an idea Boeing had in the back of his head. Work progressed simultaneously on both planes.

It was about the middle of June, 1916, when the first "B&W" was pushed out on the ramp and made ready for its maiden flight. There were those who said it looked very much like a Chinese copy of the Martin.

A jokester called it the 3-M. "It's got a little bit of the Maroney, the Martin and the Munter in its configuration," he explained.

And it was true. Each of the other planes had contributed something to the "B&W", but it had a lot of Boeing in it, too. And for those who had built it, the plane was a thing of pride and beauty.

First Boeing design, the "B&W", is readied for launch. Its fuselage profile greatly resembles that of Martin seaplane.

The "B&W" was a biplane with a wing span of 52 feet, the upper wing slightly longer than the lower wing. It had a fuselage 31 feet in length with two cockpits in tandem for pilot and one passenger. The engine was a Hall-Scott rated at 125-horsepower, mounted in the front end of the fuselage ahead of the wings and driving a two-bladed propeller. The radiator, front view, looked like a Model-T. The plane rested on a pair of sleek. lightweight, mahogany plywood pontoons.

Herb Munter was supposed to fly it for the first time on June 29, 1916. Boeing had hired Munter as his personal pilot. On the day set for the initial flight, for some reason, Munter was delayed. Boeing and those who had worked on the plane waited at the Lake Union hangar for Munter to show, until finally Boeing got impatient and decided to make the flight himself.

He climbed into the rear cockpit, tested the controls, and waved a signal to the mechanic to swing the propeller. The engine coughed, sputtered, and rent the air with its staccato blasts. He taxied the plane out into the middle of the lake. There, the plane stopped momentarily, rocking gently on its twin floats. Then, it started to move slowly.

Faster, faster, faster it gained speed, sending up spray and leaving tracks in its wake like skis in the snow. In a surprisingly short distance it lifted off the water. Boeing held

Another view of the "B&W" shows twin pontoon arrangement, the long upper-wing span, shorter lower wing. "Skis" on lower wing were unusual idea, replacing the more conventional wing-tip floats. They helped steady plane in take-offs and landings.

it steady in a straight line, climbing slowly to an altitude of about 100 feet. That was good enough.

The "B&W" was a flyable craft.

Still keeping it in a straight and level attitude, he started to descend, alighting gracefully on the surface before the lake ran into the shoreline. Turning the plane around, he taxied back to the launching ramp.

Munter, who had finally arrived, was the first to greet him.

"How was it?" Munter asked.

Bill Boeing was all smiles.

Replica of "B&W" recreates first flight from Lake Union during ceremonies commemorating 50th anniversary of The Boeing Company.

"We're in the aircraft manufacturing business," he said.

III

THE world situation at the time, probably more than anything else, made him decide to stay in it. The Great Powers of Europe had been at war for more than two years, and there was a new dimension of warfare in the skies over the Western Front. At first, the flying machine had been used only as an observation platform in the sky, or for taking photographs of enemy positions and troop movements. Then, suddenly, it had emerged as a fighting machine. Both sides began equipping their planes with guns. The aeroplane became a warplane. The first World War was destined to become the first "*War In The Air*."

Things were happening in the skies above the River Thames, the Seine and the Danube that would bring a new kind of activity along the shores of the Duwamish, even though London, Paris and Berlin were thousands of miles from Seattle. Boeing and Westervelt were well read on the turn of events, day by day, and both were certain the conflict overseas would sooner or later involve the United States. When this happened, they were sure the U.S. would have to develop an aerial fleet of its own to be ready for whatever might happen abroad.

The impact of Europe's war struck home even sooner than expected. Commander

Westervelt got orders to report to Washington. The "B&W" partnership was dissolved.

Several weeks later Boeing received a letter from Westervelt. In it, Westervelt said he didn't believe the U.S. could stay out of the war. And he intimated that the Navy might be interested in the "B&W" or a design similar to it as a training plane. The Fleet was bolstering its Air Arm.

Boeing cranked up the "B&W" and took it up for a flight, alone. He wanted to think about things. Up there in the big sky was a good place to look at the world; big things became small things, and somehow, it was easier to get your ducks in a row.

When he came down, he had made up his mind. A whole year had passed since his first flight with Maroney. In that time, he had become more convinced than ever about the future of flying. The events in Europe's skies fired that conviction. The aeroplane was no longer a luxury, it was a necessity. His country needed planes, and Boeing decided to build them.

On July 16, 1916 he founded the Pacific Aero Products Company. Incorporated for $100,000, with Boeing as President, the company was licensed *to manufacture airplanes and other products, operate a flying school and engage in the transportation of passengers and freight by air.*

Claire L. Egtvedt, who worked on the "B&W" and later became Chairman Of The Board. He retired at end of World War II.

Philip G. Johnson, production "genius" who, as President of Boeing, steered company through the World War II years.

There was a young Chinese named T. Wong, an M.I.T. graduate whom Boeing had hired, and he put Wong to work designing a training plane for the Navy. Then, Boeing went looking for new talent. At the University of Washington he found two promising young engineering students. One was Philip G. Johnson. The other was Claire L. Egtvedt. To get them, Boeing made a deal with the dean. He promised to build the University a wind tunnel to stimulate more interest in aeronautical engineering.

The trio "dug in" and the Model-C trainer was born on paper. It was a pontoon-equipped biplane slightly smaller than the "B&W", and the design had some revolutionary features. There was a lot of stagger to the wings, the upper wing far ahead of the lower wing, said to provide more inherent stability. Certainly, that was essential for trainees. There was another new feature; the horizontal stabilizer in the tail was eliminated, replaced with a large moveable elevator, more controllability, it was be-

One of the Model-C seaplanes built as trainers for the U.S. Navy. Wing plan-form was similar to that of the "B&W", but upper wing was "staggered" forward of lower wing. This particular model was modified over production trainers to be Bill Boeing's personal plane.

lieved. For their period, both ideas were new.

But it was part of Boeing's philosophy not to be afraid of trying out new ideas. The tough job, however, is getting an idea into the factory. Boeing had all the wherewithal; the shipyard building, the hangar facility, spruce, the best wood for aircraft structures from his own lumberyards, craftsmanship among the men and women who had worked on the "B&W", and the money to hire more workers, if all went well with the Model-C, and he should decide to go into production. That decision, of course, depending upon the Navy's interest.

Thanksgiving time rolled around. It was November 23, 1916 and the first Model-C was ready for its test flight. Herb Munter, now full-time test pilot was at the controls. The whole factory force turned out to watch with anxious eyes.

They saw the plane lift off without any trouble. He climbed to about two hundred feet and tried a bank. The wings dipped too sharply, and he had to fight the controls to get it level again. He tried the same maneuver again, and the plane almost went into a spin. By the time he recovered, the machine was only a few feet above the water. He slapped it down hard and taxied back to the ramp.

Herb Munter didn't like the unconventional elevator in the tail. He said he wouldn't fly it again until they changed the configuration.

The Model-C didn't fly again until January, 1917. They had made some changes and after several flights, Munter told Boeing he thought it was "Okay". It was time to demonstrate the Model-C for the Navy. Boeing ordered two more of the machines built for the tests to be held at the Naval Air Station in Pensacola, Florida.

The United States had declared war on Germany and the war machinery was getting into high gear by mid-summer when Munter finished the tests in Florida's skies for the Navy. Boeing, in Washington, sent back word that the Navy had ordered fifty of the planes.

Big things started to happen on the banks of the Duwamish. The whole operation was

Original building where Boeing Airplane Company began in 1916 still stands. In this photo it has been all painted up for the 50th anniversary celebration. But it was here that the first Boeing designed and built aircraft, the "B&W" seaplane was born.

moved to the E. W. Heath shipyard, and before long a cluster of buildings appeared in the mud flats. A new sign was painted above the door of the two-story building. The sign read – BOEING AIRPLANE COMPANY.

IV

The Model-C, first mass-produced Boeing design, however, was not considered one of the better wartime trainers for a variety of reasons, and the Navy's business never got beyond the initial order for fifty of these planes. But the Navy did give Boeing another contract to build Curtiss-designed HS-2L flying boats. These were big planes for their day, a wing span of 74 feet and gross weight in excess of three tons. The "know-how" was like money in the bank.

The HS-2L's were moving along the assembly line when the Armistice was signed, November 11, 1918, but the Navy promptly cancelled half the order. When the first 25 of the flying boats were completed, Boeing had no more airplane business.

In the immediate post-war period we find the company doing anything and everything to stay alive. The factory, for a while, turned out chairs and desks and other pieces of furniture. Then, under a licensing agreement with the Sea Sled Company of Boston, Boeing turned to building the Hickman Sea Sled, a powered craft that might well be called the forerunner of the famous World War II PT-boats. But despite this diversification, the company was running deeper and deeper in the red.

There was a time, about a year after the war ended, when Bill Boeing reluctantly said – "We're going to have to close shop."

Then, came a surprise order from the Government for rebuilding fifty of the fa-

First Boeing Airplane Co. production line shows Model-C trainers under construction. Fuselage frame was built of spruce, probably from Boeing's own timber reserves. It is interesting to note the automobile-like "steering wheel" on the control columns.

mous wartime DeHavilland biplanes (The DH-4 "Flaming Coffins") and it was enough to keep things going and make a small profit.

But if Boeing were to stay in the aircraft manufacturing business, something bigger had to come along.

The Air Mail brought good news.

New assembly building was built for fabrication of Navy HS-2L Flying Boats. Planes were Curtiss-design, not Boeing's. For their day, they were considered very large aircraft. Boeing Airplane Co. started early to gain experience in big airplane structures.

During the early "twenties" Boeing built these modified DeHavilland biplanes. Designated the DH4-M, the plane was an improved version of the World War I famous, or infamous, "Flaming Coffins" , as pilots called them. Later some of DH's were used for flying the mail.

CHAPTER TWO

"Running Fast In The Right Direction"

SINCE it was organized in 1789, the Post Office Department has been dedicated to moving the mails in the most expeditious manner. In the process it has been instrumental in furthering many forms of transportation. The early Post Roads, the Stage Coach, the Pony Express, the "Iron Horse", each of these has played its own role in carrying the mails and each, in turn, brought about many improvements in their respective modes of travel. It was inevitable, perhaps, that the airplane because of its freedom of movement and its great speed would become the ultimate mail carrier. Today, for example, the majority of all first-class letters moves in the cargo compartments of 600-mile-an-hour jetliners. But it must be remembered that the birth of the Air Mail, in effect, was the beginning of scheduled air transportation in this country.

On May 15, 1918 a group of high government officials and many curious observers gathered at the old Polo Grounds in the nation's capital for the start of the first scheduled Air Mail Service in the United States. President Woodrow Wilson and Mrs. Wilson were present for the ceremony. The official party also included such dignitaries as Postmaster General Albert S. Burleson; Second Assistant Postmaster General Otto Praeger; the Assistant Secretary of the Navy, Franklin Delano Roosevelt and the Postmaster General of Japan. There was considerable excitement and anticipation among those who watched the great experiment. The future of the whole idea of flying the mail hung in the balance.

The Post Office Department had been given $100,000 to start the service in its 1917-18 budget, but as it turned out, Army fliers and Army planes were assigned to the task under the guise that it was good training for wartime pilots. The route selected was between New York-Philadelphia-Washington because, it was believed, this would be a good test. Mail was heaviest between the financial center of Wall Street and the center of Government in Washington, D.C. If the Air Mail could speed up communications over this 218-mile route, Congress would have to look favorably on the experiment.

Everything was ready. There were three planes taking part, one at each of the terminal points. Appropriately, with the President watching, the first plane was to take off from Washington with the northbound mail for Philadelphia and New York.

At about 10:00 A.M., the scheduled time for departure, four sacks of mail were stowed in the forward cockpit of the wartime Curtiss "Jenny" trainer plane which had been modified slightly to carry the mail. There was a little ceremony as dignitaries present posed with the pilot, Lieutenant George Boyle. Then, Boyle climbed into the cockpit and waved to his mechanic to give the propeller a turn and start the engine.

Nothing happened. The engine wouldn't

VIP's at Air Mail inaugural ceremonies in Washington, D. C., Franklin D. Roosevelt is second from left, President Wilson, extreme right.

Major Ruben Fleet (left) and Lt. George Boyle, pilot, check first Air Mail route map. Plane is wartime "Curtiss "Jenny"."

start. The Air Mail was off to an embarrassing beginning. Somebody had forgotten to put gas in the tanks!

This remedied, the plane finally did get away. Only, pilot Boyle made the wrong turn. The northbound mail was heading south. Ironically, the first innaugural Air Mail sacks were grounded and reached Philadelphia by train.

The Southbound experiment did much better. Leiutenant Torrey Webb left New York's terminus, the old Belmont Race Track, right on schedule and arrived an hour later at Bustleton Field serving Philadelphia. There, Lieutenant James Edgerton was waiting in another plane already warming up. The mail was transferred quickly to Edgerton's "Jenny", and two hours and twenty minutes later, Edgerton delivered the letters to the Washington Postmaster.

Despite the inauspicious beginning in Washington, the first Air Mail was pronounced a success. Soon, the service was completing better than 90 percent of schedules with time-table reliability, and three months after it was started, (August 12, 1918) the whole operation was turned over to the Post Office Department. The Air Mail was no longer a "training school" for Army fliers, but had a status of its own. The Post Office was authorized to buy its own mailplanes and hire its own pilots.

What happened had its direct effect on the Boeing Airplane Company and its future.

II

BILL Boeing had his own role to play in the pioneering days of the Air Mail Service. It was probably due to his association with a wartime flyer named Edward Hubbard that Boeing got directly involved in the Air Mail program. Boeing had hired "Eddie" as chief test pilot to replace Herb Munter, who had left to start a small flying business of his own. Boeing and Hubbard hit it off well together. The latter was one of those "idea men" that Boeing liked to have around him.

It was Eddie Hubbard who came to Boeing one day with a proposition that sounded way out.

"Mister Boeing," Hubbard declared, "I think I know how to bring the Orient a whole day closer to Seattle."

The way he put it whetted Boeing's interest.

"How's that, Eddie?" he asked.

"Well, I've been watching the arrivals and departures of the big ships from and to the Asian ports," Hubbard explained. "Did you know that every one of the inbound ships and the outbound ships stops at Victoria, British Columbia?"

Boeing nodded. He was aware of the steamship time-tables.

"My idea is to fly across the Sound to Victoria and intercept the ships arriving from the Orient, pick up the important mail, and fly it back to Seattle," Hubbard continued. "That way these letters would get here a full day's time ahead of the ships' scheduled arrivals. The plane could also pick up last minute mail in Seattle, a day after the ships' departure times, and still catch them at Victoria."

Boeing nodded in agreement, and they talked more about Hubbard's idea. He told Eddie to look into the matter more thoroughly with the Post Office Department, then come back and they'd give it more consideration.

Strangely, a few days after he had talked with Hubbard, Boeing took a phone call from a businessman in Vancouver, British Columbia. In Vancouver they were holding an exposition, and the businessman wanted to know if Boeing would fly a plane up there and fly back a bag of letters to commemorate the exposition. Boeing agreed to do this.

On March 2, 1919 with Boeing as a passenger and Eddie Hubbard at the controls of the Model-C, they took off heading for Vancouver. The weather was anything but desirable, with dark low-hanging clouds and the threat of snow. An hour out they ran into the snow storm. The air was rough, and they almost got lost in the blinding snow. Finally, they had to land at Anacortes where they spent the night. But the next day they went on, landing at the Royal Vancouver Yacht Club Basin.

There, they picked up a special pouch of letters authorized by both the U.S. and Canadian Post Office officials and started back for Seattle.

Bucking headwinds all the way the Model-C ran low on gas and they had to

"Eddie" Hubbard (left) and Bill Boeing in front of Model-C in which they flew first International Air Mail to Vancouver in 1919.

land for more fuel at Edmonds. But three hours after leaving Vancouver the plane was parked on the ramp at Lake Union.

History would record they had carried the first International Air Mail.

After the flight, Boeing and Hubbard talked more about the idea of the Victoria-Seattle mail route.

"What we need is a bigger plane," Eddie Hubbard suggested. He said he already had cleared the idea with the proper postal authorities.

"The B-1 could really do the job," Boeing interjected.

The B-1 was a seaplane patterned much like the Curtiss HS-21 flying boats only much smaller. And it was strictly a Boeing design. The plane was nearing completion in the shops.

It was a biplane with a span of fifty feet for the upper wing, a single-engine, pusher-type, capable of carrying a payload of about 1400 pounds. They called it a mail/passenger flying boat. The fuselage was a boat-hull with two tandem cockpits ahead of the wings; a small single-seat in the nose for the pilot and a two-seat arrangement in the rear cockpit for passengers or mail. With a range of 400 miles and a speed of about 90-mph, the B-1 was ideally suited for the Seattle-Victoria mail run.

When Hubbard and Boeing made their historic flight with the first International Air Mail, the B-1 was just going into the shops. It wasn't ready for its first flight until December 27, 1919 when Eddie Hubbard took it off from the waters of Lake Union. Claire Egtvedt and a young engineer named Louis Marsh who had worked on the hull design, were with Hubbard on the flight.

B-1 flying boat was Boeing Airplane Company's first commercial design. Originally, it was built as a sport-plane, but idea didn't "catch-on." Hubbard bought a plane, and used it to fly the mail between Seattle and Victoria, B.C.

Actually, that flight was a kind of fluke. They were really just out for a taxi run. But the B-1 leaped out of the water and became airborne.

There were some "bugs", but these were ironed out and everybody was convinced they had a good little seaplane. Boeing tried to sell the design to the Navy, but they turned it down. Finally, the only customer he could find was Eddie Hubbard.

The Post Office had given Hubbard a contract to fly the Seattle-Victoria route. Hubbard Air Transport bought the B-1 and started operations. Hubbard had left Boeing, but we will hear from him again later.

The B-1, however, in the history of the Boeing Airplane Company was a significant milestone. It was the first aircraft built by Boeing and sold for commercial purposes.

"The B-1 clinched the reputation of Boeing as a plane builder!" wrote historian Henry Ladd Smith in his prize-winning book about air transportation entitled AIRWAYS.

III

BUILDING planes in the early twenties, however, was not considered a very fruitful business venture. It had been expected that the thousands of war-trained aviators returning after the Armistice would rush to buy anything with wings, start their own flying schools and airline operations. There would be "pie in the sky." But the pie turned sour. The flyboys who wanted to keep flying, bought planes from surplus Army stocks for the price of a good motorcycle. Private plane builders couldn't compete. Boeing survived only because of some military orders. Even then, it was not the kind of business Bill Boeing really wanted.

Army air Service need for ground attack plane, resulted in this Boeing design, a triplane, the GAX – "Guns, Armor and X, for unknown."

Typical was a contract Boeing got from the Army Air Service to build an attack airplane. The design, called the GAX (Ground Attack Experimental) was one dreamed up by General William "Billy" Mitchell and the Engineering Division of the U.S. Army Air Service at McCook Field, near Dayton, Ohio. Boeing was low bidder and got the order to build ten of these planes which

The "GAX" shown here, was the first multi-engined aircraft to be built by Boeing. Original prototypes were built by Air Service Engineering Division, McCook Field, Dayton, Ohio. Boeing designation was Model-10. Billy Mitchell called it a "flying fortress."

never amounted to much. They were cumbersome, overweight, and pilots called them, "Mitchell's Monstrocities."

There were some things about the GAX, however, that seem pertinent to this narrative. It was the first multi-engined aircraft built by Boeing, two pusher-type Liberty engines, and the GAX, a triplane, three wings (span 65-feet, 6 inches) mounted one above the other, and its gross weight of 10,400 pounds, was considered a very large aircraft for this period.

The BIG plane concept for which Boeing would become famous even up to the present with the 747 *Super jet*, it can be said, probably was born with the GAX. Moreover, it was a plane with heavy armor plate, mounting eight .30-calibre machine guns and one 37-mm. cannon, virtually a "flying fortress." In this respect, it was twenty years ahead of its time and the famous Boeing-built B-17 "Flying Fortresses" of World War II.

About the same time it got the GAX contract, Boeing also received an order to build 200 Thomas-Morse (MB-3) single-engine fighters for the army.

Phil Johnson summed it up. "We could build planes," he remarked. "But we couldn't build Boeings."

If this trend were to continue, Johnson, who was now production chief, warned that Boeing would lose its identity as a creative aircraft design and development company, relegated to the role of merely a manufacturing facility. This certainly was not a very healthy climate in which to live for a progressive organization.

It was the year 1925, and "Billy" Mitchell was at the peak of his crusade warning about the unhealthy state of America's air power. The yardstick, because the world was at peace, was in record-breaking performances of various aircraft designs. On this scorecard, Italy held the lead with 18 world's records, France held 16, the U.S. on the international scale, rated not higher than third-rate, not lower than fifth. Mitchell screamed, "It's like poker; you can't win with a second-best hand!"

Fortunately, for America's future in the air, poker-faced Calvin Coolidge, the 30th President of the United States, listened to the pleas of his air-minded generals and admirals, and did something about the situation, Coolidge appointed a New York banker, Dwight W. Morrow, to head a special group (It became known as the Morrow Board) and Congress appointed its own investigative committee, headed by Rep. Florian Lampert of Wisconsin (The Lampert Committee) to find out what was wrong with U.S. Aviation, both military and civilian, and to come up with some recommendations.

The result was the establishment of an entirely new procurement policy for Army and Navy aircraft, and the formation of a

In post war years, women were still employed by Boeing to do "needlework" such as this scene, which shows them sewing fabric on wings of Thomas-Morse, MB-3 pursuit plane. Boeing had contract to build two hundred of these fighters for the Army Air Service.

new Army Air Corps and a new Bureau Of Aeronautics for the Navy. Congress also passed the Air Mail Act (February 2, 1925) and the Air Commerce Act (May 20, 1926) which charged the Government with the development of a safe air transportation system, and gave it able sums to buy new planes for the Army and Navy, develop a government-controlled airways system, build new airports, further the Post Office Department's efforts to improve the Air Mail Service, and encourage the development of aviation in general.

Such actions were like blood transfusions for the aircraft manufacturers, engine companies, the Air Mail effort, and the small family of airlines trying to develop commercial air transportation. The Boeing Company, of course, shared in the program. Overnight, the picture looked brighter.

The summer of 1926 was typical of the change. There were some five hundred workers busy on the assembly lines at Boeing. The plant was almost up to wartime strength. The company was building a new pursuit plane of its own design, the XPW-9, for the Army Air Corps and a counterpart version, the FB-1 land-based fighter for the Navy. Altogether business was good, the dollar sign was growing, so was the company.

Bill Boeing was pleased. But he still wasn't satisfied. There was something wrong.

He often had confessed to close friends that he got into the aircraft manufacturing in the first place because he thought flying was a great sport. Then, he saw in the airplane a swift means of transport to bring peoples everywhere closer together. In his way of thinking the flying machine should provide wings for commerce, not wings for combat. His "dream" was to see Flying

The XPW-9, Boeing-designed pursuit plane, first of a long line of fighters that would make the company famous in this field.

Clubs spring up all over the country and a system of airlines that would parallel our system of railroads and bus lines. This, he believed, was America's real future in the air.

"Can't we build anything but warplanes?" he remarked disgustedly one day as he viewed the long line of pursuits and Navy fighters in final assembly.

Perhaps, he was burned up still because the B-1 never got into production. And they had tried again more recently, in 1925, with the design and building of a mailplane, the Model-40, for the Post Office Department. But there was only one built and nothing came of a production order.

When Post Office asked for bids for mailplane, Boeing submitted this Model-40, Liberty-powered, biplane design.

Then, it happened.

Eddie Hubbard dropped in one day to talk with Claire Egtvedt, who was now first Vice-President of the company. Hubbard had another idea. He pointed out that the Post Office Department (under terms of the Air Mail Act) was turning the job of flying the mail over to qualified private operators. He explained that he had learned the Chicago-San Francisco segment of the transcontinental route was up for grabs to the lowest bidder. He was convinced he could make the route pay. He proposed starting an airline carrying *both passengers and mail* between Chicago and San Francisco. Could Boeing build the planes?

Admittedly, Claire Egtvedt was interested in Hubbard's presentation. Together, they pored over Eddie's facts and figures. Together, they took the idea to Mister Boeing.

"It's a mighty big undertaking," Bill Boeing commented. He seemed cold to the whole proposition. Hubbard was disappointed. So was Egtvedt.

Thanksgiving time approached and 1926 was drawing to a close. The deadline for submiting bids on the Chicago-San Fran route was near. Nobody had said anything more about the airline. But Bill Boeing hadn't forgotten. He had been giving the matter a lot of serious attention.

There was the Model-40 mailplane, but he was convinced this plane couldn't do the job. Built to Post Office specifications, the Model-40 was powered with a wartime Liberty 400-horsepower water cooled engine. Boeing couldn't see "hauling all that water around" and making any money with a 1,000-pound payload. But, he was thinking, if they could redesign the Model-40 around the more powerful and new Pratt & Whitney air-cooled *Wasp* engine which was going into a new experimental Navy fighter (The FB-6) then, maybe, they could haul more payload. There might even be room enough to put in a small passenger compartment. With such a plane, they just might make money.

There was just one major obstacle. The Pratt & Whitney *Wasps* were a joint P&W/ Navy development and the Navy had top priority on all the engines built until its fighter program was completed.

Boeing made a phone call to his friend Frederick B. Rentschler, President of Pratt & Whitney in Hartford, Connecticut. They had first met during the war years when Rentschler was in charge of engine inspection for the then Aviation Section of the

William E. Boeing (left) and Frederick B. Rentschler, President of Pratt & Whitney Aircraft and new "WASP" engine.

Boeing FB-6 experimental fighter design for the Navy. Plane was first to be powered with air-cooled, radial, Pratt & Whitney "WASP" engine. It set many performance records. Ever since, Pratt & Whitney Aircraft and Boeing have been partners in progress.

Signal Corps. It was Rentschler, who had started Pratt & Whitney Aircraft and brought the *Wasp* into existence.

Was there any way Boeing could get some of the *Wasp* engines? Boeing put the question to Rentschler on the phone.

There was. If Boeing would build a plane especially as a flying test bed for P&W engines (more powerful ones were coming along) Rentschler was sure he could get some engines released from the Navy to go into the modified Model-40. Moreover, Rentschler liked the idea of the airline.

Boeing hung up the phone and took the whole thing to bed with him to sleep on it.

Over breakfast next morning he talked it over with his wife. "Supposing we should bid on the Chicago-San Francisco Air Mail route?"

"Well," his wife answered, "you might sell a lot of planes."

"To whom?"

"You could buy them yourself. At least, you'd know your best customer and his needs."

Boeing smiled. It was a good idea. If they got the bid, it certainly would generate a new market for mailplanes.

He got in touch with Eddie Hubbard and Claire Egtvedt.

"I've decided we're going to bid for the mail route," he announced. "Rentschler says he can get us the engines."

Hubbard and Egtvedt winked at each other. They had previously proposed modifying the Model-40 for the job, but admittedly, they didn't know how to get the *Wasps*. They did know, however, how to get Bill Boeing. Let him solve the problem, and he'd run with it. They got the green light to start preliminary design drawings for the Model-40A mailplane.

"If we get the low bid," Boeing said, "we'll build it."

In the name of Edward Hubbard and the Boeing Airplane Company a bid was submitted to the Post Office Department. It was January 15, 1927 when Postmaster General Harry S. New opened the sealed envelopes. Hubbard and Boeing were the low bidders. Contract Air Mail Route (CAM-18) was theirs for flying the mail half-way across the continent.

The bid they had submitted was so ridiculously low that skeptics said neither Boeing, nor anyone else, could do the job at the low dollar figure quoted. Even the Post Office Department questioned the low figure. Boeing had to post half a million dollar bond to insure performance of the contract. He did so, gladly, and for the first time the company was going to produce planes for commercial purposes.

To carry out the mission of flying the mail, he formed a separate company, Boeing Air Transport. The idea, of course, was that BAT would buy its planes from Boeing Airplane Company. In a shrewd move Bill Boeing had created a market for his own product.

The order went down to the shops to start production of the Model-40A mailplane. There was a deadline to meet. Twenty-five of the planes had to be stationed at terminal points along the route and ready to start service on July 1, 1927.

Bill Boeing remembered something Fred Rentschler had told him when the first *Wasp* had passed its crucial tests.

"We're running fast in the right direction," Rentschler had remarked.

Now, for the first time, Boeing felt the same way about his aircraft manufacturing business.

IV

THE Boeing 40-A was a biplane with conventional struts and wire bracing between the wings, which were made of spruce framework, ribs and spars, and covered

When Boeing got mail contract, in January, 1927, Model-40A design got factory priority. This was the production line.

Loading express shipment in special compartment of Model-40A mailplane. Picture also shows forward passenger compartment with two windows, tandem seating, just behind the "WASP" engine, and pilot's open cockpit behind mail compartment. Note insignia.

with doped fabric. The fuselage was a steel-tubing frame; the forward half was covered with aluminum skin (a metal mail compartment to guard against fire) and the rear section was covered with fabric. Just behind the mail compartment between the wings was a passenger compartment with two cushioned seats side-by-side and windows. The pilot sat in an open cockpit aft of the enclosed cabin.

Instrument panel in Model-40A mailplane was almost too simple. Here we see barest of instruments, temperature and oil pressure gauges, turn and bank indicator, air speed indicator and clock. There was no "steering wheel", just stick and rudder bar controls.

The first "WASP", air-cooled, radial, Pratt & Whitney Aircraft engine during initial test run at East Hartford, Conn. plant. Production version developed 420-horsepower, and is credited with being "success secret" of the mail/passenger, Boeing Model-40A.

Up front in the nose was the new 420-horsepower *Wasp*, the "success secret" Boeing was banking on. The *Wasp*, much lighter than the cumbersome, heavy Liberty motor with its bulky radiator, permitted boosting the payload over the original Model-40 design by a quarter of a ton to a 1500-pound total. The plane could carry a thousand pounds of mail, but in addition, it could also carry two passengers. The way they had it planned, carrying two passengers would add about $400 revenue to each one-way trip.

The production program called for 24 of the planes to be built for BAT, the 25th for Pratt & Whitney to be used as the "flying test bed" for new engines.

Wilbur Thomas, a Pratt & Whitney service representative assigned to the project provides us with a vivid description of the Boeing plant during the Model-40A production program.

"As fast as one of the planes was completed," Thomas reported to Rentschler back in Hartford, "it was trucked 15 miles

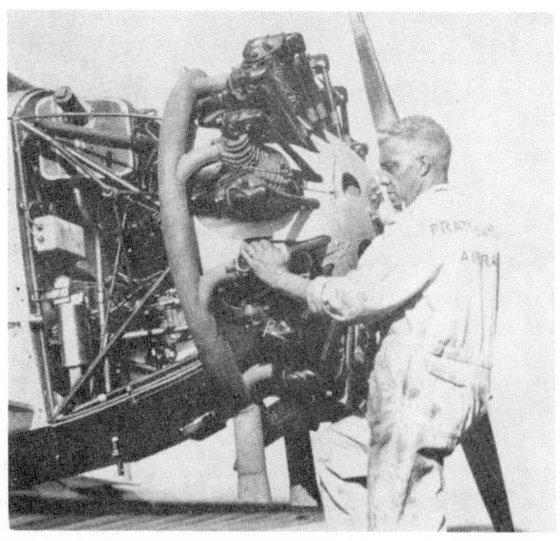

Wilbur Thomas works on "WASP" engine in Model-40A mailplane. Engine people worked right with manufacturer in Seattle plant.

One of the first Model-40A mailplanes wings its way over the treacherous mountains along Boeing Air Transport's Chicago-San Francisco route. Planes carried mail, passengers and express. They were first to fly passengers over western segment of transcontinental airway.

from the Boeing factory in Seattle to Sand Point, where a cleared pasture among the pines served as an airport. There, the plane was given a short whirl in the air and flown off to one of the ten route division points."

The first Model-40A was flown on May 20, 1927. By midnight June 30, the entire fleet was scattered along the route ready to begin flying the mail the next day.

The scene at the Omaha flying field on July 1, 1927 was typical of what happened when the mail was officially transferred from the Post Office Department's responsibility to Boeing Air Transport. There, with appropriate ceremony, the eastbound transcontinental mail was transferred from one of the Post Office planes, and stowed in the mail compartment of the new Boeing Model-40A. Minutes later the Boeing roared off into the night sky heading for Chicago.

Meanwhile, at Maywood Field, the Chicago terminus, another shining new Model-40A, with flood lights playing on it like she was the star performer on stage, took off on an history-making flight carrying the first passenger.

Reporter Jane Eads, first Chicago-to-San Francisco passenger, demonstrates inter-com system. She could talk with pilot Ira Biffle during flight. She wore helmet because of built-in earphones. Cabin was heated, there was no need to wear flying suit like Biffle's.

Strapped in the tiny, cramped cabin was newswoman Jane Eads of the Chicago *Herald & Examiner* staff. Behind her, in the open cockpit, was pilot Ira Biffle.

At 9:30 p.m., the scheduled time for departure, the *Wasp* roared to life and the plane taxied away from the ramp, picked up speed as it bounced over the grass runway, and finally lifted its wheels, pointing its nose towards Iowa City, Iowa.

The "Columbia Route" a name given to CAM-18 stretched almost 2,000 miles across plains and mountains, from the shores of Lake Michigan to the Pacific Ocean, with intermediate stops at Iowa City, Des Moines, Omaha, Nevada and San Francisco.

Pilot Biffle and passenger Jane Eads sped westward in the Model-40A at speeds of 120-miles per hour; *Running fast in the right direction.*

It was twenty-three flying hours later that a tired, but smiling Jane Eads climbed out of the cabin for her first look at the city of the Golden Gate. She told fellow reporters-"I could fly forever. I love it. Air transportation is here to stay."

And so it was. During the first full year of operations, Boeing Air Transport would carry some five hundred more aerial voyagers, pioneering transcontinental air passenger service. The Model-40A's, shuttling back and forth, night and day, set an enviable safety record. They would be remembered as having started an evolution and revolution in air transportation.

A new era was about to begin.

Three Gentlemen From Detroit

Capt. Charles A. Lindbergh and "Spirit of St. Louis" just before take-off, New York-to-Paris, May 20, 1927.

ON the same day (May 20, 1927) that the first Model-40A Boeing mailplane made its maiden test flight, a young, unknown Air Mail pilot named Charles Augustus Lindbergh, alone in his monoplane *"The Spirit Of Saint Louis,"* took off from Roosevelt Field, Long Island, and headed out across the Atlantic. His destination was Paris, France 3600 miles away, non-stop. Thirty-three and a half hours later Lindbergh landed at LeBourget Field on the outskirts of the French capital.

This epochal flight launched what has been called and, perhaps, well named "The Lindbergh Boom" in aviation circles. Certainly, history records, something like an explosion occurred within the framework of the flying community following Lindbergh's achievement. In the next twelve months, the number of applications for pilots' licenses increased 400 per cent. There were four times as many privately-owned aircraft in the skies. The number of applications for aircraft me-

After epochal Paris flight, Lindbergh flew around the country promoting aviation. He is shown here (center) with Edsel Ford, left, and Henry Ford at Ford Airport in Dearborn, Michigan. "Lindy" did much to keep Ford, "father of the Model-T", interested in aviation.

Production line at Ford/Stout Airplane Factory in Dearborn, Michigan. Planes are famous Ford trimotors, first of the all-metal airliners in this country. Pilots called them the "Tin Goose". They pioneered many "firsts" in air transportation.

chanics' certificates increased proportionately. Even the Wall Street bankers reacted favorably, and just about any idea with wings on it could get backing.

One might say in today's parlance, aviation was the going thing. Yet, a closer look at what happened, shows that although Lindbergh's flight caught the public fancy and undoubtedly stirred up a skyfull of enthusiasm, there were other factors which started the revolution and evolution in air transportation.

The truth is, the fat was in the fire *before* Lindbergh brought home the bacon. Likely of more import to the financial community, for instance, was Henry Ford's entry into the air transportation field. As far back as August, 1925 Henry Ford announced — "There seems to be a wonderful future in aviation. So we are going to build the best

Before Lindbergh's Paris flight, Henry Ford was operating his own airline with these single-engined, all-metal planes flying between Ford plants in Chicago, Detroit and Cleveland. They flew first contract Air Mail (being loaded here) February 15, 1926.

The passenger terminal building at Ford Airport was one of first in the U.S. It housed ticket counter, lounge and restaurant. Ford also pioneered airport taxi and bus service. Picture was taken after Ford Air Transport Service became Detroit-Cleveland Airline.

planes we can and if it does develop we will be ready!"

Within a year, The Ford Motor Company had its own aviation division and was producing the famous Ford trimotor, an all-metal passenger plane. Pilots affectionately called it, "The Tin Goose" because of its metallic skin. The "Goose" was put into service on a Ford-owned scheduled airline between Ford plants in Detroit, Cleveland and Chicago. The Ford Air Transport Service flew the first contract Air Mail (February 15, 1926) and pioneered such things as in-flight attendants, airport terminal facilities and limousine (a Model-T bus) service for passengers. The modern airport Ford built at Dearborn, Michigan was a "model" of things to come with paved runways, a weather reporting service, and even an embryonic traffic control system. And all of this was in operation *before* Lindbergh made his flight to Paris.

It is pertinent here because, undoubtedly, Bill Boeing was well aware of the Ford interest and operations when he made his decision to start Boeing Air Transport. He might well have been thinking – *if Henry Ford can put his money into this thing, there must be something to the future of aviation.* Likewise, the Lindbergh flight came at just the right time

Fabulous Model-T, "Tin Lizzie", got into the act when Ford built this glistening Air Transportation Service mail truck.

to give a big boost to the Boeing Air Transport operation. Enough so, at least, to make Boeing bend his efforts to putting top priority on improving the Model-40A, the design and development of a much larger passenger plane, and the formation of an air transport combine that would ultimately become today's largest domestic scheduled air carrier — UNITED AIR LINES.

The house that Bill Boeing, lumberjack, built put U.S. air transportation into a position of world leadership that it would never relinquish to this day, with the latest Boeing 747 *Superjet*, a shining symbol of progress catching up with progress.

Interestingly, Boeing, Ford and Lindbergh were all born in Detroit, Michigan, the Motor City, automobile capital of the world. Yet, the three gentlemen from Detroit probably did more than any other trio to give the world wings and not just wheels.

Of the three, Lindbergh alone is still living. He is today a member of the board of directors of Pan American World Airways, the first airline customer to buy the 747 *Super jet*. Undoubtedly, as a technical advisor for Pan-Am, Lindbergh had a great deal to say about the decision to place the first 747 order.

But what Bill Boeing did forty years ago, probably more than anything else, gave the *Super jet* the proper environment in which to live.

In 1928 he made a trip east to see Fred Rentschler at Pratt & Whitney about getting some more powerful engines. At the time Boeing was P&W's best customer. It was a team that would never break up through the years, even as the 747 *Super jet* is powered with P&W Turbo-fan engines, forty years later.

Boeing and Rentschler saw eye to eye in their assessment of the aviation industry one year after Lindbergh's Paris flight. It was time, they agreed, to jump in with both feet. They started to talk about a merger. Before it was over there came into being a gigantic holding company, United Aircraft & Transport Corporation with William E. Boeing as Chairman of the Board and F. B. Rentschler as President.

The new company encompassed Boeing Airplane Company that produced planes, Pratt & Whitney that produced the engines for the planes, Hamilton Propeller Company that made the propellers for the engines, and Boeing Air Transport that bought the finished product and put it into airline service. Overnight, the business of air transportation became BIG BUSINESS.

Before long, they had the eastern leg of the Transcontinental Air Mail Route (National Air Transport) in their fold, and also had acquired Pacific Air Transport (PAT) extending the airline operation north and south from Seattle to San Diego. It was this airline group within the combine that would become today's United Air Lines system.

There would come a time in the near future when the big United Aircraft & Transport Corporation Boeing and Rentschler had founded would be broken up. But for about five years it produced great technological advancements in aircraft design, powerplants and success rules for how to run an airline.

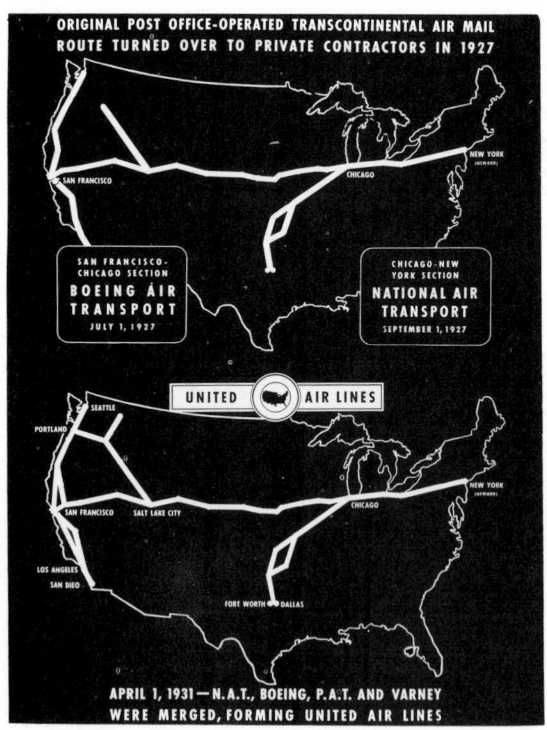

Route maps show how Boeing Air Transport, under Boeing and Rentschler, grew into coast-to-coast, United Air Lines.

Boeing Model-40B mailplane roars westward over the snow-capped mountains. The larger 40-B carried four passengers instead of two although configuration was the same as earlier 40-As. It was powered with improved Pratt & Whitney "Hornet" engines.

II

IN the first two years of the Boeing Air Transport operation, the Model-40As flew more than 5,500,000 miles, delivered over 1,300 tons of mail and carried some 6,000 passengers. BAT was making money, and Bill Boeing did not "lose his shirt" as some of the so-called aviation experts had predicted. Part of the reason for this profit factor was the extra revenue derived from the passenger business. With this in mind, Boeing concentrated on a modified version of the Model-40A designed to carry more passengers.

Sideview of Model-40B shows larger windows in passenger compartment and how mail/express compartment was moved forward, different from Model-40A. Tail wheel replaced tailskid for smoother taxiing. Also note streamlined wing lights.

The Model-40B series was born. There was a more powerful engine available, the P&W 525-horsepower *Hornet* which gave the Model-40B a speed 20 mph faster than its predecessor. The new planes were also built with room for four in the passenger cabin, with the mail compartment reduced to 500-pound capacity. These were the major changes. Outwardly, the configuration was the same except for the two windows on each side of the fuselage instead of the one window in the original Model-40A concept.

There were, however, some minor details that clearly show the emphasis on passenger comfort. Windows were openable to "air condition" the otherwise stuffy and cramped cabin. A tail wheel replaced the tail skid to make taxiing less bumpy on the riders. There was also a special shielding in the pilot's open cockpit area which permitted the installation of a radio for ground-to-air and air-to-ground communications.

And thereby hangs a tale for which the Boeing Model-40s will always be remembered in the annals of air transportation.

First and foremost in the design and building of his planes and the operation of his airline, Bill Boeing was concerned with the element of safety. He knew there was also a certain amount of risk involved in flying, the price you pay for going places in a hurry. Like running, instead of walking; there is a greater chance of getting hurt. But Boeing was dedicated to cutting the risk factor to a minimum, as evident today in the company's huge jetliners as it was in beginning.

The Model-40s were safe airplanes, design-wise and structure-wise, tested tried and true. In the first 5,500,000 miles of flying there were only three fatalities. The weather, not the planes, was the big bugaboo, particularly over the rugged western segment of the BAT route; through the Rocky Mountain passes and over the saw-toothed Wasatch range. The weather could go from bad to worse in a matter of minutes.

Throp Hiscock, a wartime flyer and "ham" radio operator who had married Bill Boeing's sister-in-law, broached the idea of radio communication, ground-to-plane to give pilots a running report on the weather ahead. The result was two-way radios for the planes which Hiscock designed and built, and first tried in the Model-40s.

Throp Hiscock, "ham" radio operator, who designed ground-to-plane and plane-to-ground radio communications systems.

Nor did it stop there. Flying in a Model-40B from Seattle to Medford, Pilot J. R. Cunningham got caught in a snowstorm and he was lost. But all the while, Cunningham on his two-way radio kept talking

Equipped with Hiscock's two-way radios Boeing Air Transport planes pioneered advanced weather reporting for pilots.

The competition gets tougher. Amelia Earhart christens Ford trimotor, "City of Columbus" in New York's Grand Central Station for start of air/rail, coast-to-coast service in 1929. At left is Grover Whalen, New York's "official greeter" in Jimmy Walker era.

to the operator on the ground at Medford. He noticed there were times when the ground operator's voice would come in loud and clear. Then it would fade out almost altogether only to come back again. He reasoned he must be flying in circles, and decided to try out a theory. He tried holding onto the voice when it was loudest, and a whole new technique of aerial navigation was in embyro — "riding the beam."

The storm got worse and Cunningham finally lost all radio contact and mushed-down on a mountainside. But he was so

To compete with TAT's Ford Trimotors, Boeing introduced its own trimotor, the 12-passenger, Model-80 super deluxe biplane.

near Medford he walked to town after the snow had stopped. And he was sure his "theory" had worked.

Cunningham and Hiscock got together. Out of this came the electronic beacons and the modern system of air traffic control that works like the block signals of a railroad or the stop-and-go lights in city traffic.

The marriage of the radio and the airplane in the Boeing Model-40 mailplane was the seed of safety, which probably more than anything else, made air transportation a scheduled operation and took a lot of fear out of flying.

The author remembers flying in one of the Model-40s and hearing a fellow passenger remark – "It's nice to know we're tied to the ground, even if it is an invisible line."

III

MORE and more passengers climbed into the four-passenger Boeings until it got so that the mail became almost a secondary source of revenue. It was time to build a bigger plane and really go after the passenger business. And there was competition. A new transcontinental airline (Transcontinental Air Transport) backed by big railroad interests and General Motors, and with Lindbergh as a stockholder and advisor, had started flying the all-metal Ford trimotors from New York to Los Angeles. Boeing had to do something to stay in the running.

Actually before "The Lindbergh Line" (TWA used the slogan taking advantage of the Lindbergh name) started operations as an air/rail service, July 7, 1929, Boeing Air Transport had a big new passenger plane flying. Designated the Model-80, it was a 12-passenger, biplane, a trimotor in the 15,000-pound weight category, the first commercial transport of any real size built by Boeing.

"The last word in travel comfort," the airline's advertising called it.

Inside the 80s had carpeting, colorful wall decor, cabin lights, soft, upholstered seats and a small lavatory. There were four single seats along the right-hand side of a narrow aisle, and four rows of two-abreast seats on the left-hand side of the cabin. Six large windows on each side of the fuselage gave passengers a splendid view of the terrain below. The plane had a cruising speed of 115-mph, faster than the Ford trimotors.

In the nose of the 80 was an enclosed cockpit for a pilot and co-pilot, and there was space in the tail for about 1,000 pounds of mail and cargo. Fuselage and wings were of aluminum and steel tubing frame covered with fabric. Boeing had not yet entered the all-metal construction phase, although the vertical tail on the first Model-80s was covered with corrugated skin. Painted all silver with an orange trim, the planes, nevertheless, had a metallic look.

There was an improved, more streamlined Model-80A with a slightly longer fuselage providing accommodations for 18 passengers and a crew of three. This

Inside, the Model-80 was very "posh-posh", with carpeted floors, parlor-car seats, fancy curtains, even flower vases on the walls.

Bigger Model-80A could carry 18 passengers. Outboard engines were fitted with NACA cowlings which increased speed slightly. For first time on "80s" the name United Air Lines began to appear. Also note the covered passenger loading ramp, air travel come of age.

bigger plane was one of the first to use the NACA (National Advisory Committee for Aeronautics) ring-cowlings around the engines which added 10 miles an hour to the cruising speed. And for its day, the Boeing Model-80A was the largest, fastest, and "most luxuriously appointed" airliner. For some reason, the price tag of $75,000 apiece, instilled confidence. At that price, the public concluded, the plane must have everything that the state of the art could provide.

The passenger business on the Chicago-San Francisco run which used the Model-80s, exclusively, increased substantially when the bigger airliners went into service. The planes, themselves, were not the only reason.

The third crew member aboard the new airliners was a registered nurse, who rode in a small jump seat in the back of the cabin. And the Model-80 will be remembered as introducing the flight stewardess to the air traveler.

Pilots didn't like the idea of "a frail female as a crew member," but the idea caught on and a whole new profession for women came into existence.

Paradoxically, the Boeing 747 *Superjet*

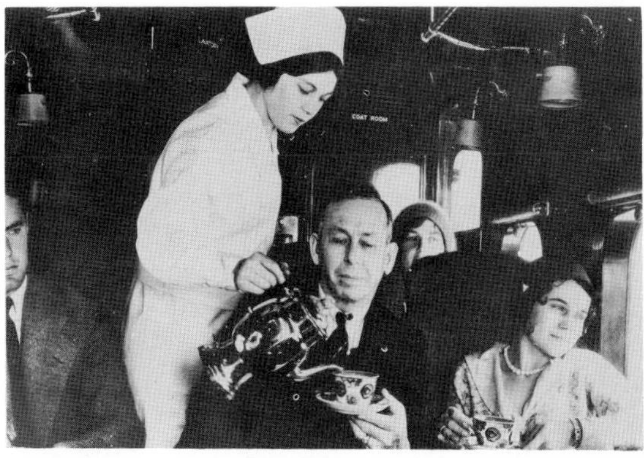

The "80s" probably will be remembered most for introducing the "flight nurse", and for their big "cathedral" windows.

What made "flying great" was when Boeing Air Transport introduced the air traveler of the '30s to stewardesses on board. Here is first group, left to right – Jesse Carter, Cornelia Peterman, Ellen Church, Inez Keller, Alva Johnson, Margaret Arnott, Ellis Crawford and Harriet Fry.

of the 70's, forty years later, will have approximately sixteen cabin attendants on board to attend to and pamper its 350 to 400 passengers. More stewardesses aboard the 747 than the entire passenger capacity of the first big Boeing commercial airliner, the Model-80 series! Certainly, that is an indication of the growth of air travel.

Perhaps, of even more significance, the Boeing Airplane Company in producing the Model-80 in the late twenties, was gaining know-how in the design and construction of large airframes which would make it a leader in the large commercial airliner field, culminating with today's 747 *Super jet*.

CHAPTER FOUR

First Of The Modern Airliners

WITH the stock market crash of 1929, and the following years of economic depression, 1930-33, the aircraft industry went into a tailspin. Many airframe manufacturers never recovered, and went out of business. The same was true of many members of the small family of fledgling airlines; people in the breadline couldn't afford an airline ticket. Yet, the Boeing Airplane Company did not only survive during this period, it showed a growth trend, emerging as the depression ebbed, stronger than ever before. Certainly, its image was one of reserve and reputation. The work force remained fairly constant, while great strides were made in aircraft design and manufacturing methods.

Boeing had the "know-how" with a background of more than fifteen years in the business. It had financial stability through the big United Aircraft & Transport Corporation and its many fields of interest, including the United Air Lines group, whose fast mail/passenger Model-40Bs and big, roomy, comfortized Model-80s were flying coast-to-coast in the "model" airline operation. And new military business, pursuits for the Army Air Corps and carrier-based Navy fighters, enhanced its reputation to a point where it virtually dominated this field. The famous P-12 series Army Pursuit planes and the Navy F4Bs were, in fact, regarded as the best military fighters in the world. And they were, as their performance proved time and time again, at Air Meets and during military maneuvers.

But this "fighter image" was also distressing. There simply was not the time nor factory space available to devote proper effort to the development of commercial-type aircraft, a field Bill Boeing wished to dominate rather than be primarily a military plane builder. Between the Model-80A, the 18-passenger luxury airliner, and the next major design configuration for an airliner, the Model-247, the company designed and built only five models for commercial operation. It was time for a change. With it came a whole new concept in aircraft design and manufacturing techniques.

In the process, the biplane gave way to the monoplane. The tubular-frame fuselage and the rib and spar wing structures covered with fabric, were abandoned in favor of the *monocoque* fuselage and the *cantilever* wing with all-metal skin.

The Boeing *Monomail* (Model-200) was the company's first effort in this direction so far as a commercial aircraft was concerned, although it must be admitted, experience in the design and construction of a high-wing pursuit (the XP-9, Model 96) was a contributing factor. A result was, however, that the *Monomail* would lead the company into a position, which would in the short span of two years, give it leadership in the transport field with the introduction of the first truly modern airliner.

First all-metal aircraft to be built by Boeing was this XP-9, Model 96, Army pursuit. Construction was entirely new process.

In the history of the Boeing Airplane Company, the design and development of the *Monomail* was the crucial turning point, comparable only to the decision of Conrad Westervelt and Bill Boeing in 1916 to build the "B&W" which put Boeing in the aircraft manufacturing business. Paradoxically, the "B&W" was the only Boeing-built aircraft never given a Model-number designation, and the Model-200 (with the copyrighted name *Monomail*) was the first Boeing-built aircraft to be given a name as well as a model designation. The latter would have another distinction – the last

"Monomail" took advantage of many new streamline techniques which gave it improved performance characteristics over the Model-40B biplanes. Absence of struts and wires cut down on drag, as did the engine cowling and partially retracted wheels.

single-engine commercial-type aircraft to be built by Boeing.

II

EDDIE Hubbard, who had become vice president of the Boeing Air Transport operation, died suddenly in December of 1928. But before his death, "Eddie" had stirred up considerable interest in a new plane for the airline. It was he who said: "The 80s are too damn big. It's like flying a barn door. I'd rather have a fleet of smaller planes, and faster. Speed is the showcase of air transportation . . ."

Eighteen months after his death, the kind of a plane he dreamed of came true, the *Monomail.* The project had been kept secret for months, but one day in the spring of 1930 a strange procession made its way from the plant site on the banks of the Duwamish to the new hangar at Seattle's King County Airport (appropriately named Boeing Field) which would become the center of Boeing's flight test operations. They were hauling the wings and the fuselage of the *Monomail* to the new hangar for final assembly.

What people saw didn't look like anything Boeing had ever built before. The fuselage was almost round. The wings were thick and tapered.

When the parts came together and the completed plane was rolled out for flight test, she was a thing of beauty and awe, a revolutionary design with streamlined features that looked like she could shoot through the air like an arrow. Even her color scheme was shocking – green fuselage, grey tail, orange wings. And on the side of her fuselage was the name MONOMAIL.

It was different, all right. No struts. No wires. The long conical fuselage cradled in the thick tapered wing, faired together like they were one. The single cockpit was located just in back and above the trailing edge of the wing. Enough space in the tube-like forward section of the fuselage to carry almost half her gross weight (8,000 pounds) in cargo and mail. Up front was a 575-horsepower Pratt & Whitney *Hornet* engine, hidden inside a streamlined cowling to give her a top speed of 158 miles per hour, almost as fast as the pursuit planes.

High-speed wings for the new five-cent Air Mail Stamp, that was her purpose and mission.

There were other features, too, that would come to light when she made her maiden flight on May 6, 1930. One of Boeing Air Transport's best pilots, Captain Edmund T. Allen (Another "Eddie" who would be-

Edmund T. "Eddie" Allen, Boeing test pilot. He believed test flying should be a science, not just "seat-of-the-pants" reaction.

come a legend at Boeing) was at the controls. And just about all Seattle turned out to see the first flight of this revolutionary new aircraft.

Curious eyes experienced anxious moments. Her propeller had an adjustable pitch feature for its blades. They could be set to take different sized "bites" of air to give the airfoil its greatest aerodynamic efficiency at various altitudes depending upon the density of the air. The *Monomail* was a test-bed for this innovation, a creation of the Hamilton Propeller people, part of the United Aircraft & Air Transport Corporation combine. It almost ruined her reputation before she had a chance to prove her prowess.

She got up and away like a beautiful bird. The pitch of the prop blades set for maximum lift for take-off. But upstairs, she was like a race horse chomping at the bit; she couldn't get up and go. The pitch was wrong for high speed, the "bite" of her prop blades ineffective. But the idea was far ahead of its time, beyond the state of art. And it did set men to thinking, contributing to the development of the controllable-pitch propeller that would solve the problem.

A new state of the art was beginning to emerge. The new plane dictated her own time for change.

Others, on the ground had some ideas that would alter the configuration of the *Monomail* and stimulate thinking in another direction. The new plane had not yet made its first flight when Congress passed the McNary-Watres Act (named for Senator Charles D. McNary of Oregon and Representative Lawrence H. Watres of Pennsylvania) an amendment to the famous Air Mail Act of 1925, which changed the whole rate-of-pay structure for the private operators flying the mail. Under the new law, mail pay got off the "rate-per-pound" scale. Henceforth, the operators got paid a fixed fee for base mile rate with a lot of extras for such things as two-way radio, passenger carrying capacity, over-the-mountains flying, night operations and other variables.

Original "Monomail" was exclusively a mail carrier. A later model was modified to carry passengers and mail. This United Air Lines "Monomail" carried four passengers and pilot. A stretched version could carry six. There was also an eight-passenger model.

Passengers boarding the "Monomail" endured some inconveniences, as shown here. Inside, too, the cabin was cramped. Even though the planes offered greatly increased speeds over the Model-80s and other bigger planes, the "Monomail" never caught on as popular airliner.

The *Monomail*, designed to carry mail exclusively, was virtually obsolete overnight. If it couldn't – and it couldn't – carry passengers, Boeing Air Transport was robbing itself of a lot of the fruits and all the gravy under the new Air Mail diet.

They stretched the fuselage and put in six seats, and they stretched it again to carry eight passengers. But only two planes were built. Put into service on the Cheyenne-Chicago segment of United Air Lines, the planes, despite their high-speed performance, drew criticism from passengers. They were too small, the quarters too cramped. Confinement was not compatible with comfort.

The idea for a larger airliner began to jell, a plane incorporating the streamline features, all-metal construction and performance of the *Monomail*, but designed for passenger comfort. To firm up the concept, Boeing Air Transport pilots were asked for their ideas of what the ultimate airliner should be like.

The survey produced some interesting ideas. Some said they preferred a trimotor like the 80 or the "Tin Goose" or the Fokker transports which seemed to be attracting more and more passengers. But they wanted all-metal construction with a streamline look, and sound-proofing, and high-performance. There were many pros and cons; possibles and impossibles.

One thing was unanimous: If they were

"Monomail" series was unique for Boeing in that planes never really went into a production model. There were many experimental versions, although basic configuration and structure were the same. This Model-221A tried out non-retractable undercarriage arrangement.

going to stay in the air transport business using Boeing-built equipment, they had to come up with something new and different.

The decision came down to go ahead with a new transport, and various design studies began to appear on paper. There were many influencing factors.

III

THE concept of the new airliner started out to be a trimotor, powered with a trio of the new Pratt & Whitney *Hornet* engines, a third again as much power as that of the *Wasps*. And they were talking about a plane of about 16,000 pounds gross weight, capable of carrying 12 passengers, a super deluxe cabin with plenty of space for mail and cargo. In one configuration it was a high-wing monoplane like the Ford trimotor and the Fokker. In another configuration it was a biplane like the Model-80 only it would be all-metal construction. Neither of these design studies got beyond the drawing board.

Pilots "flying the line" for Boeing Air Transport didn't like the idea of the 8-ton airliner, complaining that it was too heavy for the fields then in existence, unsafe for landings. They were also "sold" on the *Wasps*; the new *Hornets* were "too much for one guy to handle." Good for a bomber, maybe, but not for a transport. In respect to their judgment, plans for the new transport were scaled down – 12,000 pounds gross, 10-passengers, *Wasp* engines.

Perhaps, more than anything else it was a new bomber concept that in the end dictated the finalized configuration of the proposed new transport.

The project had been kept highly secret, but about the same time they started thinking seriously of building a new transport, the company had started building a revolutionary new bomber for the Army Air Corps. On April 12, 1931, the experimental bomber made its first flight.

Designated Model 215 (The Air Corps called it the XB-9) the plane was a twin-engined, low-wing monoplane. Outwardly, the XB-9 showed many resemblances to the *Monomail*. The wing span was greater by about 20 feet, and the fuselage about 10 feet longer. But in plan form the wings looked like that on the *Monomail*. The fuselage was round, "cigar-shaped" and structurally it was very similar. The rudder was almost identical.

But the twin-engine concept, with the engines mounted in nacelles sticking out of the leading edge of the wing, was revolutionary. In wind-tunnel tests at the NACA (National Advisory Committee for Aeronautics, forerunner of today's NASA) laboratory at Langley Field, Virginia, this arrangement indicated an aerodynamic "breakthrough". It increased propeller efficiency, a smoother flow of air over the airfoil without disruptive perturbance from a big bulky fuselage as with the *Monomail*. Performance proved the point.

On a flight from Seattle to Dayton, Ohio via Cheyenne and Chicago the XB-9 averaged 158 miles per hour. Turned over to Army Air Corps test pilots at Wright Field, the new Air Corps Materiel Division and test center, the plane hit a top speed of 185-mph, faster than the fastest pursuit plane of that period.

In early 30s Boeing introduced this low-wing, twin-engined, all-metal bomber design, the XB-9 called the "flying cigar." Prototypes were entirely company-financed. Design and its performance surprised even Air Corps people, who bought it.

Original XB-9 was modified to include retractable landing gear, different rudder and many new streamlined features. Designated, YB-9A (shown here) the new bomber, overnight, virtually made old Air Corps biplane bombers obsolete. Note "trim tab" on rudder.

There is no question that the XB-9 revolutionized military thinking about bomber designs. Of more import to this narrative, perhaps, it thrust the Boeing Airplane Company into design and development of larger planes. The "Big Plane Concept" was growing. At a gross weight of 13,600 pounds, the XB-9 was the biggest plane Boeing had ever built up to that time.

The truth is, it created an "engineering enigma" at the plant on the shores of the Duwamish. There was great anticipation and expectation of a sizeable production order for the XB-9 design. That meant gearing up for big plane assembly. At the same time, the performance of the XB-9 threw out a new kind of challenge. If the bomber were faster than the pursuits for which Boeing was famous, it meant coming up with a better, faster pursuit plane. It was a time for big decisions.

What happened had its irony. Glenn Martin came into the picture again. If Bill Boeing and Conrad Westerveldt in 1916 could "copy" the old Martin seaplane to a great extent in their design of the "B&W", then Martin could "copy" the XB-9 fifteen years later. And Martin did.

In an Air Corps competition at Wright Field, a new twin-engine, low-wing Martin entry, the XB-10, won the big production order for bombardment aircraft. The Boeing B-9, for all its high-performance and revolutionary ideas, was relegated to a secondary role. Boeing got the scraps from the table; a small production order for several

In competition at Wright Field, Martin XB-10 bomber won over XB-9 design, and later version, B-12 (above) went into production to become "backbone" of bombardment service squadrons in mid-thirties. Martin had very unusual "bird-cage" bombardier/gunner position in nose.

This famous Boeing P-26 low-wing pursuit plane was the last of a long line of fighters. Boeing turned to bombers.

service-test YB-9 bombers. The twin-engined bomber died almost before it learned to live.

But the twin-engine concept did not die.

With the know-how and production experience gleaned from the bomber project, there emerged new thinking about the transport proposal. *Why not a twin-engined transport along the lines of the bomber?*

If you could start a revolution in bombardment aviation, why not start a revolution in air transport?

The decision had already been reached to go ahead with a new pursuit plane to catch the Martin B-10 and B-12 high-speed bombers and keep pursuit aviation alive. It was a low-wing design, the prototype of the famous P-26s destined to become our front-line air defense, and maintain Boeing's prestige in the pursuit plane category.

The decision to build the new transport came when the big United Aircraft and Transport Corporation, with Bill Boeing still at its helm, began to feel the competition in its airline venture. The United Air Lines group was being challenged by a new coast-to-coast operator, Transcontinental & Western Air, Inc. (the former TAT "Lind-

New coast-to-coast airline, Transcontinental & Western Air, Inc. was challenge to United Air Lines group. Bigger, improved Ford trimotors like this one with ring cowlings, outsped Boeing 80s. For first time TWA began to appear in big letters on planes.

Competition got even rougher when TWA introduced large four-engined Fokker F-32s like this Universal Airlines' plane. Note arrangement using pusher and tractor engines mounted in nacelles hanging from struts under wings. The F-32s were covered with plywood and fabric.

bergh Line") starting to operate bigger and faster Ford trimotors and four-engined Fokker F-32s which outclassed the Model-80s. The airline business was getting to be a dog-eat-dog operation. To maintain its top position the UAL group had to do something.

Boeing accepted the challenge.

IV

SHE was a thing of beauty, the new passenger transport that took to the sky from Boeing Field on February 8, 1933 and winged out over Puget Sound. They called it the Model 247, Boeing's answer to the competition. An outgrowth of the *Monomail* and the XB-9 bomber, she was sleek and trim and her metallic grey skin glistened in the bright sun's rays. The Model 247 was a complete break with the past, the ultimate in streamlining techniques, sheer luxury aloft, the prototype of wings to come. Air Travel would never be the same; today was catching up with tomorrow.

She was the first streamlined all-metal, twin-engine transport, slightly smaller than the Ford trimotors, the Fokker trimotors and the Boeing Model-80s, but what she lacked in size she made up for in performance and the innovations she brought to transport design. Capable of carrying ten passengers – five seats in a row on each side of a center aisle in a sound-proofed cabin – a pilot and co-pilot up front in an enclosed cockpit and a stewardess, she was the airline operator's "dream plane" come true.

Her twin engine arrangement (Pratt & Whitney *Wasps* ranging in horsepower from 550 to 625-hp as the model series pro-

Boeing Model 247 was truly first of modern airliners. When United started flying 247s, the plane was fastest airliner in the sky.

Inside the 247 there were two rows of seats, five on each side of a narrow aisle. Cabin was sound-proofed and considered very "posh-posh" for its period. Large windows were a delight. Main wing spar ran right through cabin, and aisle-walkers had to step over it.

gressed) proved to be more economical than the trimotors.

The engines were mounted in streamlined nacelles ahead of the leading edge of

"Up front", Model 247 carried a crew of two, pilot and co-pilot in side-by-side seating arrangement. Instrument panel (above) was more complex than that on the old Model-40A, as one can see. Plane incorporated latest flight aids and navigational equipment.

Passengers boarded the 247 through door in right side of fuselage. This model had special ring-type cowling. It was first plane to go into service carrying passengers, even though, it was still classed as "X-perimental". Boeing Air Transport, Inc. emblem was still in use.

the wing (an aerodynamic advantage gleaned from the XB-9 bomber design) and they were enclosed in the latest NACA cowlings, the two features combining to give her a cruising speed 50 to 70 miles per hour faster than any other airliner of her period. She was also one of the first airliners to have a retractable landing gear (like the *Monomail*) and she was equipped with one of the first controllable-pitch propellers in an air transport. She had de-icing devices on the leading edge of the wings and horizontal tail surfaces. And she was the first airliner to have an automatic pilot installation, a third, unseen, crew member up front as insurance against pilot fatigue.

Upon closer observation, there was something else, a Boeing innovation that can well be called the "key" to future big plane designs. They called it "trim tab control." Small moveable surfaces (tab-like) on the

This was scene at Boeing factory when 247s went into production. Other planes are Navy fighters. United Air Lines' order for sixty planes was biggest commercial airline equipment investment up to that time. It was beginning of new era for air transport.

United Air Lines' fleet of 247s, made the "mainline" operation the largest and best equipped in the air transport industry. In this photograph, three of UAL's planes are flying in close formation over Chicago. Each Model-247 cost approximately $68,000.

elevators, ailerons and rudder which used the airstream itself to help move the large control surfaces. Pilots no longer would have to be Supermen to move the control column (stick) and rudder pedals, irregardless of the size of the control surfaces. A small thing, it was nevertheless, one of her greatest contributions to the state of the art.

But it was really her speed that changed things. Overnight, she cut the coast-to-coast travel time from 27 hours to 19½ hours with seven stops across the continent. In this respect, alone, she put the spotlight on air transportation with its tremendous advantage in time-saving over all other forms of transport.

For the Boeing Airplane Company, she was just what the doctor ordered to heal the hurt of the lost bomber competition. United Aircraft & Transport Corporation (the Boeing/Rentschler combine) placed a $4,000,000 order to buy sixty of the new planes as standard equipment on its coast-to-coast airline. The cost was $68,000 per plane, but the advantage was wellworth the capital risk.

When United Air Lines replaced its Model-80s with the new fleet of Model 247s, it virtually "monopolized" transcontinental air travel. Passengers flocked to the ticket counters to take advantage of the new "three-mile-a-minute" airliners. There was nothing in the skies that could offer anything comparable in service, safety and speed.

The future never looked brighter. It was Bill Boeing's shining hour. For the design and development of "the modern airliner", a stellar achievement in aircraft design and manufacture and the furthering of air transport, he was recipient of the Guggenheim Medal, one of aviation's highest awards.

About the time the first Model 247s went into scheduled service in the summer of 1933, Boeing decided to retire from active participation in the company he had founded. It was the fulfillment of a promise he had made to himself — to retire when he was fifty and catch up on his hunting and fishing and sailing. He was fifty-one when he stepped down as head of the United Aircraft & Transport Corp. activities. It was up to Fred Rentschler, Claire Egtvedt and Phil Johnson and others to carry on. They faced some unexpected developments.

V

"THE impact of the 247 on the United Air Lines group had the effect of a boomerang," Fred Rentschler would say later. "It was so far ahead of its time that it virtually obliterated all competition." To keep in the race other airlines, namely TWA, had to do something to improve their now obsolete equipment. Logically, they turned to Boeing wanting to place an order for the new trans-

TWA's answer to the United Air Lines' high-speed 247 transports was this Douglas-built, DC-1 airliner. It was twelve-passenger, low-wing, all-metal transport, bigger and roomier than the Boeings. Plane here, "Old 300," was first of a long line of DC-family airliners.

port. The answer was NO, not until the sixty planes were completed for United Air Lines.

As a result,TWA turned to other manufacturers to come up with a competitive design. There was the boomerang. The Douglas Aircraft Company of Santa Monica, California accepted the challenge and introduced in a very short time, its DC-2 airliner, faster and roomier than the 247. There

Interior of the DC-1 (prototype of the DC-2 airliners) was more spacious than cabin of the Boeing 247. Wide aisle, the absence of wing spar bisecting cabin, and height of cabin made the DC skyliner very popular. Douglas transports were also faster than 247.

Only one of the Douglas DC-1 was built. But TWA was quick to put into service improved DC-2s which were larger and faster. The DC-2 could carry fourteen passengers, a crew of two up front. Its size, speed and luxury appointments made 247s virtually obsolete.

followed an even larger, DC-3, 21-passenger Douglas airliner. Lockheed Aircraft Corporation also got into the picture with its twin-engined 10-passenger *Electra* and the 14-passenger *Lodestar*. And the race was on to build the best commercial airliner in the spirit of the American free-enterprise competitive system. In time, it would give the United States undisputed leadership in the air transport field and help forge today's world-wide system of air transport.

It has been said, and rightly so, that the Model 247's greatest contribution was to "light the fuse" that brought into being the new and revolutionary transport designs. Indeed, the Douglas and Lockheed designs looked very much like puffed-up versions of the original 247 design. But each in its own way introduced features that improved the end product of air transportation. The modern airliner was here to stay. With it a whole new industry was born, the business of scheduled air transportation.

For its pioneering effort and splendid safety record, the Boeing 247 earned its rightful place in Aviation's Hall of Fame. Altogether, there were 75 of the Model 247 series built. One was a "flying test bed" for new Pratt & Whitney powerplants. Others

In 1935, American Airlines, a new transcontinental competitor, introduced the popular DST, Douglas Sleeper Transport. It was 21-passenger dayplane, the popular DC-3. As a sleeper, it provided Pullman-sized berths for 14 passengers. More than 1500 DC-3 are still flying.

Modified Boeing 247-D called "Nip and Tuck", piloted by famous flyer, Colonel Roscoe Turner, shown here, won world-wide recognition in 1934 London-to-Melbourne Air Derby. Turner and Clyde Pangborn completed flight, but placed behind British and Dutch entries.

were sold to private companies as executive aircraft and for promotional purposes. Another won recognition when it placed third in the famous London-to-Melbourne race piloted by Colonel Roscoe Turner and Clyde Pangborn. Still another, with armour plate and machine guns, was sold to a Chinese war lord.

During World War II, thirteen were modified as cargo planes designated C-73s and performed as personnel transports and cargo carriers. There are claims even, that two of the planes sold to the German *Lufthansa* airline, in the mid-thirties, never did go into airline service, but were taken apart piece by piece and studied closely to influence the design of a twin-engined Nazi bomber.

Here at home during the war years, United Air Lines used another as a research airplane to study static interference and probe thunder storms with resultant improvements in airborne communications and meteorological forecasting.

As late as the summer of 1968, the author flew in one of the remaining 247s operated by Island Airlines of Port Clinton, Ohio. Others are reported still flying in South America.

What a plane she was, that Boeing Model 247 that made her first public appearance on static display at the "Century of Progress," the Chicago World's Fair in 1933.

She was in herself a symbol of progress.

If there was anything wrong with her, it was too much progress in too big a dose. There were cries of "monopoly", and the finger was pointed at the United Aircraft & Transport Corporation. She stirred up a "hornet's nest."

The bigger planes, the DC-2s and DC-3s and others she forced into creation, served their purpose, too. They taught Boeing a lesson which probably more than anything

During World War II, some Model-247s were designated C-73 cargo planes, and used by Air Transport Command. They flew from bases all over the world. Repeated many times was this scene as ATC pilots prepare to take off. So far as is known two of the planes are still flying.

else one day would have its influence in the decision to build the 747 *Super jet*.

It was Phil Johnson, whom Bill Boeing had hired to work on the first production

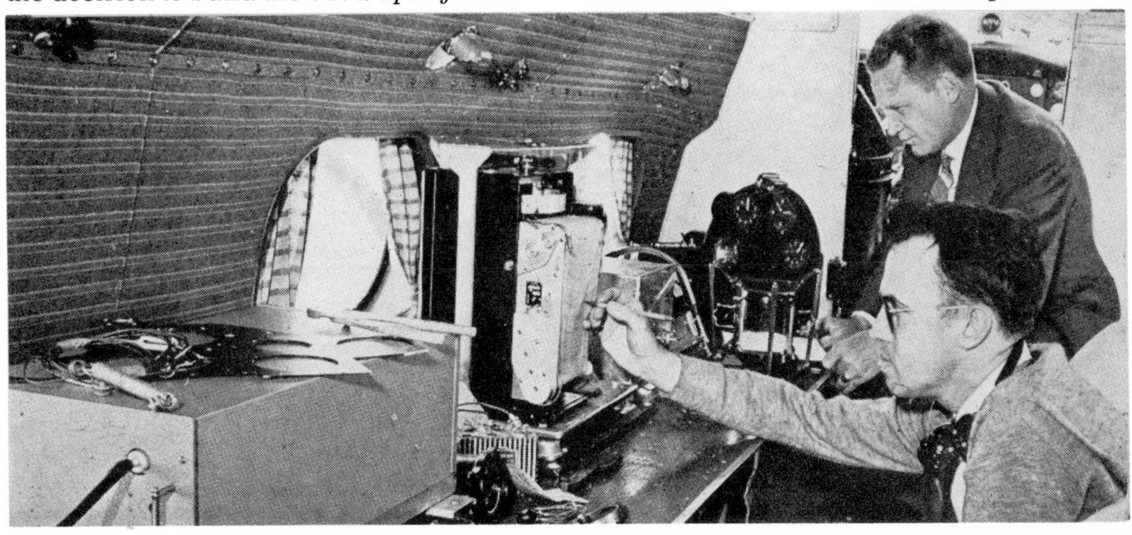

During late thirties, United Air Lines equipped its last Model-247 as a "flying laboratory" to study effect of electrical storms on airborne radio communications. Crew of scientists in this plane chased thunderstorms all over the sky to get the answers.

Inside United Air Lines 247, "flying laboratory" the "storm chasers" used special equipment and instruments to check various atmospheric conditions and effects on radio communications. They found many unknowns, which later contributed to safer flying for everybody.

Model-C trainers for the Navy back in 1917, who bore the brunt of the lesson learned. Johnson was head of the United Air Lines group when the plans for the Model 247 were jelled. Perhaps, even then, he saw the handwriting on the wall.

"When we scaled down the proposed transport design from the twelve-passenger plane with the more powerful P&W *Hornet* engines," Johnson would say in reflection, "the 247 was doomed almost before it left the drawing board!"

In the near future, all he could do to "soup-up" the 247s wasn't enough to meet the competition of the new Douglas skyliners. Never again would Boeing be afraid to tackle a big plane concept. And the chance would come sooner than anyone expected. But first, there was some very rough air ahead.

CHAPTER FIVE

Four Engines Instead Of Two!

"GENERAL," said the President of the United States, "I think I've got a job for your boys, if you think they can handle it."

Franklin Delano Roosevelt was talking.

Across from him in the White House sat Major General Benjamin D. Foulois, then Chief of the Army Air Corps. "Benny" Foulois, whom the Wright Brothers had taught to fly in the first military airplane, outwardly, was excited and delighted to be there with his Commander-in-Chief. It was the first time since taking office in 1933 that Roosevelt, a former Undersecretary of the Navy, had shown any personal interest in the air arm of the military services.

The President noticed this pleased attitude in his air chieftain and got right to the point.

"Remember, Benny, when the Army Air Service innaugurated the scheduled air mail back in 1918?" FDR asked, recalling that he had been present to see the first mail plane takeoff.

Foulois nodded, puffed pridefully, his small stature growing suddenly tall even though he had not been personally involved.

Maj. Gen. Benjamin D. Foulois, who was Chief of The Army Air Corps in 1934 when army fliers took over job of flying the mail.

Roosevelt continued: "Well, Benny, I want your boys to take over, and start flying the mail again. Are they ready?"

"Yes, sir," Foulois replied. He knew it was an order.

It was an answer he would later regret. But at the moment the General was thinking only of the welfare of the service he so dearly loved. The Air Corps, long a stepchild of the Army and Navy, desperately needed more appropriations for new equipment, public recognition and moral support. And here was an opportunity, Foulois believed, to show Congress, the President and the people his men and planes were in readiness for any emergency, and worthy of more financial attention in future budget considerations. The General was anxious to prove a point.

"How soon can you begin?" Roosevelt wanted to know.

"In about ten days . . ."

The meeting broke up shortly after that, but the same afternoon, Friday, February 9, 1934, Roosevelt drafted White House Order No. 6591 and signed it. The order cancelled all domestic Air Mail contracts in the hands of private airline operators, created its own national emergency in this respect, and directed that army fliers fly the mail. The deadline for the civilian operators to turn over the reins was midnight, February 19.

It was an unprecedented move, but one the President had been wanting to make ever since the New Deal had come into power, and he had learned there was a possibility of another "Teapot Dome" scandal which he could blame on the previous Republican Administration. FDR was playing politics; at which he was most adept.

In recent months, a Senate investigation, headed by Alabama's Senator Hugo L. Black (The Black Committee Hearings)

"Teddy" Roosevelt was first U.S. President to take an airplane ride with Archie Hoxsey at St. Louis Air Meet in 1910. Here, 22 years later, Franklin D. Roosevelt deplanes from Ford Trimotor to attend Democratic Convention in Chicago, and accept nomination, 1932.

had turned up some highly explosive information regarding the awarding of lucrative mail contracts to the civilian air carriers under terms of the McNary-Watres Act of 1930. During the hearings, there were cries of "graft," "collusion," "profiteering" and "favoritism" which convinced FDR's advisors there was enough evidence to warrant clipping the wings of the culprits. In the air postal service, politicos saw an excellent whipping post.

The cancellation order involved more than 27,000 miles of air mail routes flown by privately-owned airline companies, among them, of course, the United Air Lines group. Unfortunately, the directive came at a time when The Boeing Airplane Company and its business partner, United Air Lines, were already having big problems. In Seattle, with the production order for sixty Model 247s almost finished and an unexpected reversal of interest in a new Army pursuit plane and Navy fighter which turned thumbs down on both designs, they were laying off men. First quarter earnings for United Air Lines were heading for a half million dollar loss; the new Douglas DC-2 transport was taking customers away from the slower and smaller 247. Business was bleak.

There were plans for a larger two-engined transport, and some discussion about a new bomber model. But FDR's order dropped a bomb into the scheme of things. It threw the air transport industry into a state of chaos and confusion. Likewise, the airframe, engine and propeller manufacturers were also affected. Nobody was sure of anything, and all Hell broke loose.

When the Army fliers did start flying the mail, things got worse, not better. In the first week, five pilots were dead, six others critically injured, eight planes completely washed out; property damage was more than $300,000. Over-anxious to make a good showing, Army officers had sent their brave fliers up in the worst flying weather on record for a decade, a week of blinding blizzards and vicious gales.

The public was shocked, stunned, horrified, and Congress was buried under an avalanche of protests demanding something be done to stop the slaughter. General Foulois ordered his men to fly only

Public reaction to army fliers flying the mail brought this kind of editorial comment: McClelland Barclay's interpretation of "death toll" and sacrifice is depicted in this illustration. The drawing appeared in Aero Digest magazine during period of Air Mail cancellation.

during daylight hours and only under favorable weather conditions. Still, there were more crashes, more deaths.

Finally, on March 10, one month and a day after he had signed the cancellation order, FDR announced the abandonment of the Air Mail Service. All planes were grounded for eight days for the installation of new equipment. He also announced that flying the mail would be returned to civilian operators as soon as a satisfactory arrangement could be worked out.

The Army had done its thing; but flying the mail wasn't its bag. Notwithstanding the loss of life (twelve pilots were killed altogether) the Army experiment cost almost $4,000,000. It has been called FDR's first big blunder. But if there was anything good that came out of it, the tragic record of the Army flying the mail pin-pointed the need for new Air Corps equipment. And it caused Congress to take a closer look at the commercial aviation picture, and pass new laws.

The Black-McKellar Bill (The Air Mail Act of 1934, passed June 12 of that year) for better or worse, calmed the turbulent sky, at least temporarily. But even so, it was pretty mixed up, giving air transportation three bosses: (1) The Post Office Department to determine routes and schedules. (2) The Interstate Commerce Commission to fix rates and payments for flying the mail. (3) The Bureau of Air Commerce, as in the past, to be responsible for the airways system, license planes and pilots. Moreover, the new Act ordered the airline companies to completely separate themselves from any affiliation with aircraft manufacturers.

The latter was the blow that hit Boeing the hardest. The big United Aircraft and Air Transport combine – the "dream" of Bill Boeing and Fred Rentschler which had done so much to improve planes, engines and propellers and build a profitable airline system – had to be broken up. Out of it came three new companies, each independent corporations – United Air Lines, United Aircraft Corporation and The Boeing Airplane Company which also included Stearman Aircraft in Wichita, Kansas.

Ironically, it was The Air Mail Act of 1925 that lured Boeing into the airline business with the formation of Boeing Air

Transport, and it was The Air Mail Act of 1934 that made Boeing give up its air carrier operation. Boeing of Seattle was back where it had started, solely in "the business of building planes."

Once more the company was almost broke, could hardly meet its payroll. Claire Egtvedt, who had taken over as head of the company when Bill Boeing retired less than a year before, had a big job cut out for him.

It would almost take a miracle.

II

THERE was a "miracle" in the making. In Washington and in Dayton, Ohio at the Air Corps Material Division, the latter charged with the design and development and testing of all new army aircraft and equipment, a group of far-sighted Air Corps officers were taking a long look at future air power requirements. Nor were they, like most of the country, blind to some strange happenings around the world. Trouble in the Orient, where Japan had invaded Manchuria. Germany had quit the League of Nations and had a new leader in Adolf Hitler, whose Nazi Party was stirring up things. The threat of an Italian invasion of Ethiopia was imminent. Mussolini was rattling the sword. Aware of these events, the "youngbloods" of the Air Corps were thinking of a different kind of air force – long-range bombers to protect our territorial possessions of Hawaii and Alaska. Everything was *top secret*, but the die was cast.

We find Claire Egtvedt in May of 1934 in Dayton, invited there by the Air Corps chiefs to talk about a new bomber project. He could hardly believe what he was hearing. The Air Corps wanted a plane with *a range of 5,000 miles, capable of carrying 2,000 pounds of bombs, heavily armed to fend for itself without a fighter escort.* The Air Corps people had some money they could spend for engineering studies for such a plane. Both Boeing and Martin (because of the B-9 and B-10 bombers) were invited to submit plans. If so, they had thirty days to come up with a design proposal. The best design would win the contract to build this "super dreadnaught" of the skies. One plane, strictly an experiment, to see *how big* was practical and possible.

There was $600,000, "all our eggs in one basket," said the Air Corps planners, for the winner in the design contest.

"Project A", they called it, and back in Seattle behind closed doors Boeing engineers kept the midnight oil burning to meet the deadline. To get the range, which meant a gigantic plane for fuel space, alone, there was no choice with existing powerplants, but to design around *four engines instead of two!*

Right on schedule, the plans were ready for Air Corps consideration. It was the biggest, boldest step yet – a plane with a wing span half the length of a football field, a total of 4,000 horsepower, four engines of 1,000 horsepower each, a plane that would weigh (gross) in the neighborhood of 70,000 pounds. Boeing Model 294, "the impossible dream."

The word came back. Boeing had won the contract.

Project A, the XBLR-1 (Experimental Bomber, Long Range, Number 1), Boeing Model 294, became the XB-15.

Work had barely started on a wooden "mock-up" when there was another request from Wright Field. Wanted: *A new bomber to go into production. Range, 1,020 miles, top speed of 250 miles per hour, a 2,000-pound bomb load, a crew of four to six.* Not the size of the XB-15, but a plane that could meet these requirements, and there would be a production order for 220 planes awarded on a competitive test basis. But this time, the companies interested, had to put up their own money for design and engineering and construction of the first plane. Entries had to be on the flight line at Wright Field by August, 1935. Boeing wanted to take a crack at that competition, too.

Money was scarce, but they'd get it from somewhere. A design study was started, Model 299. What happened, we'll discuss in the next chapter.

But first, let's take a closer look at the XB-15 project and its impact on The Boeing Airplane Company and the future of air power and air transport.

The "mock-up" was an indication of the size of the task. A fuselage 87 feet, 7 inches long with a *flight deck*, not just a *cockpit;* places for a pilot and co-pilot, a radio opera-

Highly secret, "Project A" emerged as Boeing Model 294, later designated as Army Air Corps super bomber, XB-15. It was first of really BIG modern aircraft designs. Only one was ever built. Plane carried 30-ton payload to set world's record at Wright field, 1939.

tor, navigator, and a *flight engineer* at his own console to assist the pilots with engine operation and other auxiliary functions like flaps, a retractable landing gear, de-

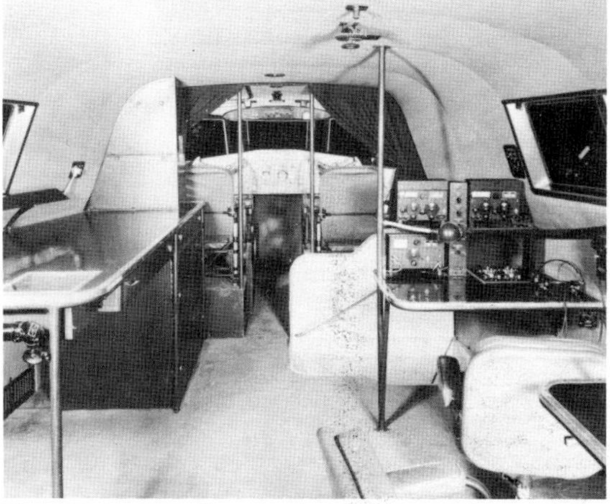

The XB-15 was first Boeing design to incorporate "flight deck" for crew, pilot, co-pilot, navigator, radio operator and flight engineer.

icers, cabin heating, "booster" controls. Bunks for the crew members. A kitchenette or "galley", six machine gun turrets, lavatories. Such things had never been built-in before ("too fantastic") but there she was, a virtual "flying battleship," curtained-off for secrecy, the wooden-mock-up was being

XB-15 bristled with armament, truly a "battleship of the air." Men working on top turret give idea of tremendous size of plane.

Barling bomber of the mid-twenties was "dream plane" of famed Billy Mitchell. Note the multi-wheeled undercarriage to spread the weight.

turned into a metal monster. The wing, 149 feet long in final form, was coming together in two huge panels. "The big spars, stressed and braced with structural members looked like Bridge beams," said one Boeing engineer. "Scaffolding around the wings and fuselage made the whole place look like a shipyard, not an airplane factory."

BIG planes weren't new. As far back as 1913, Igor Sikorsky, a Russian engineer, (who in 1940 would become the "father of the modern helicopter") designed and built a giant four-engined biplane, the *Grand*, for Czar Nicholas. It had a 92-foot wing span and weighed over four tons. The early twenties saw the first "super bomber" in the lumbering, six-engined Barling (three wings mounted one above the other) built for the U.S. Air Service, a "dream" of Billy Mitchell's. Underpowered, the Barling never amounted to much, ended up as a gunnery target. Biggest plane of the early thirties, about the time the Air Corps brass started thinking of "Project A", was the Swiss-built, Dornier DOX, a 169-passenger flying boat sponsored by the German airline Lufthansa. The DOX had a wing span of 157 feet, was powered with twleve engines (six pushers and six pullers in tandem pairs) and weighed 105,000 pounds.

Igor Sikorsky, better known as the "father of the helicopter" built this huge plane, "LeGrande" for Czar Nicholas of Russia in 1913.

Germany's Lufthansa airline, first foreign carrier to buy the 747 had ideas about trans-Atlantic air service as far back as 1929 when it sponsored development of this Dornier DOX flying boat. Plane also had "flight deck," and it could carry more than 160 passengers.

One of the engine nacelles on the Boeing XB-15 bomber was larger than the fuselage of biggest pursuit plane in 1939. Special doors permitted mechanics to crawl into nacelle and make repairs. The XB-15 was flying "test-bed" for first 1,000-hp radial engines.

But the XB-15 was different. It was really the first of the big planes to use the latest state of the art; new manufacturing techniques, modern streamlining and high performance powerplants. In this respect, it was a new concept, a new challenge from drawing board to delivery apron.

Men had never worked before in forming such large metal parts. They had to design special tooling, of course, and sometimes, the tooling design was tougher to whip than the aerodynamic problems with the plane itself. Large, grotesque machinery appeared in the Seattle facility on the Duwamish. Boeing was tooling up to build big planes. XB-15 was the big test.

Could they build a plane this big? Would it fly?

They did, and it did. On October 15, 1937 – 42 months almost to the day after Boeing's plans for the XBLR-design competition were submitted at Wright Field – XB-15, with test pilot Eddie Allen on the Flight Deck at the controls, lifted off the runway at Boeing Field. The XB-15 was a very remarkable airplane. And in the months ahead she passed every test demanded of her with flying colors.

But her greatest contribution was providing the "know-how" to build big plane structures. In this field, the Boeing Airplane Company with its experience gleaned from *Project A,* jumped way out ahead of other manufacturers.

In building BIG planes there was a big future ahead.

III

JUAN Terry Trippe and William Edward Boeing both were educated at Yale University; Boeing with the class of '04 and Trippe seventeen years later. Whether they were brought together in future years by this old school tie is probably debat-

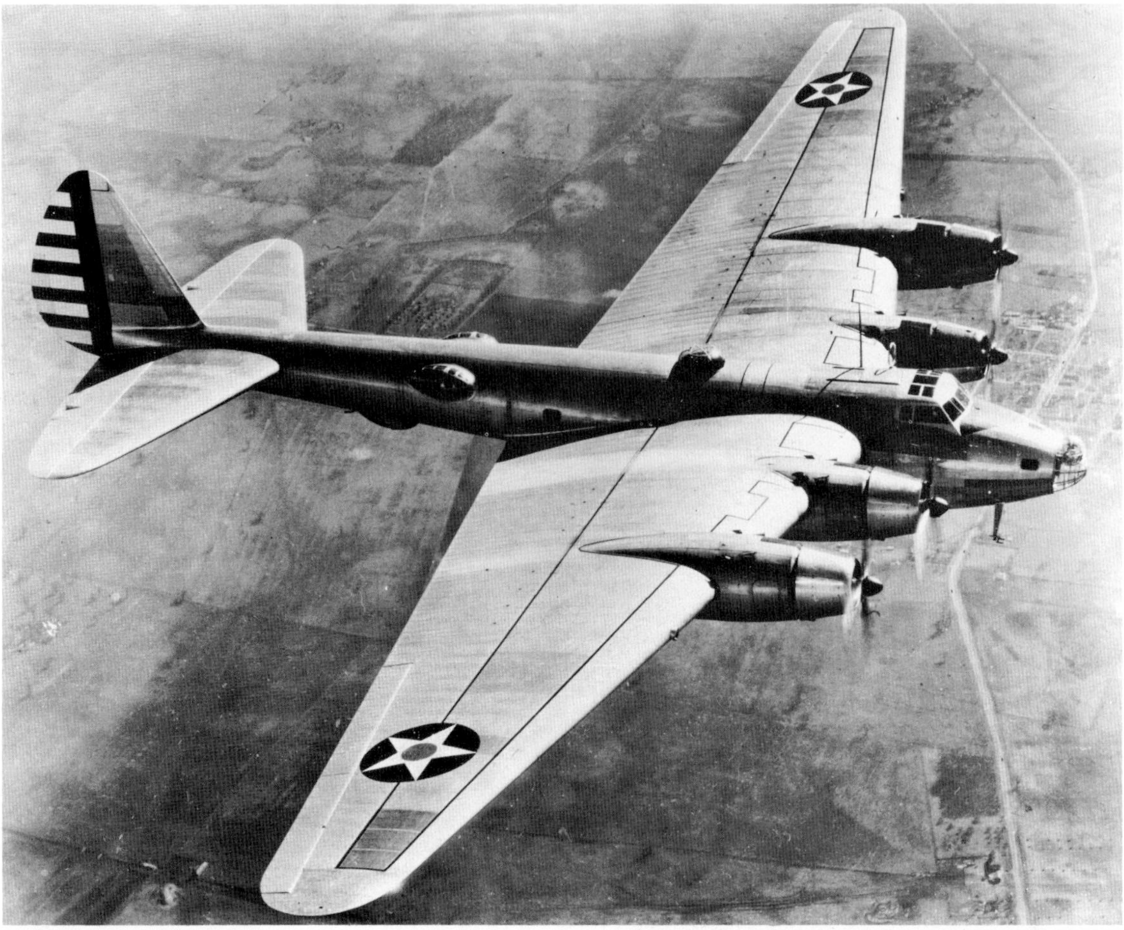

XB-15 was first flown in fall of 1937. Although it was first Boeing four-engined design to go into the shops, it flew after the famous XB-17 "Flying Fortress." The massive wing and nacelle arrangement, shown here, were later used in design of famous "Flying Clipper" series.

able, but it seems likely that each followed the other's career in commercial air transport, particularly in the formative years of our fledgling airline system. Bill Boeing, as we know, formed Boeing Air Transport in 1927 and about the same time Juan Trippe took over the helm at Pan American World Airways. By 1934 Boeing Air Transport was a leader in the domestic field of air transport and Pan-Am was blazing air routes around South America and planning air service across the Atlantic and Pacific Oceans. And even though Bill Boeing had retired from active participation, the Boeing Airplane Company and Pan-Am were destined to get together. The latter was looking for a large flying boat design for its transoceanic conquests. It seems safe to assume that Boeing and Trippe (through their Yale Alumni relationship, if nothing else) talked about the idea.

Pan American World Airways' Juan Trippe (left) and Charles A. Lindbergh, played major role in selection of Boeing Model 314 flying boats.

Model 314 Boeing "Clipper." Cabin was divided into "step-level" compartments to conform to hull shape. Wing and engines were same as those on XB-15. Pan Am sponsored development with $3,000,000 order. Big planes pioneered regular scheduled Atlantic service.

At any rate, on June 21, 1936, Pan American World Airways signed a $3,000,000 contract with the Boeing Airplane Company for six large flying boats with an option for six more.

That order launched the Boeing company in the production of super transports for commercial operation, a role it would never relinquish even up to the present time. And significantly, it was thirty years later that Pan American announced it was buying 25 747 *Superjets* which undoubtedly influenced The Boeing Company to put the new "queen of the skies" into production.

But let's go back for a moment and see what happened in 1936 to get the first really big plane production program rolling with the design and development of the Boeing Model 314 flying boats, first of the line of the famous Pan-Am *"Flying Clippers"*.

The XB-15 (Project A) was the key that opened the door to the new opportunity. Even as the huge *Superbomber* went together, engineers were thinking how the big wing could support a flying boat hull, and already there were more powerful engines that could meet fuel and payload requirements for a transoceanic sky ship. Moreover, they were confident now of working with big plane structures.

Then, too, there was that old haunting feeling that the company was getting back into the same old rut of building nothing but military planes. Why not use the XB-15 *know-how* to build a king-sized airliner? Those big wings should be airlifting passengers, mail and cargo, not a payload of bombs.

As always there was the problem of money to finance such a project. But wasn't the XB-15 experience, money in the bank?

The reorganization of Boeing Airplane Company (forced by the new Air Mail Act that broke up United Aircraft and Air Transport) had put some new "idea" men in high places. Among them was Wellwood Beall, a graduate of the Guggenheim School of Aeronautics at New York University and chief engineering instructor at the Boeing School of Aeronautics in Oakland, who moved up from sales to engineering where he probably should have been in the first place. And Fred Collins, who had done so much to force the Model-80 into being, was now promoted to sales manager. Both were pushing Claire Egtvedt hard for a new commercial airliner project.

Beall, on his own time, started working up some preliminary designs for a flying

Wellwood Beall, who is generally credited with engineering design of first Boeing "Clipper" models. He pushed hard for big boats.

boat; the XB-15 wing and nacelles and tail gave him a good start. Competition spurred him on. Glenn Martin was in the picture again, building a big boat for Pan American. If Boeing were to get in the race, now was the time.

"Go ahead," Claire Egtvedt said.

Beall's boat became a reality.

Flown first on June 7, 1938, Model 314, the new Boeing "Clipper," had a wing span of 152 feet, the same airfoil and plan form as the XB-15 wing. Her boat-hull fuselage (106 feet long) looked like a giant whale. She had a Flight Deck, engineer's station, bunks for the crew. And she could carry 74 passengers in one configuration; 40 passengers as a sleeper. A crew of ten, and there was plenty of room for cargo.

Designated Boeing Model 314 she had a gross weight of 82,500 pounds, more than the XB-15, a better than 15-ton payload in fuel, passengers and cargo. More important, she had a range of 3500 miles and a crusing speed of 180 miles per hour.

There were several changes in her basic configuration; a single tail at first, then a double tail and finally she emerged with three rudders. That latter, Model 314A, had more powerful engines and could carry 1200 gallons more fuel, increasing the range. This latter factor gave her the lead role in pioneering Trans-Atlantic air travel.

These Boeing Clippers cost about $700,000 apiece. They took some 350,000 man-hours to build. But they were worth all of this and more. For Pan-American on the Trans-Atlantic run they saved the day.

In race for Pan American orders Boeing had red hot competition from Glenn Martin. This four-engined Martin flying boat pioneered Pan Am Pacific routes. Martin was building much larger flying boat at the time that Boeing Model 314s appeared, but Boeing got contract.

Model 314 "Clippers" went through many changes even in the experimental stage. This is "NX" basic design, but with triple rudder arrangement. Note also, the similarity of the "flight deck" with that of the XB-15 bomber. Passenger accommodations were luxurious.

Juan Trippe had made a deal with Portugal so Pan American could fly the southern route across the Atlantic via the Azores to Lisbon, about 2400 miles. With its Sikorsky and Martin Clippers Pan-Am was already flying this distance from San Francisco to Honolulu and then island-hopping – Midway, Wake, Guam, Manila and on to Hong Kong. The "China Clippers" linked the Western World with the Orient. Mail and passengers could fly from San Francisco to Manila in five days. It took three weeks by surface vessel. But the Atlantic offered a new challenge.

On the westward flight, the Martin flying boats proposed to start the service, simply didn't have the range without a stop at Bermuda. That is, and carry any kind of payload.

But Trippe could not get landing rights for Bermuda from the British government.

The new Boeing Model 314 flying boats delivered late in 1938 could beat the British ban. They had the range, these super Boeings, to by-pass Bermuda. Moreover, they could carry a crew of ten (the long flight required crew shifts) and 24 passengers on the flight from the Azores to New York. At last, regular scheduled trans-Atlantic air service was possible.

On May 19, 1939 a certificate of "public convenience and necessity" required by law was granted to Pan American for the new Boeings to start operation. Next day with Captain Michael Laporte in command *Yankee Clipper* (a Boeing Model 314) took off from a dock facility near LaGuardia Field, New York on the first scheduled commercial flight to Lisbon, Marseilles and Southamption. The flight was com-

Boeing Model 314 flying boat, "Atlantic Clipper" carried VIPs, including Winston Churchill, across the Atlantic in World War II. One Boeing "Clipper" made historic round-the-world flight to escape capture by Japanese after Pearl Harbor attack. Ships were slow but could carry big payload.

pleted without incident.

Juan Trippe, according to his biographer Matthew Josephson (*"Empire of the Air," Juan Trippe and The Struggle for World Airways, Harcourt Brace & Co., 1944)* would say: "Think of it, now we have the right of way to fly around the world. The papers are in a safe up at the office."

He might have added, "and the equipment to make it possible" with a nod of thanks to the Boeing Airplane Company for the development of the Model 314 which at the time was the largest in-production commercial airplane.

Trippe would also prophecy — "People will fly to London in ten hours for $100!"

And Dr. Edward P. Warner, the noted aviation authority and vice-chairman of the Civil Aeronautics Board would say about the same time: *"It is perfectly possible to build a leviathan of an airplane weighing 400,000 or more pounds and carry 400 passengers across the Atlantic . . . Two such planes departing from opposite shores each day could carry twice as many people as ever crossed this ocean annually in cabin and first-class steamers!"*

Was the 747 *Super jet* in his vision?

We know better, but Mr. Warner certainly was unafraid to make such a prediction, staggering the imagination three decades *before* the first 747 would begin regular trans-Atlantic service.

Perhaps, in 1939, when he looked at the Boeing *Yankee Clipper* — a leviathan for her day — he saw fantasy and fact coming closer together.

The day of the sky giants was here to stay.

Meanwhile, there was a new high horizon to conquer.

CHAPTER SIX

We Ride The Stratosphere

ON September 5, 1862, two daring English aeronauts, James Glaisher and Henry Coxwell in a hydrogen balloon ascended to an altitude of 37,000 feet above the earth.

When about five miles high, both became senseless, caused by lack of oxygen in the thin, rarified air. Glaisher passed out completely, but Coxwell managed to open the descent valve with his teeth, and miraculously, they lived. But ever since, man has faced the problem of sustaining life at high altitudes.

At first, those who accepted the challenge, thought it was lack of oxygen, alone, that caused physical discomfort and, sometimes, death in the upper-air regions. But as they climbed higher and higher with the aid of oxygen masks, and carrying their own supply of breathable air with them, men learned there was another danger. At extreme altitudes, nitrogen forms bubbles in the blood unless oxygen is *forced* into the bloodstream. They call this *aero-embolism*; it can kill you the same as lack of oxygen when you venture too high without the right protection.

Really what was needed was a kind of "submarine of the air," an aircraft fuselage with sealed joints, a kind of "shell within a shell" capable of withstanding the pressure differentials between the interior and exterior skins. Strangely, men learned from the structural design of the underseas craft, the secret of how to build an aircraft to ride the stratosphere.

The fuselage had to be air-tight, and that meant designing new type doors and windows, a structural problem. Then, too, there had to be some system of supercharging the cabin air for pressurization. Probably more than anything else "the big plane concept" influenced Boeing engineers to tackle the problem. Admittedly, the smaller planes and the tremendous expense and complicated structural requirements for a pressure cabin held back the development. But with huge planes like the XB-15 and the "Flying Clippers" the picture changed.

It is not difficult to see the designer's imagination running wild; the shell-like fuselage of the XB-15, almost as long as a submarine, one could envision, transformed into a "*Nautilis*."

And think of what it would mean: The 10-man crew of the *Super-Dreadnaught* of the skies being able to work in their shirt-sleeves at altitudes where the bomber could not be seen nor heard. The big "Clipper Ships" capable of flying high enough to get above most of the adverse weather conditions and turbulence on their transoceanic runs. Certainly, this was the next logical step.

The XB-15 and the "Clipper" Model 314 were still under construction when the decision was made that Boeing would build a new transport to be a *pressurized cabin airliner*.

They drew up the plans. They gave it a number, Boeing Model 307 transport. They even had an appropriate name for it – the STRATOLINER, because it could fly in the substratosphere, above 20,000 feet. That was the dream and the challenge.

But first, there was a top priority job to tend to, the "mystery ship" Boeing was building, Model 299, (see last chapter) which was nearing completion to be ready for the crucial Air Corps competition at Wright Field, deadline – August, 1935. If they could get that production order for more than 200 planes, there would be plenty of money in the bank to build the *Stratoliner*.

Nobody ever dreamed how much the two designs – Model 299 and Model 307 – would help each other.

II

FEW persons have heard of Boeing Model 299, the plans for which were laid down in the spring of 1934, and construction started a few months later. Yet, within ten years, improved versions of the basic design would trace their white contrails across the skies over Europe, and leave their mark forever on the pages of World War II his-

Boeing Model 307 was the first four-engined transport the company ever built. Plane was also first pressurized-cabin airliner to go into scheduled service. This artist's drawing shows how "Stratoliner" could be made up for night travel, with interior converted into berths.

During World War II Boeing "Flying Fortresses" introduced high-altitude, daylight bombing. This formation leader has an over-head cover of B-17s leaving contrails in the sub-stratosphere. Planes were not pressurized. Crews relied on individual oxygen masks.

tory books. Model 299 was the prototype of the famous B-17, *Flying Fortress* bomber, whose exploits must rank her among the best-known and best-loved aircraft ever built. In 1,000-plane raids over Germany she flew into immortality and glory. It is also true, that the design itself contributed many improvements for the bomber and the commercial airliner to make these planes fly higher, farther and faster.

We have seen in the last chapter how Boeing engineers tackled the problem of building the super-sized XB-15, employing first the idea of adding extra engines to carry the heavier airframe, accessories and payload. *To build bigger planes, add more engines* was a kind of rule-of-the-thumb, until the 299 came along. In their preliminary design studies engineers took a new approach. *Why not put more engines on a smaller plane and build up its performance?* The answer was, *try it and find out*, and that's what they did. In this respect, Model 299 was a revolutionary concept.

Evolution not *revolution*, might be more accurate in describing what happened. When they drew up the plans for Model 299, engineers took a long look at what they already had on the shelf. There was the Model 247 transport; the "299" took on its fuselage profile and general construction technique. There was the huge XB-15; the "299" took its circular fuselage cross-section, mid-wing configuration and plan form, engine arrangement and the same shaped rudder. What emerged was a design about half as large as the XB-15 and about half-again the size of the Model 247, incorporating the best features of both these models. This would be Boeing's entry in the upcoming Air Corps competition at Wright Field, built entirely at company expense.

"The biggest gamble we've ever taken," Claire Egtvedt would tell the Board of Directors. It would cost a quarter of a million or more to build the one airplane!

Work went on in an atmosphere of strict security measures. Guards were everywhere around the curtained-off area where the "299" was taking shape. Only authorized, carefully screened personnel with proper passes were admitted. It was not just for military security reasons, that things were so tight. It was really because of the four engines. The performance potential looked to be far out ahead of twin-engined Martin B-12 and Douglas B-18 designs which, it was learned, would be entered in the competition. Thus, an aura of mystery surrounded the birth of the first *Flying Fortress*. Boeing engineers had a better idea, and wanted it kept secret.

The first of July, 1935, the "mystery ship" was rolled out of its final assembly hangar at Boeing Field. Silvery bright in the sunlight, she was more mystifying than mysterious. An incredible thing with wings. Bigger than anything Boeing had ever built before (The XB-15 was months away) and bristling with "bubble blisters" for machine

The "mystery ship" being built in Seattle in mid-thirties was this Boeing Model 299. It was prototype of famous "Flying Fortress" B-17s. First Air Corps' four-engined, all-metal bomber, the plane bristled with armament. "Blisters" on side of fuselage were gun positions.

gunners, a bombardier's "green-house" in the nose. Enough to make one observer remark — "She's a flying battleship, a veritable *flying fortress!*"

That she was. Designed to carry a crew of eight, pilot and co-pilot, bombardier/navigator, and five gunners, a bomb load of eight 600-pound bombs at top speeds in excess of 230-mph for a range of more than 3,000 miles. Much better than the Air Corps specification required — *if she could perform as predicted.*

Boeing registered the name *Flying Fortress.*

History recorded it.

Model 299 first flew on July 28, 1935 with test pilot Les Tower at its controls. She was sound in every respect, better than expected. The word got around — "We've got a winner!"

She turned the word into meaningful exploitation, lifting off Boeing Field in the wee hours before dawn on August 20, 1935, and pointing her nose for Dayton, Ohio — 2,000 miles away.

Up . . . up . . . up she climbed, her four Pratt & Whitney 750-horsepower *Hornet* engines throbbing to clear the mountain ranges. Les Tower, Henry Igo, a P&W engineer, Louis Wait, navigator, and Bud Benton, test observer — her four man crew — were exhilarated the way she climbed the ladder. Leveling off at a cruising altitude well above the highest peaks, they took time out for sandwiches and coffee. The automatic pilot did the flying.

Mountains behind them, they decided to "let her run." The *Hornets* had plenty of sting, they soon found out. At times, "299" hit ground speeds of better than 235 miles per hour!

Roaring across half a continent, she slipped majestically down out of the western sky landing at Wright Field just nine hours after she had left Seattle. No bomber of any size had ever flown so fast, and few fighters.

Claire Egtvedt was there to greet the crew. He was all smiles. Perhaps, he was thinking — *"It was worth the big gamble; the odds look better now."* He began to believe the word: They had a real *winner* this time!

All you had to do was look at her parked there on the flight line. Nearby was the Martin entry, the twin-engined B-12, and the Douglas B-18 — a bomber version of the famous DC-3 airliner — and they looked

Model 299 takes off on record-breaking non-stop flight from Seattle to Wright Field. During flight plane hit speeds faster than fighter planes of that period, 1935. Distinctive feature was the high rudder and the cone-shaped tail. Later these were changed for dorsal fin.

so small compared to the Model 299. They *were* small by comparison, about half the size of the *"Flying Fortress."*

The competition began. And in the days ahead, Model 299 passed every test with flying colors. The visionary "bomber generals," who believed the Air Corps needed a long-range striking force — just in case — watched with unbelieving eyes as they saw the *"Flying Fortress"* prove her prowess. This was the kind of a bomber that would give Air Power a Sunday punch.

Then, it happened.

On one more routine test flight, "299" roared down the runway and started to climb. She was airborne. Then, suddenly, one wing dipped sharply. The next instant, she plunged to the ground in a mass of flames. A fortress burning.

Les Tower and Major Pete Hill, chief of Wright Field test pilots, died as a result of the crash. One man lived to tell what happened. Lieutenant Donald L. Putt, named project officer on the "299," who had been riding along as a test observer, survived the crash. Suffering severe burns and shock, it was Don Putt, who had rushed again and again back into the flaming wreckage trying to get Tower and Hill out. And it was Putt, who muttered from the hospital bed when they thought he was dying — *"Don't blame the airplane . . ."*

Later, he filled in the pieces to help crash investigators pin-point the cause: Model 299 had a new feature, locks on the big control surfaces to keep them from flapping in the wind on the ground and ripping off. And the locks had *never been released.* It was no fault of the design, structure or powerplant.

But because of the adverse publicity surrounding the crash, the whole concept of the four-engined *"Flying Fortress"* was almost scrapped. Critics, who knew little about the circumstances and refused to listen, pointed out the big bomber was too much airplane for one man to handle. Despite the pleas of men who had flown the "299" to go ahead and put the *"Flying Fortress"* into production on the basis of her splendid performance record during the trials, the conservatives won. For the time being, at least, the "big bomber concept" was shot down in flames.

There was no back-up Model 299 to finish the in-service utilization trials with bombardment squadrons. The Douglas Aircraft Company of Santa Monica, California with its B-18 bomber was awarded the production contract.

Boeing did, however, get a contract to build thirteen modified "299s," the first of the B-17 series, for service test, a thin ray of hope that gave the *"Flying Fortress"* a second chance.

In Seattle, Boeing engineers picked up the pieces of their broken dream and bent themselves to the new task at hand — gearing up to produce the second generation *"Flying Fortresses,"* the thirteen serv-

Boeing entry, Model 299, in competition at Wright Field crashed in flames and this Douglas Aircraft Company entry, XB-18, a twin-engined bomber was awarded 200-plane contract. The B-18 was outgrowth of the Douglas DC-3 airliner. It had DC-3 wings and tail surfaces.

Army Air Corps gave Douglas single-plane contract to build this super, super bomber, the XB-19. Wing platform looked very much like that of the XB-15, but plane was almost twice as big. Mechanics could crawl inside wing to nacelles to make engine repairs in flight.

ice test YB-17s and one other for structural tests.

Work on these YB-17s stirred new thinking on the development of the proposed four-engined transport, Model 307. The prototype *"Flying Fortress,"* Model 299, even though it died an ignominious death had left a rich legacy. Its wings, powerplants, nacelles, empennage (tail surfaces) were ready-made for the *"Stratoliner."*

When they could come up with the right configuration for the 307 fuselage and pressurize the cabin, the pieces would fit together. In this respect, Boeing had the jump on other aircraft manufacturers who were building a four engine transport plane.

It was known, for instance, that Douglas Aircraft was working on a super deluxe airliner, a giant of a plane capable of carrying 42 passengers. And Douglas was getting "big plane know-how" with the help of an Air Corps contract to build a super bomber, the XB-19, almost twice the size of the Boeing XB-15. The proposed transport, desig-

First Douglas four-engined transport was this DC-4E, a joint airlines/Douglas Aircraft Company project. Plane was not pressurized, but it was first of really big, luxury airliners. Prototype had triple tail. Later versions became famous DC-4 and DC-6 commercial airliners.

nated the Douglas DC-4E, it could be expected, would be a commercial version of the big bomber.

There was also a rumor that Lockheed Aircraft Corporation at Burbank, California, had plans for a four-engined, high-altitude commercial airliner. It was no rumor that Lockheed already had a contract to build the XC-35, a modified version of its high-speed ten passenger, twin-engined "Electra" airliner, in service with some smaller airlines. And the XC-35 would have a pressurized cabin!

The Douglas DC-4E, from best information available was not projected to have a pressurized cabin. But it posed another kind of threat to the "*Stratoliner*" concept. One-time Wells Fargo banker, turned airline executive, William Allen "Pat" Patterson, a Boeing Airplane Company and Boeing Air Transport alumnus, now head of United Air Lines (no longer a part of Boeing) had put together a group of airlines to help underwrite the cost of the new Douglas commercial transport. United Air Lines, TWA, Pan American, American Airlines and Eastern Air Lines, the "Big Five," had agreed to share in the development costs of the DC-4E which incorporated many of their ideas for the "ideal airliner." And they had promised not to go elsewhere to buy another design in the same weight category (50,000 pounds gross) until they gave Douglas first crack at potential orders.

United Air Lines' President, William A. "Pat" Patterson, ironically, a one-time Boeing Air Transport executive promoted first Douglas DC-4E.

The competition was getting tougher and rougher, the way they played the game. Probably as much as anything else this factor put the pressure on to get the "*Stratoliner*" out of the factory and into the sky.

Boeing had no choice. It had to get going.

The Model 307 pressure cabin "*Stratoliner*" could well be the company's last chance to stay in the commercial airline field for a long time.

III

THINGS began to happen, not just talk. Construction was started on the "*Stratroliner's*" fuselage. Engineers had decided to make it a perfect circle in cross-section because air under pressure expands equally in all directions. When completed, it looked like a sealed-tight railroad tank car with a bulbous nose and tapering off in a conical tail. Air-tight bulkheads sealed off the forward crew compartment and the main cabin, sealed windows and doors. All that was needed was to add the B-17 wings and engines and tail assembly to make it an airplane. That was simple, the business at Boeing was building airplanes. The problem was to "pressurize" the cabin; compress the air inside to make it a liveable environment at altitudes where the air outside was thin and scarce and death from lack of oxygen lurked in the atmosphere. That was not so simple.

The key to the problem was a device called the supercharger.

Let us digress a moment: The internal combustion engine which was the main source of power for aircraft until the advent of the jet engines, is dependent on the air it breathes. The engine needs just the right amount of air mixed with just the right amount of gasoline ignited by a spark to cause an explosion, the force of which makes things go round, the wheels to give an automobile motion or the propeller to give an airplane thrust. In this respect, the engine is like a human, it needs oxygen to live. At high altitudes, engines suffer the same ill effects as humans. They gasp for oxygen that isn't there in sufficient quantities, and they sputter and die out.

For years this factor kept airplanes from flying at high altitudes, which accounts for

Boeing Airplane Company was one of first aircraft manufacturers to build its own pressure chamber on the ground to simulate high-altitude conditions. In this tank-like affair engineers worked out many problems that led to the successful development of pressurized cabin.

man's first invasion of the upper air regions in balloons and not aircraft. The balloon has no such limitations, but rises of its own accord because its heated gases are lighter than air.

Not until the first supercharger came into being could the aircraft engine operate at high altitudes.

Fortunately, superchargers were available for the engines on the *"Stratoliner"*, and Boeing engineers carried the idea a step farther. They rerouted some of the

When first "Stratoliner" fuselage was built, engineers devised the "soap and water" test looking for air leaks. Here, workers cover fuselage with soapy substance, the idea being that when pressurization was turned on, any leaks would cause bubbles, easily descernible.

The "Stratoliner's" fuselage was perfectly round and shaped like a huge cigar, as one can see in this factory scene. Overhead crane moved whole fuselage section into position for wing attachment. Only ten 307s were built – four for Pan Am, five for TWA, one for Howard Hughes.

supercharged air being supplied to the engines into the cabin to give it a "pressurized" atmosphere.

They had the pressure cabin. They could go ahead now and take the B-17 wings and other components "off and the shelf" and make the "*Stratoliner*" a reality.

The pieces came together quickly, and what a beauty she was there in final assembly. Four engines with the superchargers capable of giving her a service ceiling above 26,000 feet. A wide cabin, air-conditioned and pressurized, with plush decor and seats for 33 passengers, a "flight deck" up front for the crew. There was nothing like her, so far as was known, anywhere near completion.

In test after test they pumped air into the fuselage of the first "*Stratoliner*" there inside the factory. The scene was almost grotesque. A silvery, elongated, wingless tube being pumped up like a sausage balloon, you could almost see the skin expand. And the fuselage was covered with a thin layer of soap to see if any bubbles formed indicating leakage. Then, they hung weights and applied torsion wrenches to the fuselage, twisting it, warping it, to test its structural strength under pressure. The fuselage held. There was nothing like it.

Well, there was the DC-4E. But it didn't have a pressurized cabin. The "*Stratoliner*" would make it obsolete before it got into the air.

The airline people thought so, too, when Boeing salesmen showed them the brochure about the "*Stratoliner.*"

Pan American and TWA were "very interested." Juan Trippe of Pan-Am and Jack Frye, President of TWA saw a chance to get into the air first with an "over-the-weather" super-sized, super deluxe transport. They would be pioneering a whole new concept in air travel.

Interior of "Stratoliner" had a row of single seats on left-hand side of cabin and berths (Pullman style) on right.

But how much did the *"Stratoliner"* weigh?

The airline people remembered their commitment to Douglas. Even though things weren't going too well with the group effort on the DC-4E – costs were skyrocketing and the prototype seemed to be getting out of hand – there was still that agreement to be honored.

The *"Stratoliner"* weighed in *under 50,000 pounds gross.*

The door was open. Pan American ordered four of the Boeing Model 307 *"Stratoliners"* and TWA ordered five.

Boeing had "got going" in time.

IV

THE first *"Stratoliner"* flew on December 31, 1938, and she was everything expected of her. Initial testing completed by Boeing crews, the airline people flocked to see the new "Queen of The Skies" and fly it. Both Pan-Am and TWA were anxious to get their planes, and Boeing was bustling. The

Prototype "Stratoliner" demonstrates how plane could fly on only two of its four engines. Note, starboard propellers "feathered" in this photo. First plane crashed during test flight and almost spelled end of 307 program. First plane had very small vertical fin area as did first B-17s.

ALO ALTO, Calif. (UPI) — iam C. Mentzer, retired ted Air Lines official and deer of the world's first sucsful multi-engine plane for rseas flight, died Thursday Stanford Medical Center. He 64.

entzer retired last May as ted's senior vice president engineering and maintece because of failing health.

* * *

ENVER (UP

moving down the line vice-test YB-17s. They h plane to be specially d Hughes who planned orld and break his 1938 a feat virtually assured s splendid performance ısing speed in excess of ..ere was the prospect of more orders from foreign airlines.

Because of the plane's performance, particularly because of a supercharger, Boeing got a contract to equip the one YB-17 destined for structural tests with superchargers. Designated YB-17A, this project, the Air Corps said, if it were successful might lead to more orders for more of the high-altitude *"Flying Fortresses."* The huge XB-15 was also flying. And the first of the Pan-Am "Clipper" flying boats was about to make its maiden flight. More flying boats were on the line, and the factory was bursting at the seams. Farther up the Duwamish, at the Boeing Field site, construction was started on a new factory addition. Things never looked brighter.

The design staff was even talking about another "dream," a pressurized fuselage for the *"Flying Fortress"* which would mean a bigger bomber. At the moment, however, the Air Corps wasn't interested.

There was a bad crash, and they lost the first *"Stratoliner,"* but out of it came some changes, namely a big dorsal fin for the tail which made it a better airplane. When the modifications were made, the first *"Stratoliners"* were delivered to the airlines and went into service.

Pan American was first in the air with the Model 307, and before long, its *"Stratoliners"* were flying high over the Andean Peaks on its South American routes. Short-

Later model 307s incorporated the famous B-17 dorsal fin shown here, which greatly improved plane's stability. Although "Stratoliners" had supercharged cabin, they were not equipped with turbo-superchargers. Geared superchargers provided breathable air for passengers and engines.

One of Pan American World Airways first 307 "Stratoliners" flies high above the Andean peaks of South America. Note how wheels are not fully retracted, similar to arrangement on the Boeing 247 airliner. "Stratoliner" was last of two-wheel/tail wheel airliners.

ly thereafter, TWA got its planes, and started a much publicized "over-the-weather" domestic service, coast-to-coast with stops at Chicago, Kansas City, Albuquerque, Los Angeles. As expected the *"Stratoliners"* attracted more passengers, who wanted the experience of flying four miles or more above the earth, in the roomy, luxuriously appointed, pressurized cabins. Because their high-altitude environment helped increase their speeds, the *"Stratoliners"* were also time-savers, thus exploiting air transportation's greatest product – *speed.*

Indeed, the new Boeings offered a new experience for the air traveler. The author remembers well his first flight in one of TWA's *"Stratoliners."* Compared with riding in the DC-3, which once we felt was delightful, the ride in the *"Stratoliner"* was deluxe. The difference between riding in a coach on the train, and riding in a Pullman.

Here was sheer luxury aloft. Wide, comfortable seats, three abreast in a row of eight along the right side of the aisle, single seats on the left. Plenty of leg room to stretch out. Plenty of height to walk around without thumping your head, even for a six-footer. Plush carpeting on the floor, a decor of bright, comforting, solid "safety" colors. Air-conditioning, sound-proofing, so quiet the drone of the engines was almost a lullaby. Individual lights and ash trays for every seat.

Modern conveniences, a "Ladies' Lounge" in the tail, wash basin, lavatory, even a vanity table. The "Men's Room" up front complete with electric shaver, itself a novelty thirty years ago.

Berths, if you liked, for the night traveler. The seats were convertible like a Pullman's. A galley, hot coffee, food warmers; no more box lunches. Two hostesses, not one, to serve you.

All of this and a flight, the smoothest I had ever experienced. Very little turbulence, riding the sub-stratosphere, above most of the storms that cause rough air.

And the view, I'll never forget. The whole world, it seemed, was spread out below from 16,000 feet, the altitude at which we were flying, well above the highest peaks of the mountain ranges between Albuquerque and Los Angeles. The highest I had ever flown without an oxygen mask. The temperature outside, 28-degrees below zero; the temperature inside, a comfortable 70-degrees, and zipping along at better than three miles a minute.

So fast, we saw the edge of night rimming Albuquerque at take-off, but we were still in the purple twilight landing in Los Angeles!

The dawn of a new age when man would see two sunsets crossing the continent in less than 15 hours was about to begin.

The *"Stratoliner"* had raised the curtain. She was the harbinger of wings to come.

Wings above the Duwamish had put man in a comfortable environment, on the first step, on his way to the stars.

CHAPTER SEVEN

Superforts And Stratocruisers

HIGH above the snow-capped peak of Mount Ranier, altitude, 14,410 feet, one of the first Boeing *Flying Fortresses* glistened in the bright morning sunlight. At its controls was Captain J. D. Corkille, and beside him in the co-pilot's seat was Lieutenant P. H. Robey, Air Corps officers from Wright Field. A sergeant mechanic and two Boeing flight test engineers completed the crew. They were on a very important test.

Originally slated to be a structures test model for ultimate destruction, this (YB-17A) was first to test successful turbo-supercharger.

Each of the YB-17A's Wright *Cyclone* engines had a new type supercharger. Called the turbo-supercharger, the device was developed by Dr. Sanford Alexander Moss, a Cornell University Phd. as far

In this LePere biplane Lieut. John Macready (left) set high altitude record. Dr. Moss, father of turbo-supercharger, stands next to Macready.

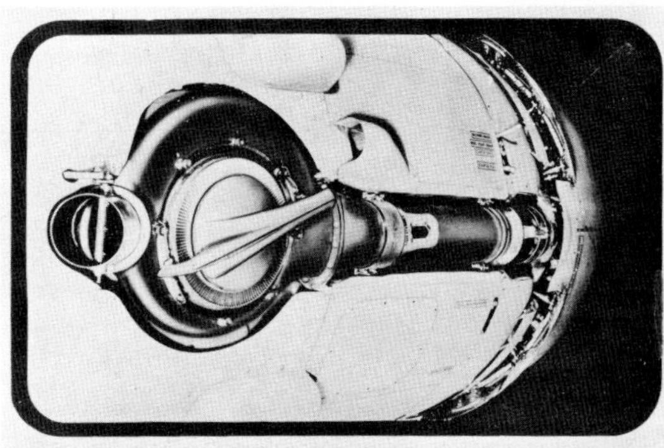

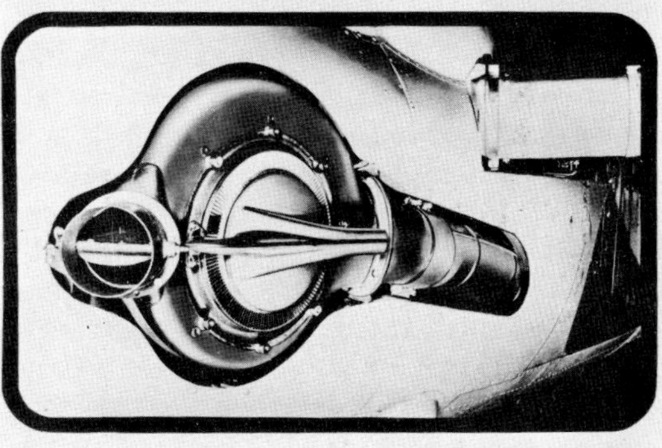

Turbo-superchargers were mounted on top of engines. They were like "artificial lungs" feeding pressurized air into combustion chambers.

back as 1917. The first turbo-supercharger was tested on a World War I Liberty engine atop Pike's Peak in the fall of that year. And later, Army fliers at McCook Field set new altitude records in a LePere biplane equipped with a Liberty engine and turbo-supercharger.

For the first time, the airplane invaded the upper air regions. But the early turbo-superchargers were not too reliable.

Chiefly, the science of metallurgy held them back. The way the turbo-supercharger works was the big bugaboo. It is really a small jet engine. Exhaust gases from the big aircraft internal combustion engine, through a system of ducts, spin the turbine wheel or fan which compresses fresh air sucked into a small chamber and, then, feeds this air back to the engine to let it "breathe" normally. Dr. Moss, himself, once explained it to this writer – "The turbo-supercharger kids engines at high altitude into thinking they are at sea-level."

In early developmental stages, the hot exhaust gases were too much for the metal in the turbine wheels whose tiny "buckets" or "scoops," because of the excessive heat blew to pieces. Not until the mid-thirties, when General Electric turned Dr. Moss loose in its big laboratories, did the turbo-supercharger get a new lease on life. GE-metallurgists whipped the problem.

The YB-17A "Flying Fortress" high in the sky over Mount Rainier that day in March, 1939 was testing the latest GE model turbo-superchargers. If all went well, the B-17 would become the world's first high-altitude bomber.

"Johnny" Corkille had the throttles pretty well forward, engines pulling with a resounding roar, as the plane climbed higher and higher, until the altimeter registered 25,000 feet, two miles above Ranier's crest. For a couple of hours, the crew in their oxygen masks and electrically-heated suits flew in circles at the same altitude. Then, they raced the B-17 over a predetermined course and clocked its speed. Everything worked perfectly.

The plane hit 311 miles per hour ground speed; 100 miles an hour faster than any bomber of its size ever had flown before. At that altitude, it was also faster than any fighter plane had flown. Such performance would change many things.

Back on the ground, Paul Robey, who was project officer on the turbo-supercharger project, sent a hurried teletype to his commanding officer at Wright Field. The message was in code, and a puzzled operator at the other end read – *"She climbed like a mountain goat, and ran like a deer."*

It was an historic message because it

Success of turbo-supercharger gave new life to B-17 "Flying Forts," and the four-engined bomber went into mass production. This was scene at Boeing plant in Seattle showing B-17 forward fuselage sections on assembly lines. Note Pearl Harbor banner in background.

insured a new life for the turbo-supercharger, which the military had once thought of abandoning. And it resulted in more orders for more *Flying Fortresses.* Who said the Model "299" was dead?

The first high-altitude flight of the B-17 had even greater significance for this narrative:

(1). Boeing engineers felt that flight crews on high-altitude bomber missions should have the advantage of the pressurized cabin, and almost immediately design studies were started to make the B-17 a pressurized bomber. The result was a much larger aircraft, a "super bomber type," and the company went ahead with its own design and mock-up to present to the Air Corps.

(2). Success of the turbo-supercharger — as the flight proved — meant that, at long last, engineers had solved the metallurgy problem with turbine wheels which could withstand the red-hot temperature stresses. It was the "key," as we shall see, to the development of the successful jet engines for aircraft.

One day, in the distant future, the giant eight-foot diameter turbo fans of the four Pratt & Whitney JT9D engines, each developing more than 43,000 pounds of thrust, would make possible today's incredible Boeing *Super jet,* the 747.

Perhaps, it is stretching a point, but it can be said, that flight of the first high-altitude *Flying Fortress* in March of 1939, began an era of progressive development of super bombers and super transports that would give Boeing the edge in *know-how* to design and develop and deliver the 747, first of the really big commercial jetliners.

There will be arguments, pro and con, about the impact of World War II and the resultant technological evolution, but the fact remains, in the XB-15, the *"Flying Fortress,"* the *"Stratoliner"* — all flying *before* Hitler marched into Poland, September 1, 1939 — Boeing took the big step in the design, development and production of truly large aircraft.

History tells us that by the end of World War II more than 12,000 *"Flying Fortresses"* had been built, and the B-17 became a shining example of the "arsenal of democracy" at work. A bomber, designed

A formation of three Boeing B-17 "Flying Fortresses" drops its sticks of bombs on German target. These late models have nose gun turrets, the famous ball turret in belly, and tail guns. The "Forts" were so heavily armed, they flew without fighter escort.

The famous B-17 "Flying Fortresses" were considered to be the most rugged aircraft ever built. Time and time again, during peak of bombing effort over Germany, they flew home after suffering unbelievable damage. This "loner" was struck by our own bombs, but returned safely.

and originally built by Boeing, built during the war by Douglas and Lockheed, normally competitive airframe manufacturers. The plane's engines, designed and built originally by Wright Aeronautical Corporation, built by Studebaker, an automotive manufacturer. General Electric turbo-superchargers, built by Allis Chalmers, the farm machinery people. Nacelles for the engines, built by a brassiere manufacturer. The end product: An Air Armada the like of which the world had never seen before.

Flying Fortresses, which before the conflict was over would drop 640,036 tons of bombs on the enemy in the European Theater of operations and in the Pacific Theater of operations. *Flying Fortresses* that would shoot down almost as many enemy aircraft over Europe as all other American warplanes combined, including fighters!

Where else could this happen, but in the land of the free and the home of the brave?

II

THE European war was less than four months old when in January, 1940, the Boeing Airplane Company along with several other aircraft manufacturers received a War Department circular (R-40B) setting forth specifications for a new four-engined bomber. Even though the U.S. was still a neutral country, there were those in high places, who feared we could not remain so for long. President Franklin D.

After World War II, TWA converted one of B-17s into airliner configuration. Fuselage was very cramped. (Gordon Williams Photograph)

This B-17 played unusual role. It was flying testbed for B-29 engines. Modification permitted mounting big engine in nose of the aircraft.

Roosevelt already had declared a state of national emergency. There were signs that once again, as America had done in 1917-18 she might have to come to the aid of England and France. Our Two former allies were taking a terrible beating from Hitler's forces. The Maginot Line was crumbling. Britain was being bombed relentlessly. If France and England should fall, the United States would be Hitler's next target; Nazism and our way of life were not compatible. To be prepared, our military planners warned that neither the *"Flying Fortress"* nor any other plane of its size could adequately defend our shores. There was needed a plane with much greater range and more striking power. The War Department circular asked for such plane. It was marked URGENT.

In Seattle, Boeing already had "on paper" the pressurized version of the B-17, Model 334. They had even built a mock-up.

Air Corps generals shook their heads. "It doesn't go far enough," they said. What was wanted was a bomber with a range of 5,000 miles, capable of delivering 2,000 pounds of bombs at the half-way point; a plane that would operate at altitudes of 30,000 feet or more at top speeds in excess of 300 miles per hour; capable of defending itself, heavily armed and heavily armored.

It was a big order, and whatever was done had to be done in utmost secrecy. Such a plane, decidedly, must be classed as an *offensive weapon.* The "isolationists" would certainly fight it from every angle. Interested companies would have to go ahead on their own, awaiting a more favorable Congressional acceptance of the real danger that lie ahead.

Boeing went ahead on its own. By midsummer, 1940 it had a new design, Model 345, still an "on paper" airplane, which it presented to the Air Corps people.

Meanwhile, the war situation had worsened. Italy had joined Germany in declaring war on France and England. And France had fallen to the Nazi. Time was running out.

Boeing's "paper" airplane was the best we had; a $3,600,000 Air Corps contract said *go ahead;* build two prototypes for flight test, and a third for static testing.

The official Air Corps designation was – XB-29.

Boeing called it, the *"Superfortress."*

Design-wise and production-wise, the B-29 program was a radical departure from any previous operation. Certainly, it was not just a king-sized version of the B-17 models. About the only true adaptation from the B-17 design was the shape of the rudder and the distinctive dorsal fin. Otherwise, the B-29 was an all new airplane, although its construction techniques, except for size, used conventional materials – all-metal with control surfaces fabric-covered. There were, however, many "firsts" in engineering design and fabrication methods.

Prototype XB-29, first of the "Superfortresses." At this stage, plane didn't have any armament, and was equipped with three-bladed propellers.

B-29 had a wing span of 141 feet, a third again that of the *"Flying Fortress,"* and the wing itself was an entirely new and revolutionary airfoil, much thinner than the B-17 wing, with solid panels and "honey-comb" bracings for strength replacing the spar and rib construction previously used. Use of trailing edge flaps which increased lift for take-off and slow-speed landings, but which hid themselves in flight to give increased speed by cutting down on airflow resistance, was something never tried before in a plane of this size. The principle, carried even further, would one day appear in the 747 design. The B-29 was the "flying test bed." It was also this new wing structure that permitted storage of vast amounts of fuel in the wing, a key to long-range operation for bomber or transport.

Another innovation introduced by the B-29 which would contribute much to the fabrication of big planes in the future, was the use of a "production joint," a new technique used in joining together sections of the fuselage. The B-29 was actually broken up into five sections for major assembly. The "production joint" enabled these sections to be joined together by bolts, using a torsion wrench, thus, eliminating the necessity for splicing of beams, or "stringers." No more skin overlaps as was customary in conventional airframe construction.

In the process, small clips tied the former to the long "stringers" inside the fuselage. Rivet holes on the clips were prepunched, full size, as were the matching holes on formers and stringers. The operation was comparable to working with an erector set. Boeing ingenuity thus permitted utilization of thousands of unskilled workers in the airframe industry. True assembly-line production, like that in the great automotive plants, was just a step away.

On the basis of wind tunnel tests, and faith in Boeing design, engineering and production capabilities, the Air Corps in an unprecedented action placed an order for 250 of the B-29s *before* fabrication of the *first* plane was even half completed. That order came in May of 1941, six months *before* Pearl Harbor. A month after the Japanese attacked Pearl Harbor in that "Day Of Infamy," December 7, 1941, the production order was increased to 500, and by the end of the war, 3,970 *Superfortresses* had been produced. In the war emergency, the Boeing Airplane Company became the focal point of a sprawling aircraft manufacturing complex the magnitude of which was far beyond the imagination of the wildest "dreamers" inside or outside the aviation community.

At peak production, more than 150,000 persons, men and women were working on the B-29, in Seattle at a greatly expanded Plant Two, in Renton, Washington where another new plant was built, in Wichita, Kansas, Omaha, Nebraska, and

Biggest of World War II bombers, B-29s move down the assembly line at Boeing's plant in Wichita, Kansas. The circular fuselage, like that of the "Stratoliners," helped in pressurizing the big bomber. A long pressurized "tunnel" ran over bomb bay, which was not pressurized.

Marietta, Georgia, where huge government-built plants suddenly sprang into being. Boeing built the planes at Seattle and Renton and Wichita; Glenn Martin Airplane Company built them in Omaha; Bell Aircraft at the Marietta facility. Never before, and never since, did Uncle Sam pour so much money into a single project.

In the beginning, shortly after the Pearl Harbor attack, at a secret meeting in Washington, Wellwood Beall, then chief engineer at Boeing, sat across the desk from General Oliver P. Echols, chief of the Air Corps Materiel Division planning, in charge of all U.S. aircraft design, development and production. The first B-29 was still in mock-up stage; they were still making changes to improve its performance expectancy.

General Oliver P. ("Red") Echols, who signed contract that put the B-29s into production long before first prototype spread its wings.

"Is that B-29 of yours really as good as you say it is?" Echols and Beall were eye-ball-to-eye-ball. "We've got to know; the fate of the country might well rest in this weapon."

"We believe it is," Beall answered. "We'll make it so. You give us the facilities and materials and a free-hand to run the test program, and we'll guarantee it."

The conversation went on like that as the two men discussed the many problems that had to be worked out.

"Red" Echols, one of the first engineering officers to be given the rank of general, excused himself to go in and talk with his chief, General Henry H. "Hap" Arnold, now commanding general of the Air Corps.

When he returned Echols told Beall that the United States Government was committing itself to spend more money on the B-29 project than any other project of the whole war planning – a three *billion* dollar gamble.

Boeing could go ahead and "run the show."

The XB-29, prototype of the "*Superfortress*," lifted its wheels off Boeing Field on its initial flight, September 21, 1942. It was pretty much just "skin and bones," raw airplane. Engineering-test pilot, "Eddie" Allen, who had done so

Prototype XB-29 comes in for landing at Boeing Field, Seattle after initial test flight. First models were built in Seattle plant, where B-17s were still moving down assembly line. It was 21 months later, that first formation of "Superfortresses" hit targets in Japan.

much to help design its high-lift wing, was at the controls.

It wasn't like other "first flights." Only a few persons knew about it, and were permitted to see it happen; the whole area was under the tightest military security, a guarded fortress not an airplane factory.

After the flight Allen's comment was terse.

"She flies," he said.

After that the "growing pains" and the "proving pains" were terrific. The brand new Wright 2,200-horsepower engines had never been flown before in an aircraft of any size and weight. There were a lot of engine "fires," until a cowling flap device helped solve the problem. At high speeds and because of its size, control taxed the strongest man's strength, until they combined the "tab" innovation introduced on the Boeing B-9 (see chapter four) with a "booster" system and a patented aileron and elevator hinge feature. At high altitudes, under pressure, the side gunners' plexiglass fire-control stations "popped out," causing the discomforts of decompression and the danger of crew members being "sucked" out of the fuselage – until they beefed up the structural members. One problem after another developed; one problem after another was solved, and all the while, the production line kept growing in Seattle, Renton, Marietta, Omaha as rapidly as the facilities were made ready.

And all the while, the turn of the war in Europe and in the Pacific kept dictating changes. Now, they were talking about double the range (10,000 miles), more firepower, a 20,000-pound bomb load. What had started out to be an 80,000-pound airplane suddenly became a 60-ton giant with equal demand for performance increases. Boeing had its task cut out to make good on Beall's promise to Echols – to America.

But there was no turning back. And finally, there she was, 120,000-pounds of

Production model B-29 was vastly improved version having first flush-mounted, remotely-controlled gun turrets and .20mm cannon in tail. More powerful engines were available and four-bladed propellers, which made planes the fastest and highest-flying bombers in the world.

Example of B-29's firepower was this remote-controlled turret atop forward fuselage section. Turret mounted five .50-caliber guns.

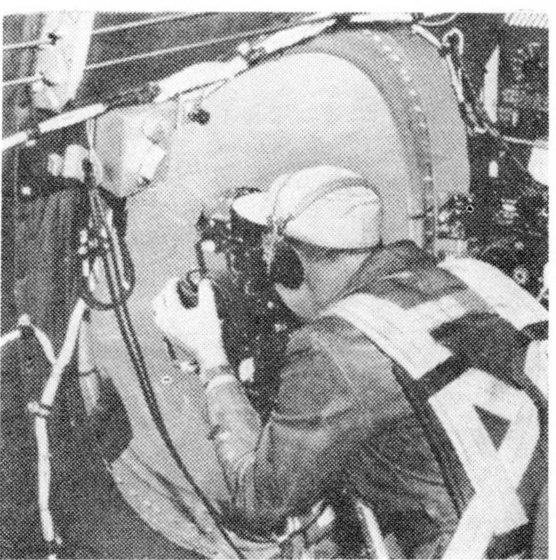

The "Superfort's" gun turrets were controlled from plexi-glass-enclosed sighting stations (like this) inside the long tube-like pressurized fuselage.

airframe and engines and armament, the first *big* aircraft pressurized for its crew of 10 for an operational altitude *above 30,000 feet;* the first aircraft in its weight category to go into mass production; the first bombardment aircraft to incorporate remote-controlled sighting stations, the fire-control of a battleship applied to a skyship, bristling with flush-to-fuselage turrets, ten to twelve .50 caliber machine guns covering every angle of attack, a .20mm cannon in the tail; two bomb bays capable of carrying two 4,000 pounders, eight 2,000 pounders, eighty 100-pound bombs depending upon the purpose of the mission; a speed of better than 365 mph maximum; and she had the promised range with the help of in-flight refuelling techniques being developed.

Such was the big plane that was being turned out at the rate of better than three-a-day in mid-1944 at a time when the Allies were mounting their offensive in all theaters.

In-flight refuelling techniques worked out, with B-29 "tankers" feeding B-29 "bombers" gave the "Superfortresses" long range capabilities.

The day before the greatest invasion force of history hit the beaches of France (D-Day, June 6, 1944), the first "*Superfortresses*" bombed Bangkok from secret bases in China. And ten days later, sixty-eight B-29s dropped their bombs on steel mills in Yawata, Japan.

There was more to come; much more.

Perhaps, more than any other aircraft, the B-29 would leave its mark in history.

On August 6, 1945, it was a B-29, the *Enola Gay* that dropped the first Atomic Bomb on Hiroshima, and three days later another B-29 named *Bockscar* dropped the second bomb on Nagasaki.

The world would never be the same again.

The Big Plane Concept had given us the delivery weapon for a new kind of *force* which, for better or worse, depend-

This specially modified B-29, the "Enola Gay," was probably most lethal aircraft of World War II. It dropped first Atom Bomb on Hiroshima!

ing upon its use, would decide the destiny of mankind.

Japan surrendered, and it seems safe to say that the B-29 and the Atomic Bomb probably avoided the need for the expenditure of a million lives had we tried to conquer Japan with an invasion force and conventional weapons.

One high-ranking Japanese Air Officer after the war would tell an interrogator: *"You won because of those terrible B-29s!"*

"Those terrible B-29s," he repeated. "How did you possibly get them in time?"

One answer, perhaps, was on the lips of a Hoosier-born seaman first-class aboard one of our naval vessels on patrol in the Pacific when a flight of our first B-29s went into action from Okinawa. His ship was rolling along in untroubled waters when suddenly there was an alert.

"Planes approaching . . . Planes approaching . . . Battle stations . . . Battle stations!" the alarm spread quickly.

The gob from Indiana with his buddy, crouched in their gun parapit ready for action.

The drone of the approaching planes grew louder and louder. Then, suddenly, they came into view.

The sailor threw off his steel helmet, and lit a cigarette.

"Put that out," yelled a superior officer. "They might be enemy planes."

"Hell, no," said the sailor. "They ain't. Nobody could build any thing that BIG and make it fly but us."

In Seattle at Boeing, they knew what he meant.

III

THEY had learned how to build large airplanes, and how to mass produce them. There were bigger planes flying by the end of the war, but none would ever be produced in such quantities, and none equalled the over-all performance of the *"Superfortress."* Indeed, no other aircraft manufacturer had had so much experience in building planes in the size category of the B-29. That, alone, would play the decisive role in the post-war future of the Boeing Airplane Company.

Phil Johnson, who as President had led the company through the war years, the master-mind of the B-17 and B-29 production lines, died of a stroke suffered in September of 1944. Too much, pressure, they said. Claire Egtvedt, wartime Chairman of the Board, who had been with the company for almost thirty years, had stepped in once more to run the company's destiny. It was up to Claire to chart the course.

And Egtvedt could look back at what happened after the Armistice in 1918. He could see the plane production dwindling. Who needed bombers in peacetime? Already they were moth-balling B-29s at Davis-Monothan Air Force Base in Arizona. The more than 5,000 *"Superforts"* on order before VJ-Day had been cancelled. The same thing had happened with the then *big* order for the Navy flying boats after World War I. History was repeating itself. Boeing, to survive, faced another crisis.

Perhaps, with a shake of his head, he dismissed the idea of making office furniture or turning to the manufacturing of Sea Sleds, as Bill Boeing had done two decades before. To move in that direction was unthinkable. There was some consideration given, however, to building automobiles. But the answer always came out the same. The business at Boeing was building aircraft. The problem was to look around and find out what kind of planes were in demand. Then, come up with the best product, and go ahead and build it.

The "look around" was through a very small window.

There was need for an improved long-range, high-performance bomber like the B-29. And that got top priority.

A "seventy-five per cent NEW" bomber, the B-50, came into being. Basically the same configuration as the B-29, the new model was fabricated of much stronger metal which increased its weight up to 170,000 pounds; it had 50 per cent more

Replacement for the famed B-29 was this B-50 bomber which had more powerful engines, was built of stronger metals, and could carry A-bomb.

horsepower, using the latest Pratt & Whitney 3,350-horsepower engines. The B-50 was 20 to 30 miles per hour faster than the B-29, and with applicable refuelling techniques it had unlimited range.

During the immediate post-war period, the B-50 became the prime delivery vehicle for the A-bomb, and as such, the backbone of the Strategic Air Command until the bigger Consolidated B-36, six-engined, 260,000-pound giant was available. Orders for the B-50 in sizeable quantities kept the production lines going for a time. But the end of the line was in sight.

Biggest bomber to come out of World War II was Consolidated B-36 (at right), a six-engined giant that dwarfed the B-50 shown here beside it.

There must be another need.

What about a jet-powered bomber? Boeing had studies "on paper" for using the recently developed turbine engines, either to drive propellers (a turbo-prop B-50) or as a pure jet, capable of half-again the speed of any piston-powered aircraft. But the Air Force wasn't interested.

"No range," said the Air Force procurement people prodded by the Strategic Air Command generals. "Until the jet progressed, you couldn't fly from Seattle to San Francisco and back again with any sizeable payload!"

What about a new transport? The basic design was there already, three prototypes moving down the line. They called it Model 367, a long-range, king-sized military cargo plane. Its genesis was a story with a familiar ring. In the same manner that the famous "*Stratoliner*", Model 307, had come out of the B-17, the new transport had come out of the B-29.

The wings, tail, undercarriage and powerplants in the "*Superfortress*" gave engineers a head start in the design and fabrication of the new cargo plane. Only the fuselage was different – a giant figure "8" in cross-section with the upper lobe much greater in diameter than the lower, to provide for more cargo space. "She looks like a pregnant B-29", some wag remarked.

The "pregnancy" gave birth to many revolutionary ideas in the design and capabilities of a military logistics transport. The "figure 8" was separated by a heavy cargo floor. In the upper fuselage she could carry 134 fully-equipped combat troops, almost three times as many as any other World War II troop carrier aircraft. They could also put aboard three loaded one-and-a-half ton trucks, or two light tanks – driving the vehicles up a special ramp through clam-shell doors in the bottom of the fuselage just ahead of the recognizable B-29 dorsal fin in the tail. Moreover, in the lower fuselage she could carry bulk cargo loaded through

This seating arrangement in upper lobe of C-97 military transport permitted carrying more than 130 fully-equipped airborne soldiers.

This C-97 military transport, cargo plane version of the B-29 could carry heavy motorized equipment, ramp-loaded through doors in tail.

fore and aft doors. And there were built-in cargo hoists to expedite loading techniques. In this respect, she was probably the first specifically designed "aerial freighter".

Such was the military air transport presented to the Air Corps people about the same time that the B-29 was taking shape. But the pressure was on to build the long-range *"Superfortress"* and the cargo plane was of secondary importance. The military did, however, order three prototypes, designated C-97s, and the first of these flew on November 15, 1944.

Two months later, on January 9, 1945, the C-97 made a spectacular flight, non-stop from Seattle to Washington, D.C. She was at that time, the first transport plane of her size and capacity with a pressurized cabin, and capable of speeds at high altitude of better than 350 miles per hour!

By war's end, the new Global Air Forces had ordered ten service test models, enough to keep the C-97 program from being scrapped.

And suddenly, she had a new role in the post-war planning. With modifications, she became the KC-97 a "flying tanker," to refuel the B-50 *"Superfrotresses"* on 24-hour "global patrol" to keep the peace. Altogether more than 600 of the C-97 series in various configurations were produced.

The C-97 military transport was modified as a "flying tanker" designated the KC-97. Note the long gas boom in the tail, a Boeing development.

The post-war picture brightened. Boeing was still in the aircraft manufacturing business. But unfortunately, the business was all military . . . . .

Until the basic C-97 became a plushed-up commercial airliner, Model 377, to be called — the Boeing *"Stratocruiser."*

IV

THE role of the B-17 *"Flying Fortress"* was to carry the war to Hitler's Germany. Boeing built the vehicle which in turn revolutionized aerial warfare, making possible high-altitude, precision bombing. Round-the-clock bombing and thousand-plane formations of B-17s knocked Germany out of the war. The role of the B-29 *"Superfortress"* was to carry the war and the A-bomb across the Pacific to Japan. The B-29s did the job, and it is said — "shortened the war by many months, if not years." The record, however, would not be complete without mention of the Boeing *"Clippers"* and the *"Stratoliners"* in their wartime operations. The big Boeing Model 314 Flying Boats flew Churchill and Roosevelt and many other VIPs to secret meeting places early in the war to make possible a much closer partnership. "Winged Diplomacy" had its beginning. And the Boeing Model 307 *"Stratoliners"*, flown mostly by civilian airline crews, were the first landplanes to blaze new sky trails across the Atlantic and the Pacific, pioneering the post-war air routes. Thus, did a *pre-war* commercial airliner help change the whole concept of air transportation for the post-war era.

The double-deck fuselage of the military C-97 transport, Boeing engineers felt, could be easily adapted for a commercial airliner. This artist's cut-away-drawing shows the result. The conversion, which required many modifications, became Boeing Model 377, called the "Stratocruiser."

Did the planes make the times? Or did the times make the planes?

Perhaps, the question will never be answered. But the time was ripe for the introduction of the "*Stratocruiser.*" The post-war air traveler wanted more than the pre-war DC-3 airliner.

The war had shown the versatility and utility of air transport. It was a certainty the airplane had "arrived" as the common carrier for people and things. Anything and everything had moved by air during World War II. *Airlift* was the "aerial lifeline" of the Allied Forces and the enemy. It would play the same role in the commerce and trade of a peacetime world.

Where was Boeing in this peacetime air world?

It was true, some of the "*Stratoliners*" had been returned to their airline owners. But there had been only ten built. Even so, they pioneered the first "air coach" services, slashing fares to bring air travel within reach of many more pocketbooks. These planes, with their high density seating arrangements, were not pressurized, and they became obsolete almost before they were put into service by Trans World Airlines, the new TWA which planned round-the-world operations. Already they were superceded by newer and larger airliner-types, the prototypes of which had come into existence during the war. Indeed, the entire scheduled airline industry, worldwide, was rushing to buy the passenger plane versions of the military transports.

Post-war Model 307 "Stratoliner" which TWA converted into high-density aircoach. Cabin pressure system was removed to permit more seats.

TWA, for example, was exploiting its new Lockheed "*Constellation*" a 69-passenger, four-engined, 300-mile-an-hour, pressure cabin airliner which had been produced in limited number as the C-69 troop carrier. Lockheed Aircraft Company also had a stretched version, the "*Super Connie*" almost ready to fly.

Then, there was Douglas with its commercial version (DC-4) of the C-54 "*Skymaster*" which had done a workhorse job as troop transport and cargo carrier in all theaters of operation. And right behind it, already moving down the line in Santa Monica, was a deluxe DC-6 pressurized airliner, larger, faster.

Lockheed "Constellation," shown here, was really pre-war design. But military took them over as (C-69) cargo transports for wartime emergency.

Single-tailed DC-4 was post-war version of the C-54 military transport. It was outgrowth of Patterson's "dreamplane" DC-4E of 1939.

Consolidated Aircraft Corporation of San Diego, builders of the famous B-24 "*Liberator*" bombers, the replacement for the B-17 (which it never really did) had entered the picture with a new twin-engined *Convair* 240, the white hope to replace the popular DC-3. Glenn Martin Company of Baltimore, builders of the fast B-26 *Marauder* medium bombers had its entry; the twin-engined Martin 202 airliner. Even Republic Aviation, builders of the rugged P-47 *Thunderbolt* fighters had its airliner design – the four-engined "*Rainbow*", transport version of the XF-12 photo recon ship. There was also Curtiss-Wright with its commercial adaptation of the twin-engined C-46 "*Commando.*"

This was the situation in September of 1945, when Claire Egtvedt turned the reins of the Boeing Airplane Company over to William M. Allen, newly elected president. A time when employment was decreasing, Air Corps contracts were being cancelled right and left, and the big plants loomed as potential ghost factories. A time when B-17s and B-29s were being blowtorched into scrap aluminum to become pots and pans; a time when somebody had to make the decision for Boeing to get back into the commercial airliner business, or face the future as strictly a military plane builder.

Allen knew and so did everybody else, the *"Stratocruiser"*, Model 377, offshoot of the B-29 and the C-97, was the only hope for Boeing to get back into the civilian air transport picture.

Nobody, however, expressed much interest in the proposed airliner, because its price tag ran above the million dollar mark. The competition, building transports while Boeing had been building bombers, had a head start in the race with military transport assembly lines comparatively easy to convert to airliner production, keeping costs down. Moreover, the airlines were already committed to buy DC-4s, DC-6s, Martin 202s, Convair 240s and Lockheed *"Constellations."*

The *"Stratocruiser"* would have to be something out of this world to get into the sales ring.

Boeing, if it wanted to maintain its pre-war reputation as a leader in the design and development of the modern airliners (Chapter Four: "First Of The Modern Airliners") and the first high-altitude pressurized cabin *"Stratoliner"* (Chapter Six) a pre-war development, must take the gamble, alone.

Bill Allen decided to go for broke.

"We're going ahead and build fifty *'Stratocruisers',"* he announced. It was one of his first official acts as the new company president.

At the time there was some interest in the Model 377 from several of the airlines, but nobody was willing to sign on the dotted line. The *"Stratocruiser"* went into production without any firm orders. The only commitment was the one Boeing made — to build it.

"The chips are down," Allen told his Sales people. "If you don't sell the 377, a lot of people will be out of jobs, and Boeing

Boeing's answer to post-war competition in air transport field was this double-decker "Stratocruiser." Model 377 was outgrowth of the B-29 "Superfortress" and C-97 military transport. Plane had "spiral staircase" leading down to first-class lounge in lower fuselage.

Factory scene changed from military to commercial transports as Boeing's first post-war airliner, the Model 377, moved down the line.

could be out of business!"

The first protytype *"Stratocruiser"* flew on July 8, 1947 and by that time, the Sales staff had done its job well.

Pan American World Airways was committed to buy twenty of the Model 377s – an order totalling more than $24,500,000 including spare parts. It was the biggest contract, dollar-wise, any privately-owned air carrier corporation ever had placed up to that time. PAA President Juan Trippe was betting on Boeing again. He announced the big planes would operate on the Trans-Atlantic and Trans-Pacific runs. Pan-Am called them – *"StratoClippers"*.

A new Trans-Atlantic air carrier, American Overseas Airways part of American Airlines, Inc., largest U.S. domestic airline in 1946, ordered eight *"Stratocruisers"* to start its trans-ocean service. Other carriers fell in line, (SAS) the Scandinavian Airlines System, British Overseas Airways Corporation (BOAC), Northwest Orient Airlines, United Air Lines, all placed orders for the *"Stratocruiser"* bringing the total above the fifty mark.

Bill Allen's "big gamble" paid off.

The *"Stratocruiser"* had saved the day for Boeing as a builder of commercial airliners. And when the first of the planes went into service, almost overnight, they became the "showcase" for post-war air transportation.

Main cabin of the "Stratocruiser" was divided into sections and was much larger than any of the other post-war airliners. Male passenger in back of hostess, is descending "spiral staircase" to lower lounge. Trend toward "spaciousness" began with Model 377.

The "Stratocruiser," converted into a sleeper plane with 28 full-sized Pullman berths. As dayplane it could carry up to 100 passengers.

You had to see it, and ride in the *"Stratocruiser"* to believe it was happening.

She was king-sized and super deluxe!

Inside the cabin, you almost forgot she was an airplane.

V

I REMEMBER the first time I saw one of Northwest Airlines *"Stratocruisers"*, and boarded her for a short trip from Chicago to St. Paul. It was in the spring of 1949 – 20 years ago – and the double-decker airliner parked on the apron at the Chicago terminal seemed to dwarf the United Air Lines DC-6 and the TWA Lockheed *"Constellation"* which were parked nearby. And the others were considered BIG airliners. But the *"Stratocruiser"* had a 20-foot greater wing span, her fuselage was 15 feet longer and her fat fuselage was by comparison like the shape of a whale alongside a shark. She was, indeed, the Big Plane Concept exemplified.

There were many configurations with regard to seating capacity in her cabin, depending upon the individual airline, but she could carry from 55 to 100 passengers. As a "sleeper" there were 28 upper and lower berths. But the feature nobody will ever forget was the spiral staircase in the center of the cabin that went down to a 14-passenger lounge. And the view from there, below the wing, gave one the feeling of riding in a glass-bottom boat.

This lower lounge was the "thing" that made her the talk of the airlanes. For the first time, if you got tired of sitting, you could get up and "go downstairs." There was something about just being able to do it, that gave air travel a new image.

I remember, Northwest's time-table had a sticker on its front cover. The sticker read: "ENJOY THE LOUNGE . . . ONE DRINK TO ST. PAUL . . . TWO DRINKS TO SEATTLE!"

That was part of the "new look", too.

Somebody even dubbed her – *"The Statuscruiser."*

Sometimes, there were as many as five cabin attendants, the number varied. Flight crew consisted of pilot, co-pilot and flight engineer on domestic flights. For overseas operation she carried a navigator and radio operator.

She didn't have a cockpit, she had a "Flight Deck". Back in her day (BH, Before hijacking) they would let you stand in the doorway and look at the flight crew at work. Up front, there was plenty of room; big windows, good visibility. And the pilots' compartment was equipped with the very latest electronic aids, for safe flight operation, communications and navigation.

Performance-wise her design and powerplants (four Pratt & Whitney 3500-take-off-rated-horsepower engines) gave her a cruising speed well above 300-miles-per-hour at altitudes between 20,000 and 25,000 feet. Even so, better than five miles up, her cabin atmosphere was kept at sea-level pressure, and she was completely air-conditioned. Her empty weight was about 75,000 pounds, and she could carry almost that in payload. She had a range in excess of 3000 miles.

Several of Pan American's *"Stratocruisers"*, modified to carry additional fuel, introduced the first non-stop New York to London service.

In many ways she was air travel – high, wide, and then some.

Unforgettable feature of the Boeing "Stratocruiser" was the first class lower lounge. Here, we see the famous "spiral staircase" which years later would be incorporated in the 747 "Super Jet." Note the small bar in rear. Passengers liked opportunity to move around.

Her greatest contribution, perhaps, was to bring a kind of "spaciousness" to the once cramped and confined passenger accommodations of the smaller airliners.

By her very size, she provoked the question – *How big will they get?*

The "front office" in the "Stratocruiser" was a maze of instrument panels and controls. Cockpit was surrounded by windows, and pilots called it "the greenhouse." Flight Engineer's panel is at right. This was Northwest Orient Airlines' cockpit arrangement for Model 377.

Biggest plane of the post-war era was this Consolidated C-99 military transport. It could carry up to 400 troops. Only one was built.

There was already flying at the time the "*Stratocruisers*" went into service, a much larger transport-type aircraft – the Consolidated XC-99 designed to carry 375 combat troops, a 265,000-pound, six-engined sky giant. Only one was built. Its performance fell short of expectations attributed, primarily, to the existing powerplants. Two engines . . . four engines . . . six engines! There would be a time when you would run out of wing and a place to put any more horsepower. What was needed was a whole new kind of power source.

The "*Stratocruiser*" was the last of Boeing transports designed around the piston-engine and the propeller.

But we shall see her basic fuselage configuration again in the first U.S.-built jet transport, a design Boeing had "on-paper", and had started building in 1956 when the last of the "*Stratocruisers*" was delivered to the airlines.

The era of jet propulsion was about to begin.

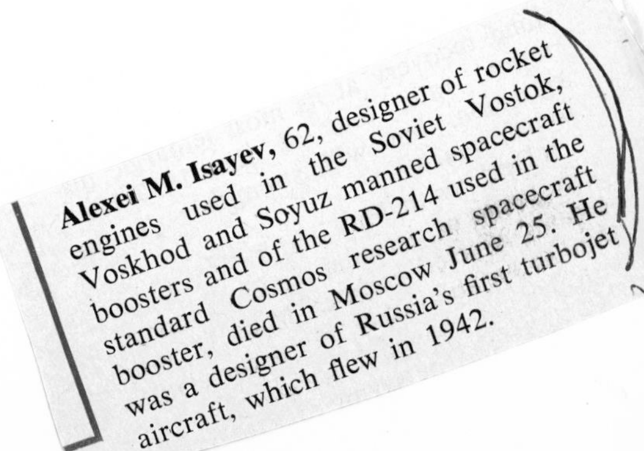

Alexei M. Isayev, 62, designer of rocket engines used in the Soviet Vostok, Voskhod and Soyuz manned spacecraft boosters and of the RD-214 used in the standard Cosmos research spacecraft booster, died in Moscow June 25. He was a designer of Russia's first turbojet aircraft, which flew in 1942.

CHAPTER EIGHT

A Whole New Kind Of Power!

BACK in 1922 while tests were being conducted on Dr. Sanford Moss' turbo-supercharger U.S. Air Service engineers at Mc Cook Field requested the Bureau of Standards to investigate the practicability of jet propulsion motors for aircraft. Ironically, a study prepared by Edgar Buckingham and later published by the National Advisory Committee for Aeronautics, concluded: *"Propulsion by the reaction of a simple jet cannot compete, in any respect, with airscrew propulsion at such flying speeds as are now in prospect."* Needless-to-say, the idea went "pfft," like when you let the air out of a toy balloon and it goes "jetting" around the room – the basic principle of jet propulsion. And it was not until 20 years later that the U.S. had its first experimental jet-propelled aircraft. The breakthrough came about almost simultaneously in England, Italy and Germany.

In 1928 an Englishman, Frank Whittle, had written a thesis on the potential of gas turbines in aircraft and jet propelled flight. Whittle carried his idea farther and took out his first patents two years later. The British Government officially showed enough interest, and Whittle formed Power Jets Ltd. in 1936 to build a turbojet engine.

About the same time in Germany, Hans von Ohain, who had been doing research in the same field, applied for his patent on a turbine engine for aircraft. Meanwhile, in Italy, Ing. Secondo Campini had the idea of hooking up a piston engine to drive a three-stage compressor, burning the exhaust gases in a tailpipe, thus producing jet thrust. The next logical step was to apply these powerplant developments to aircraft.

What happened was a well kept secret because of military security reasons during World War II, but it seems pertinent to relate here briefly, because it led Boeing and other aircraft manufacturers in this country to the threshold of the Jet Age. The Englishman, the German and the Italian with their ideas of jet propulsion thrust Boeing and others into the era of jet propulsion.

On August 27, 1939 a German Heinkel (He-178) aircraft powered with a turbojet engine (von Ohain's principle) was successfully flown – the first jet-powered aircraft in the world to fly. The following year Campini's engine in a Caproni-built Italian aircraft was also flown, but with disappointing results (little more than 100 mph speed) because of the piston engine driving the jet, although in principle it was jet-propelled, one of the first aircraft to fly without a propeller. Then, on May 15, 1941, Whittle's engine in a British Gloster airframe made its maiden flight. Because England was our ally, and Italy and Germany our enemies, American military men were advised of the Whittle engine, and the suc-

Sir Frank Whittle (right) was knighted for his development of first successful British jet engine. Whittle started experiments in 1928.

After end of World War II, captured records revealed Germans had flown this Heinkel (He-178) with von Ohain turbine engine in 1939.

Caproni — 1940
Gloster — 1941
Messerschmitt - 1941 ?
Bell 1942

Italians had this Caproni-built propellerless aircraft flying in 1940. It employed jet principle with piston engine driving compressors.

cess of the first Allied jet-propelled aircraft.

Among the first to know the secret was General Henry H. Arnold, Chief of the U.S. Army Air Forces, and when "Hap" Arnold heard about it he flew to England to take a closer look. When he came home, Arnold called a special meeting of his top engineering people. General "Red" Echols was there, the man who had done so much to help further the B-29 project, and Brigadier General Benjamin W. Chidlaw and Brigadier General Frank O. Carroll of the Engineering Division at Wright Field, along with key civilian engineers from General Electric Company (builders of the turbo-superchargers for the B-17s) and Bell Aircraft Company, builders of the P-39 *Airacobra* fighters. Assistant Secretary of War, Robert A. Lovett was also present.

After some preliminary discussion General Arnold took a packet of blueprints from his brief case and announced: "These, gentlemen, are the plans for the Whittle

British "Gloster" fighter with Whittle jet turbine was first Allied jet propelled aircraft. Plane was flying months before Pearl Harbor.

General Henry H. "Hap" Arnold, Chief of the United States Air Forces in World War II, pushed hard for U.S. to get into the jet engine race.

Engine. Your job, is to build one like it and better and, then, design an airframe around it. Now, let's get to work."

A few days later, Colonel Donald J. Keirn, chief of the Powerplant Laboratory at Wright Field, received a set of strange orders. The orders read: *"You will proceed . . . to determine the desirability of adopting package power plants and to investigate late developments of sleeve valves."*

Keirn's destination was England. Not until he reached there, did he learn that *"sleeve valves"* were the RAF's new jet plane, and *"packaged power plants"* were Frank Whittle's engine. The B-24 Keirn flew back to the U.S. had a precious cargo under its floorboards – a complete working engine of Whittle's design.

The engine was turned over to General Electric laboratories in Lynn, Massachusetts, and GE supercharger engineers went to work to carry out "Hap" Arnold's order – *build a better engine.* The result was the I-16 jet engine. Meanwhile, Bell Aircraft in Buffalo, had been at work designing a new plane to accept the powerplant. The U.S. was getting into the jet race.

Early in the fall of 1942, things out of

the ordinary started to happen at the Army Air Forces' secret test base, Muroc Lake, California – today's Edwards Air Force Base, home of the Aerospace Test Pilots School and where, at this writing, the Boeing 747 *Superjet* is undergoing extensive flight performance tests (see Chapter 14). Strangely, what happened there 27 years ago, was destined to have a great influence on Boeing's thinking to get into the Jet Age without which, the 747 might never have come into being. But it did happen, and the strange goings-on at Muroc in 1942 played an important role. The whole place was shrouded in tight security. A battallion of MPs had moved in. There was a special hangar whose windows had been covered with curtains and a heavy guard around it. Every day VIPs landed in big planes and disappeared into the hangar, to come out again, and fly away.

Even the highest-ranking officers on the base didn't know what was going on inside. An MP explained it to a General whom he refused to let in – *"What's going on inside there is the hope of tomorrow. We are coming out with a gadget that will revolutionize the sewing machine."*

The *gadget* was Lawrence Bell's XP-59 fighter design, our first jet-propelled aircraft. It was a mid-wing monoplane of all-metal construction powered with two of General Electric's I-16 turbojet engines. It had a thin laminar-flow wing design so that it would cut through the air like a hot knife through butter. But there was one thing very strange about it. There were no propellers!

On September 29, 1942, chief test pilot for Bell, Robert M. Stanley walked out to

Built by Bell Aircraft this XP-59 ("Aircomet") was first successful USAF jet plane. It was powered by two General Electric jet turbines.

the plane, now parked on the Flight Line, and climbed into the cockpit. With an observer squeezed into a special cockpit up front they tried some taxi runs and then an engine started acting up. With one engine, they raced across the desert and lifted the plane up several feet above the crust. That was really the *first flight* of a jet-propelled airplane in this country. But they didn't do much more that day.

It was October 1, bright and clear, when Stanley, alone, took the plane up for a real test. And when he came down he remarked – "This is the greatest thing that has happened to aviation since the Wright Brothers first flew at Kitty Hawk."

There followed months of testing the XP-59 at Muroc. Meanwhile, Bell Aircraft got an order to build thirteen more P-59s as trainers. GE was working on a more powerful jet engine. So was Westinghouse and Pratt & Whitney. And Lockheed Aircraft Corporation was building the "*Shooting Star*" destined to become America's first combat jet aircraft. Close on the heels of the P-80 was another jet fighter, the Republic XP-84 readied for the new Westinghouse TG-100 axial-flow compressors instead of the centrifugal-flow GE-jet engines. Consolidated Aircraft was also reported working on a propeller/jet combination powerplant for the XP-81 fighter.

Just about everybody was thinking jet power.

Where was Boeing?

Fortunately, Ed Wells, who had been project engineer on the Model 299, prototype of the "*Flying Fortress*" was present during some of the tests of the XP-59 at Muroc. Wells had worked on every bomber design since. And when he saw the XP-59 perform, he couldn't help thinking – *"Why not a jet bomber?"*

That was in September of 1943, and when he got back to Seattle, Ed Wells talked the idea over with the higher-ups. Nobody seemed excited, but nobody built any barriers, either. So Wells and Preliminary Design Chief, Bob Jewett, worked up a design for a jet-powered bomber.

Boeing hadn't built a fighter since the P-26 pursuit. The name Boeing was synomonous with *big planes*. Bombers and transports. *"Superforts"* and *"Strato-cruisers."* Moreover, it was obvious there was a limit to what could be done with conventional piston-engine-propeller powerplants. There was needed – *a whole new source of power.*

Jet propulsion was the answer.

In the beginning, the Boeing approach was to start with what they had, which meant a scaled-down B-29 design fitted with four jet engines mounted in pairs, in nacelles, under the wing. It had a thin wing, but not much different from the B-29 airfoil. The design didn't show much in wind tunnel tests.

"It was like hitching a Kentucky Derby winner to a dray wagon," said one engineer.

To use jet power effectively, you had to design a jet aircraft.

Germany's surrender and the end of World War II, signalled the beginning of a whole new approach to the design of jet aircraft. The war (in particular Germany's vast scientific alchemy of weapons which had produced the first jet fighter "Me-262," the rocket-powered fighter "ME-163," the frightening V-1 "buzz bombs" and V-2 rocket missiles) changed everybody's thinking about the shape and size and powerplants of wings to come.

Germans had Me-262s (above) flying combat in last days of Air War over Europe. Note sweptback wing, engine mountings and high tail.

Significantly, within ten years after VJ-Day the Boeing Airplane Company was producing a six-engined bomber, the B-47 *"Stratojet,"* the eight-engined B-52 *"Stratofort"* and had built the forerunner of the famous 707 series of jet transports – America's first passenger jetliners.

German Me-163 was first rocket-powered fighter. Later, it greatly influenced design of Bell X-1 first U.S. plane to fly faster than sound.

The period marked a gigantic step into tomorrow.

II

IN September of 1945, less than a month after VJ-Day, a little more than a week after Bill Allen had become the new company President, plans for a revolutionary new jet Bomber were submitted to the Air Force. This time, the design had little resemblance to the B-29 or anything else they had done in the past. It was an airplane with a highly *sweptback* wing with four jets throwing thrustpower back over the top of the fuselage and two more engines in the tail. Everybody was fired-up over the idea.

At Wright Field, critics put the fire out. "With all the engines in the fuselage," an armament expert said, "you could blow the thing up with a good burst of fifty-caliber gunfire."

"Try something else," said the Air Force.

Back to Seattle. Back to the drawing board. Back to the wind tunnel. And time was running out. North American had a medium jet bomber design. so did Consolidated Aircraft. Moreover, the Air Force had given them contracts to go ahead and build prototypes. If Boeing was to stay in the race, they would have to come up with something radically different. In Seattle, the decision was to "go way out."

The "way out" airplane became Boeing Model 450 (Air Force designation XB-47) and when preliminary sketches and models were presented this time at Wright Field even the military was excited. In April, 1946 Boeing got a contract to build two prototypes. And two months later, another experimental contract came through for a much heavier bomber, a 360,000-pound design with turbo-prop (gas turbines driving the propellers) which Boeing had been working on, paralleling the Model 450 program. It, too, had an Air Force number . . . XB-52. Both planes marked the beginning of a new era at Boeing. The post-war picture puzzle was beginning to come through much clearer.

Indeed, history was repeating itself. The whole situation was very much like what had happened back in 1934 with the Model 299 *"Flying Fortress"* and the XB-15 *"Super bomber."* With the XB-47 Boeing had a design which it was hoped would go into mass production the same as was hoped for the 299. There was every indication, sooner or later, the Air Force would have to go jet in its bomber program. It was pretty certain the first big production orders would be for a medium-size, medium-range jet bomber type. With the XB-52, Boeing – as had been the case with the XB-15 – was being given the chance to explore the potential of big planes with jet power. The hope was that history would stay in line.

As it turned out history was most obliging.

III

THE first XB-47 built at Plant Two in Seattle, birthplace of the B-17, was rolled out of the factory onto the apron at Boeing Field on September 12, 1947. Ironically, it was 24 months, minus one day, since Boeing had submitted its first proposal for a jet bomber to Wright Field for evaluation. The XB-47, unveiled for the first time, was a far cry from that original design. It was, as one observer remarked, "an extreme departure from traditional airframe design, the like of which the industry has never seen before!" The comment was well justi-

Boeing got into the Jet Age with this bomber design, the XB-47, shown here during roll-out ceremony. Swept-back wing, jet engines in pods under wing, and bicycle-type landing gear were revolutionary features. Because of thin wing, plane carried all its fuel (kerosene) in fuselage.

fied. And for those who were allowed to see it at close range — there was no public ceremony for the rollout — the reaction was one of awesome curiosity at the strange configuration. Some veteran Boeing employees had seen the first *Monomail* and that was something new; they had seen the first *"Flying Fortress,"* the 299, and that was sensational. But this gleaming thing with the drooping wings, no propellers, and a tandem bicycle-wheel undercarriage — it was *something else!*

You had to see it to believe it.

The wing! That was what made it look so extremely different. The reason was the way it came sweeping back from each side of the fuselage, at an angle so sharp it gave the profile of an arrowhead. And it was so thin, almost razor-edge like. When you looked at it head-on, there didn't seem to be any span at all. Yet, it was 116 feet, tip to tip, greater in span than the wing of the latest B-17, and in area it was almost equal to that of the B-29 *"Superfortress,"* whose wing span was 25 feet more. Moreover, it looked so different because there was no great round engine nacelles to clutter up its leading edge.

Or, was that really what gave her the "new look"? The arrangement of the six General Electric J-35 turbojet engines slung in bullet-shaped pods under the wings, to say the least, was a radical departure from normal engine mount configuration. A pair of the engines in a single pod, on streamlined nacelle and strut arrangement, were mounted to each side of the fuselage on the wing about a third of its span out. The other two engines, in single pods, were slung out near the wing tips. Some said this gave her "that droopy look," although the wings were purposely designed with this flexibility.

Take a second look. It wasn't really the wing. Or the pods and the way they were hung that accounted for her unusual appearance. Hell no. It was the fuselage and the landing gear and the fighter plane-like canopy in the nose, that made her a swinger. Indeed! In profile she looked like a king-sized, elongated P-80 *"Shooting Star,"* one of the first jet fighters.

Perhaps, it was the arrangement for her crew of three, pilot, co-pilot/gunner, and bombardier/navigator. There were three cockpits, one in the bullet-shaped nose,

On flight line at Boeing Field, the XB-47 dwarfs B-50 last of the propeller-driven bombers Boeing built for the Air Force. High degree of sweepback in wing is most evident in this photograph. Holes in side of fuselage are for JATO rockets. "Stratojet" was A-bomb carrier.

for the bombardier, below the pilots, who sat in seats on top of the fuselage, one behind the other, under a king-sized fighter-type, tear-drop shaped canopy.

Surprisingly, she was almost 10 feet longer than the B-29. Built long with a purpose. To carry a single 22,000-pound bomb with conventional explosives, and the first bomber designed to carry thermo-nuclear weapons of the post-war type. The fuselage had to be shaped like it was to permit such bomb stowage.

The XB-47's armament was also revolutionary. The *"Stratojet"* unlike Model 299 with its bristling gun blisters which earned it the unforgettable name, *"Flying Fortress"* had only two .50 caliber guns in an unmanned turret in the tail. High-speed, stripped-down B-29s in World War II had proved they were almost invulnerable except for attack from the rear. And the XB-47 was twice as fast as any wartime *"Superfortress!"* Hence, the two tail guns which could be fired manually by the co-pilot, or automatically by radar which could spot any attacker approaching the guns' cone of fire.

The way she rested on the ground, that beat anything. No main gear and tail wheel arrangement like the B-17. No nose wheel and main gear configuration like the B-29. No wheel retraction into the engine nacelles in the wings, because there were no nacelles. Instead, dual wheels on a truck mounted forward of the wing, and another set mounted to the rear of the wing, in tandem (like a bicycle's wheels) retractable into the fuselage ahead of and behind the bomb bay.

These were just some of the outward

Unique bicycle-type landing gear arrangement is more evident in this photo of XB-47. Note small outrigger wheels on inboard pods for balance.

In a cloud of smoke, XB-47 leaps off the runway using JATO rockets. Rockets were seldom used, but would permit short take-offs and increased payload for short-range missions. The thin wing is also most evident in this photograph, but engine cluster at right is due to camera angle.

innovations that made her appear so different. But the XB-47 also had some built-in features, vital to her performance. There were strange-looking tubes sticking out of the side of her fuselage, rocket exhaust stacks. Inside she was fitted with eighteen JATO (jet-assisted take-off) solid fuel rockets. Each had a 1,000-pound thrust. These rocket boosters, at a critical moment during take-off, gave her an extra push to permit operation from regulation airfields of her day. Since the first jet engines were slow to accelerate at sea-level, she needed this extra thrust to get airborne without using up too much runway.

Likewise, her extremely high wing loading, and the fact that the jet engines at this stage of development could not produce reverse thrust, made landings critical at certain weights. As a precaution against this, she was fitted with a deceleration parachute which popped out of the fuselage from a compartment under the tail, its release triggered by the pilot. The 'chute, a ribbon type, was 32-feet in diameter and served as an airbrake permitting landings to be made with greater safety.

Hidden from the eye, too, was the fact that the XB-47 carried all of her fuel inside the fuselage. The thin wing did not permit internal fuel tanks as did the more conventional designs before her.

And, of course, she was different because she did not burn high octane aviation gasoline. She burned kerosene.

Who said the Jet Age was so new? It was dependent upon coal oil, the stuff grandma used to burn in her kitchen stove.

Paradoxically, for all of these innovations which one saw in the first XB-47 there on the apron at the time of first rollout, none of them in itself was really new. The sweptback wing had been used on the Me-262 and in this country on the North American XP-86 fighter design. A Martin B-26 modified *Marauder* bomber had tried out the idea of the tandem bicycle-type landing gear. And hadn't the old Ford Trimotor used the principle of hanging the engines from a strut arrangement on the wings? The JATO system also had been used on heavily-loaded bombers during World War II and on large flying boats. And the drag 'chute had been tried on several fighters.

But the thing that was really new, a forward step, was that the XB-47 brought all of these things together in one aircraft. In this respect, she set a pattern that would dominate the design and development of jet bombers and jet transports for the next two decades.

It would, truthfully, not change until the men who had designed and built her and their successors, younger men with newer ideas, began thinking about the plane of

Drag chute blossoms as XB-47 comes in for a landing. Like JATO units for assist in take-off, the landing chute was there as built-in safety feature. Its use was not always required. As plane slows down note how wing is beginning to "droop," a distinctive feature.

the "seventies" – the 747 *Super jet.*

And even then, as someone has pointed out, they couldn't forget the "47" in designating the model number of today's jet transport leviathan of the skies.

IV

IT was 66 days from the time of the XB-47 roll-out until the plane was scheduled to make its maiden flight, December 17, 1947 – the 44th anniversary of the Wright Brothers' first flight in a heavier-than-air, power-driven, man-carrying flying machine at Kitty Hawk, North Carolina. The Flight Plan called for the XB-47 to take off from Boeing Field, fly over the Cascade mountains and land on the long runways of the Moses Lake Air Force Base. Nobody was taking any chances. There was no question about getting off. They could always use the JATO power, if necessary. Take off like a rocket. But it seemed a good measure to have the large area at Moses Lake for the landing. Away from the more populated area of Plant Two in Seattle.

Even among those who had designed and built her, there was concern and anxiety. After all, no aircraft with so large a sweptback wing had ever flown before. None of her size and weight had ever tried landing with the bicycle-type gear. Likewise, she was the largest and heaviest (76,000 pounds, empty weight) jet-powered aircraft ever built up to this time. Test pilot Bob Robbins would have at his finger tips *three times* the power of the B-29 "*Superfortress.*"

Some chariot he would be driving. Hitched up to 27,000 horses, or about the equivalent in thrustpower to horsepower ratio.

It was asking a lot of him and his co-pilot, Scott Osler. They could make or break the hopes of everybody at Boeing. This was not just another "first flight" of a conventional aircraft. The XB-47 "*Stratojet*" was the Big Plane breakthrough into the Jet Age. She was carrying the future of Boeing on her wings.

The day dawned under a grey sky. A report from Moses Lake said there was ice on the runway. But the weatherman promised clearing skies, and they said the ice would probably go away. The project engineer, George Martin, said if the weather cleared they would try it.

There had been no public announcement of the flight, but the word had got out, and hundreds of persons in their cars found vantage points around the field. Key Boeing personnel gathered around the Flight Test Operations building. This was military business, but this wasn't wartime. So, there were newsreel cameramen present, and radio broadcasters, numbers of magazine and press representatives. The weather cleared.

Shortly after lunch Robbins and Osler, wearing crash helmets and carrying oxygen masks, climbed into the bubble canopy and started running down the check list. Word came everything was OK at Moses Lake.

The six jets started with a whine, and XB-47 started whistling up a storm. At 1:42 PM Robbins started her rolling down the runway. The moment of truth was now . . .

About a quarter way down the concrete, he saw a red light flashing on the instrument. It was a fire warning. Number two engine. And he cut the power, braked the "*Stratojet*" to a rolling stop.

A check showed the alarm to be a false instrument reading, and they turned around to start the take-off once more. Robbins was sure everything was all right.

Poised and ready again, he released the brakes at 2:02 PM and the plane once more started to roll down the runway. She rolled and she rolled and she rolled, a characteristic pilots would have to learn about the jets. They were slow to lift off.

Past the V-2 marker on the runway, which meant the plane was committed to fly, Robbins showed concern. He started to reach for the JATO release. But he never did fire the rockets . . .

"You're airborne!"

He got the word from the tower, and he didn't even know the XB-47 was off the ground! They were sixty feet in the air and climbing like sixty . . .

Thump! The gear came up, and there was only the swishing of air inside the cockpit. No throbbing, irritating vibration of propellers whipping the air. Helmeted, with built-in earphones, the pilots could hear only the chatter of voices.

On the ground, observers watched the sweptwing bomber climb like a fighter. And, perhaps, they were awed by the thin trails of dark smoke in the plane's wake. The odor of kerosene fumes she had left on the ground. And the still echoing, shrieking, whistling sound and roar of her engines.

Out of sight now, high in the sky in her own domain, the XB-47 was proving to her pilots she was a marvelous piece of machinery.

Over the inter-com, Robbins commented – *She handles like a pursuit plane!"*

He tried some S-turns. Good response. Quick response.

They let the gear down. It got a little rough. But when they used the flaps to slow the plane down, she smoothed herself out.

Robbins eased back on the power to bring the ship near the stalling speed. He was relieved, she didn't have any tendency to fall off on one wing. And she gave plenty of warning before approaching the stalling speed.

Then, he shut down one engine purposely.

No sign of instability.

Then, he tried a landing in the air. Everything he'd do in a few minutes at Moses Lake – up to a point. Low thrust. Gear Down. Flaps. Everything was perfect.

This is one helluva airplane, Robbins thought to himself.

In the next few minutes they were landing at Moses Lake. The bicycle undercarriage touched down easily. Then, she wobbled a little on the outrigger wheels, but she rolled to a stop.

They didn't use the drag 'chute.

There was plenty of runway left.

Bob Robbins told inquisitive reporters – "This is a new breed of an aircraft. You have to fly it to believe it."

Months of testing proved the new breed could take it and dish it out. The Air Corps people ordered ten for service test – $30,000,000. Then, in September, 1948 the word came that the B-47 *"Stratojet"* would go into mass production at the Boeing plant in Wichita, Kansas. And before the last B-47 would roll out of the Wichita facility, October 24, 1956, more than 2,000 of the *"stratojets"* had been produced.

Boeing would have the know-how for building large jet aircraft that no other manufacturer could claim.

One day, that would be the influencing factor that would give men the daring to build a plane of the size of the 747 *Super jets.*

The Jet Age would also give us a new breed of men and the kind of machines they would create.

Gear retracted, in a shallow banking attitude, a production model B-47 (Boeing Model 450) looks more like a streamlined "king-sized" fighter than bomber that was larger than the famed B-29 "Superfortress." Shadow makes this B-47 appear to have unusual wing span. Look again!

CHAPTER NINE

America's First Jetliner

IN the fall of 1950 the Boeing Wichita factory was a bee-hive of B-47s moving down the production lines as fast as the pieces could come together. The *"Stratojet"*, vastly improved since its historic first flight in December of 1947, had set spectacular performance records, and was now regarded as the principal medium bomber in the new United States Air Force's growing global operations. A 600-mile-an-hour nuclear strike weapon that could go anywhere with newly developed air-to-air refueling techniques, she was the fastest jet aircraft of any size flying anywhere. Small wonder Boeing President William M. Allen stood there on the flight line at Wichita with a look of pride in his eyes as they rolled out one of the gleaming new *"Stratojets"*, and readied it for him to take his first jet ride. Bill Allen had been a driving force in making this baby possible. It was almost five years to the day since he had taken over control of the company, at a time when he had to make the decision to go jet power. Now, it was a good way to celebrate, see what it was like in the "front office" of Boeing's first and latest jet-powered aircraft.

Allen was suited up with slip-over coveralls, helmet, oxygen mask and parachute, and he walked out to the *"Stratojet"* whose engines were already whistling. They had the small aluminum ladder already in position so he could climb up through the bottom hatch into the ship's bullet-shaped

Jet Age manufacturing know-how was gained by Boeing when the XB-47 "Stratojet" bombers went into production. This was typical assembly line scene at Boeing Wichita. Douglas and Lockheed also built B-47s.

Boeing President, Bill Allen, who made decision to build XB-47, climbs aboard for first jet ride.

nose, where he would ride in the bombardier/navigator's seat, below the pilot and co-pilot in their bubble canopy on top of the fuselage. Pilot Doug Heimburger and co-pilot Ed Hartz were already strapped in and ready. Minutes before, a mechanic had kidded Heimburger – "Not many guys get to be higher than the boss!"

Bill Allen had heard the remark, and he smiled to himself as he climbed into the forward cockpit and the hatch slammed shut. Perhaps, he was thinking, *not many bosses get a chance to be this close to the end product and experience such a thrill of satisfaction.* It was one way, the only way, to really keep on top of things. Bill Allen is like that.

Inside the forward compartment now, oxygen mask plugged in, earphones crackling, Allen heard the pilot's voice, "All set, Mr. Allen?".

"O.K. Let's go." Allen was excited a little. He was anxious to find out what jet flight was like. He had heard so much about it.

The jet started to move, taxiing out to the end of the runway. There, it stopped. But in the next instant, with the roar of the engines behind him increasing, they were racing down the runway. Through the tiny window in front of him, Allen could see the concrete ribbon reeling in at an alarming rate. He was so close to the runway, and they were moving so fast, it almost made him dizzy.

The ribbon dropped away. Not a quiver, and they were off the ground. He couldn't believe it, so fast, so quiet, so smooth, and climbing like a fighter plane. No vibration. No noise.

Jet flight was a sensation. Exhilarating.

On the navigator's instrument panel in front of him, he could see the altimeter needle moving . . . 5,000 feet . . . 10,000 and climbing, until they levelled off at 20,000 almost five miles up in the Kansas sky. He looked out the side window and back to see the tips of the sweptback wings; the wing was perfectly straight now, no droopy look. The wing's high degree of flexibility was riding the cushions of air and smoothing out the wrinkles.

The plane banked in a sweeping arc. Then, it straightened out again on a new course, and Allen settled back to relax.

It was so quiet and smooth. Allen couldn't help thinking – *so much quieter, so much smoother* than flight in the piston-powered propeller planes in which he had flown. His thoughts wandered: *Why shouldn't everybody enjoy this kind of flying? The air traveler was being discriminated against. The airlines should have a jet transport.* He wondered how the boys back in Seattle in Preliminary Design were coming along with Boeing's proposed new jetliner design. *Hell, if the world situation would just calm down, they could be building a commercial jet transport.* The thought hit him that Boeing had just delivered its last *"Stratocruiser". Except for some on-paper studies Boeing was out of the commercial airplane market . . .*

The pilot's voice over the inter-com interrupted his thoughts. "Would you like to do some test maneuvers, Mr. Allen?" Heimburger asked.

"No. I just want to see what jet transportation will be like."

And he said to himself, "It's wonderful!"

The flight lasted for about an hour and then, they were back on the ground again, and shortly afterward, Bill Allen was sitting in the seat of a TWA *"Constellation"* enroute to Chicago, New York and then, out across the Atlantic for England to see what Europe was doing in the new world of the jets. He enjoyed flying, the comfort and the swiftness of air transportation. But this trip was different. He was nervous and irritated. Not because the flight wasn't enjoyable. But because he kept thinking about being up there in the B-47 a few hours before, and how much different jet flight was from flight in the conventionally powered propeller airliner.

There wasn't any doubt about it. Sooner or later, the airlines would have to go jet. Boeing had better do something about it.

In England at the annual Farnborough air show, he saw another reason why Boeing had better get busy. There, the new DeHavilland *"Comet"* jetliner was on display. It was a beautiful silver and white and blue airliner, a low-wing monoplane with four jet engines buried in the wing, tricycle landing gear, wide, comfortable fuselage, with room for almost 100 passengers, capable of 500-mile an hour speeds, half again as fast as the *"Stratocruiser."* Moreover, British Overseas Airways Corporation (BOAC) already had ordered the *"Comet"* and was planning to put it into service in the near future.

Just looking at the plane, Allen knew that the British could grab the lead in the commercial plane market with such an airliner. It was just a matter of time. Catching up would be tougher than Hell.

At the Air Show, reporters asked him point blank — "When is Boeing going to build a commercial jet transport?"

British took lead in commercial Jet Age when BOAC introduced this four-engined DeHavilland "Comet."

Bill Allen wished he could answer. But there were so many things to do first. The big, long-range XB-52 jet bomber had priority over everything. They would just have to wait and see what happened.

II

WHAT had happened to the XB-52 bomber project read almost like fiction. The reader will remember that the big plane had started out as a turbo-prop design (see Chapter Eight) but all of that had changed. The tremendous success of the XB-47, air-to-air refuelling techniques that had given it good range, and the prospect of much more powerful jet engines from Pratt & Whitney and Westinghouse had the Air Force people thinking pure jet power for the big bomber. The jet engine driving propellers (turbo-prop combination) was out. So it was, that Boeing engineers had reworked the basic concept into an eight-engined turbojet bomber. In October of 1948, they had taken it to Wright Field to sell.

Things didn't go the way they had planned at all. Colonel Pete Warden, a young engineer who was bombardment project officer, and who had done so much to further the XB-47 program, took one look at the new XB-52 proposal and shook his head. The state of the art had made too many advances, he pointed out. They should take a fresh look at what could be done and come up with a more advanced idea.

"Think more along the lines of the B-47 design," Pete Warden said with a glint in his eye. "And come back and see us."

That was on a Friday. Over the weekend, the Boeing Group which was in Dayton and included the company's top engineering and design talent, holed-up in a hotel room and went to work. They gave the XB-52 a greater sweptback wing, like the XB-47. They took the jet engines out of the fuselage and hung them in pods on the wings, four pods, each with a pair of engines. From data available, which they had brought along, they projected performance and weight figures. What they did showed promise: Weight, in the 330,000 pound category, a plane almost double the size of the XB-47 to permit a fuel load that would give it much more range and permit a heavier payload. Speed, "more than 600 miles per hour," the data said. They even went so far as to carve a balsa wood model of the new bomber.

When it was done, the data and the model looked so good it even startled the men who had worked up the design.

Why the Hell hadn't they done this in the first place? Aerodynamically trim and clean, big enough and with plenty of power, the XB-52 looked like the kind of a bomber nobody could turn down.

"We've got another *'Flying Fortress',"* somebody remarked. And they gave it a name – *"Stratofortress."*

Monday morning they were back in Pete Warden's office with a thirty-three page detailed proposal and the XB-52 model.

The Air Force was more than pleased, and Boeing got the green light to go ahead and build two prototypes.

Of course, all of this was secret stuff. But the author remembers talking with Pete Warden, a good friend, about that time and we were talking about the XB-47 which Pete thought was the best thing that had ever happened. He beamed with pride everytime he mentioned the *"Stratojet."* But for a minute he got carried away.

"Dammit," he said, "I can't tell you what I want to tell you. But we've got a new jet bomber that will make the XB-47 look like a miniature; it's going to be the Sunday Punch that can knock anybody down and keep them in line . . ."

Later, I learned he was talking about the XB-52.

As things turned out America needed that Sunday Punch and needed it badly, much sooner than anyone had believed possible. Shortly after the XB-52 design had jelled, the Soviets closed the gates into Berlin, and "Operation Vittles," the Berlin Airlift had to take over. By their very act, the Russians had demonstrated that from now on the U.S. must stand alone. We needed the kind of range and the striking power and speed which the new *"Stratofortress"* promised. It didn't matter how much it cost. Fortunately, by the time "Operation Vittles" was in full swing, the huge wooden mock-up of the XB-52 was already taking shape in Seattle.

The prospect of the big XB-52 which would be faster even than the XB-47 and need tremendous amounts of fuel, started Boeing engineers thinking about a new jet tanker. The KC-97 propeller-driven tankers certainly weren't suited for the job. Nor was it economical to use the C-97s converted into flying tankers, an interim solution being used to give the *"Stratojets"* the kind of range they required to fill-in as the global defensive weapon.

A "team-mate" jet tanker for the XB-52 gave birth to another thought: Why not make a proposal to the military to build a jet *tanker/transport.* That was what had happened with the KC-97. It had started out as a big cargo plane, turned into a flying tanker "teammate" for the B-50s, the super *"Superfortresses,"* wound-up as the popular commercial *"Stratocruiser."* The whole idea seemed a natural process of evolution; one already proven.

Could they sell the jet tanker idea? Not right now, the Air Force wasn't interested. Everyone was shaking in his boots. The Pentagon was talking *"Polar Concept,"* with long-range bombers (flying without refuelling over the North Pole to any potential target) like the six-engined, piston-powered Consolidated B-36s, being built in Fort Worth to be the "backbone" of the Strategic Air Command's atom-carrier "deterrant force." The XB-52 was important to replace the B-36s. So much was dependent upon its success. The tankers would have to wait until they saw the *"Stratofortress."*

III

"RUNNING fast in the right direction," the words of Fred Rentschler, Bill Boeing's partner in the big United Aircraft combine of the twenties, took on Jet Age meaning when Pratt & Whitney in Hartford, Conn., announced its new J-57 jet engine had passed every test. With these engines, each promising 10,000-pounds thrust, the XB-52 would be ten times as powerful as the B-29s or the B-50s. Winged power. Thunder aloft. Awesome. But even moreso, was the fact that the U.S. had exploded the first Hydrogen bomb. A B-47 had dropped the H-bomb over a lonely Pacific

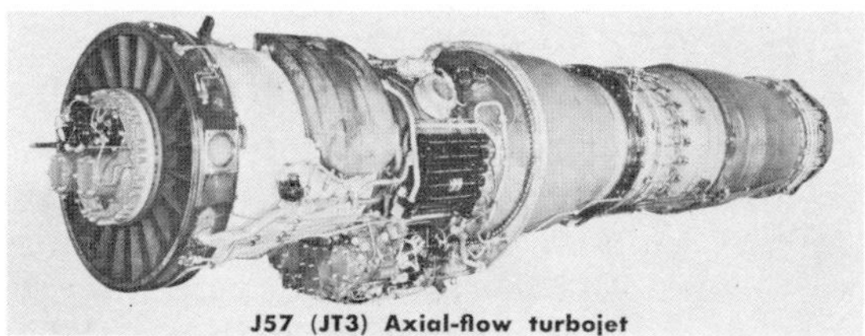

Development of this P&W axial-flow turbojet engine of 10,000-pound thrustpower, made possible XB-52.

Isle in a secret test – the new bomb was ten times as powerful as the A-bomb dropped on Hiroshima.

About the same time a B-29 flying an Arctic Mission picked up strange dust particles in the air. Later President Truman announced the Russians had exploded their first atomic bomb. Russia. Was she friend or foe? The cold war got red hot. Chinese communists crossed the 38th parallel into South Korea.

With these threats hanging over us, the Air Force pushed harder for the XB-52 development. "We need it to survive," declared a high-ranking Congressman. "To Hell with the cost." And the USAF ordered ten B-52s into production – about $15,000,000 each – to be built in the Wichita plant. The contract was signed many months before the first XB-52 was rolled out of Plant Two in Seattle. That event, everyone awaited with great anticipation.

Model 464, Boeing called it (B-52 series) the "*Stratofortress*," covered with white canvas, ghost-looking in appearance, was rolled out of final assembly, Plant Two, on November 29, 1951. There were very few Boeing workers even, who saw the thing like a big white whale being trundled over to the Flight Test Center building at Boeing Field. The roll-out was staged purposely at Thanksgiving time, to keep the B-52 secret as long as possible. There wasn't another rollout until spring, when they readied her for first flight.

April 15, 1952 was the day. And Test Pilot "Tex" Johnston, one-time Thompson Trophy winner, a pylon-pusher at the National Air Races, got the assignment to fly her. Colonel Guy Townsend, who like Pete Warden had fought for the B-47 program, was to be the co-pilot. This time, there was no keeping people from seeing

Korean crisis put cloak of secrecy around development of XB-52 "Stratofortress." On cold November night in 1951, first of the big jet bombers was rolled out "under wraps" from Seattle Plant Two.

her. The word was out about the test flight, and crowds jammed the area to get a glimpse of the giant. It was remindful of the time fifteen years, less six months to the day (October 15, 1937) when "Eddie" Allen had wheeled out the XB-15 for her maiden flight. The XB-15 was the biggest for her day. And it was true of the XB-52 in the Jet Age.

Comparing the giants for size was interesting. There were those present who had worked on both planes. Waiting for the take-off, they compared notes, tested memories.

XB-15

Crew: ten
Wing Span: 87 ft. 7 in.
Height: 18 ft. 1 in.
Length: 87 ft. 7 in.
Wing Area: 2,780 sq. ft.
Empty Wgt.: 37,700 lbs.
Gross Wgt.: 70,700 lbs.
Max. Speed: 200 mph.
Ceiling: 18,000 ft.
Powerplant: Four P&W twin Wasp, 850-hp, total 3400-hp.

XB-52

Crew: five
Wing Span: 185 ft.
Height: 48 ft.
Length: 152 ft.
Wing Area: 4,000 sq. ft.
Empty Wgt.: 160,000 lbs.
Gross Wgt.: 390,000 lbs.
Max. Speed: 550 mph.
Ceiling: 39,000 ft.
Powerplant: Eight P&W (J-57) jet engines, total approx. 70,000 thrust power. Converted: 140,000-hp.

What a giant thing she really was, this XB-52 "*Stratofortress*." The ultimate in power and design.

Poised there at the end of the 10,000-foot long runway at Boeing Field, she seemed eager to try her wings. From concept (the turbo-prop version) to creation, she represented seven years of effort.

There was a roar from her eight jet engines, and the whale started to move. Her size made her appear to be just creeping along at first, but she was gaining momentum, accelerating rapidly as the sound of her engines increased to the rumble of thunder, earsplitting, deafening. But nobody cared. There was light under the wheels . . . she was airborne.

The sight was worth the seven years.

Johnston climbed in a slow turn, then headed for The Cascade Mountains to the East, and Larson Air Force Base in the plain of Central Washington. The roar of the crowd almost matched the roar of the plane. Bill Allen was there, and Wellwood Beall, Ed Wells, Bob Jewett, Maynard Pennel, George Schairer, Bob Withington, Vaughn Blumenthal, Art Carlsen – the men who had worked up the design and made that model back in the Dayton hotel room. There wasn't any doubt now.

General Mark Bradley, Air Force Director of Procurement and Production was also a witness to the flight. Mark Bradley was all smiles. The "*Stratofortress*" was everything they had said it would be and more.

"Marvelous! Marvelous!" he said to Bill Allen.

It was less than six days later that Allen, at a special meeting of the Board of Directors, recommended the company go ahead and develop the jet-powered tanker/transport prototype. On the strength of flight test data coming in on the XB-52, he was sure the Air Force would increase the production order for more of the big jet bombers, and they would be needing the jet tanker to insure the global range.

The Board of Directors approved his request.

Boeing was going to build a jet transport. It would serve a dual purpose: A prototype for the jet tanker, but also as a prototype for America's first commercial jet airliner.

IV

EVER since the first successful jet turbines for aircraft had appeared on the scene, even in the latter days of World War II, Boeing designers had been playing with the idea of a jet transport. Quite naturally, they had turned to the basic "*Stratocruiser*" design with the idea of replacing its piston engines with turbo-props or turbojets. Remember, they had done the same thing when they first proposed the XB-52. The

XB-52 on first flight. Much larger than the XB-47, the new bomber resembled smaller sistership in profile. Sweptback wing, engine pods and tail were like features. She carried crew of five.

result was about the same. The project was abandoned in favor of a new approach with the sweptback wing and the engine pod arrangement. In short, they hung a transport's fuselage on the jet jombers' wings, keeping the same bicycle landing gear. The wind tunnel data looked pretty good. But, somehow, the design didn't look like an airliner. Structurally, the high-wing posed complications. It would of necessity, lower the ceiling in the main cabin. A tall passenger would have to duck under it, recalling to mind the inconvenience of the main spar which went through the cabin of the Boeing Model 247, the first modern airliner. Likewise, the bicycle undercarriage and the "droopy look" seemed out of place in an airliner configuration. The design group was told to come up with something new and different.

The jet tanker/transport was officially given project status on May 20, 1952, and the Board had allocated $15,000,000 to build the prototype. It was Boeing money. There was no Air Force experimental contract for the jet tanker, although just about everybody in the Air Force said they needed such a plane. Nor, was there any money coming from the airlines to help share in the development costs. Once more, Boeing was sticking its neck out. Admittedly, it was a big gamble, but it seemed good, once more, to be designing something for commercial use and not just another military airplane.

Coincidentally, the same day that the jet transport project became official, marked the 25th anniversary of the maiden flight of the Model-40A mail/passenger plane which put Boeing in the air transportation business back in 1927. It also marked the 25th anniversary of Lindbergh's take off on his epoch Paris flight. Was not this, perhaps, a good omen of things to come?

For company records, the jet tanker/transport project was designated Model 367-80 because it was the 80th configuration of the C-97 military *"Stratofreighter"* and its commercial version the *"Stratocruiser."* The project had another name, Model 707, but Boeing people who worked on it called the plane, the *"Dash Eighty"* even though in its ultimate form there was little if any resemblance to the C-97 or the *"Stratocruiser."*

Beyond this, *"Dash-Eighty,"* the jet tanker/transport protytype was an all new design. She emerged a low-wing, swept-wing monoplane resting on a conventional tricycle landing gear — dual nose wheels, and the main gear, two trucks with four wheels each, one on each side of the fuselage under

Prototype of first U.S. commercial jetliner, the Boeing 707 "Dash Eighty" is rolled out of hangar in Seattle. Note small, round windows. She was really designed as tanker/military transport.

the wing. She was powered with four Pratt & Whitney JT3, 10,000-pound thrust engines, the commercial version of the engines which powered the B-52 bombers. The engines were mounted in streamlined nacelles extending forward of the wing, but which seemed to be almost "molded" into the airfoil. She was designed to carry twice the payload of the "*Stratocruiser*" and with a cruising speed 200 miles an hour faster!

This was the prototype jet tanker/transport which was rolled out of the Renton facility where she was built on May 14, 1954 amid bands playing and prideful ceremony. She was painted a rich yellow with a copper brown trim, and she looked every inch an airliner type, not just a commercial version of a jet bomber. There were those who said they could hear her saying: "*Here, I am. Look me over. I'm everybody's jetliner . . .*"

Among those who saw her make her debut, rolling slowly out of the big hangar into the afternoon sunlight, was an honored guest. Those close to him said there were tears in his eyes.

His name was William E. Boeing.

Bill Boeing was 72, and he had little more than two years to live (He died September 28, 1956) but on this day he saw the realization of a dream. For the "*Dash Eighty,*" proud queen mother of a whole family of jetliners would make possible in a short time the kind of air transport Boeing had always wanted, wings for commerce, not wings for combat. Perhaps, he was thinking, too, of that July 4, 1914 (half a century ago) when he had taken his first airplane ride with Terah Maroney in the frail cloth and wood hydroplane. And now this . . . He watched as his wife, Bertha, christened the 707, prototype of the modern jetliner.

Bill Boeing's well-deserved *gift of prophecy.* His name proudly lettered on the fuselage.

Trailing edge wing flaps extended, gear down, "Dash-Eighty" comes in for landing. Truck-type main gear (four wheels) was later used on 747. Note upsweep of rear fuselage which resembles "Stratocruiser."

And two months later (July 15, 1954) on the 38th anniversary of the founding of The Boeing Airplane Company, "*Dash Eighty*," the 707 prototype, made its first flight ushering in the Jet Age for America.

The big question now was – *Could they sell this expensive piece of machinery? For what kind of a price tag?*

Bill Allen faced the problem squarely. "Sell the jet prototype," he told the Sales people, "or we may all have to start looking for new jobs."

The first break came when the Air Force, in March of 1955, ordered the jet tanker

KC-135 Air Force jet tanker, using Boeing-developed "boom-type" refuelling system, services B-52 in flight. Similarity of wing planform is evident. But bomber is high-wing and tanker a low-wing.

Experience in B-52 manufacture (shown here in one assembly stage) helped in setting up production line for tankers and jet transports. Many of the "Stratofortress" assemblies were interchangeable in KC-135.

version (KC-135) to go into production. There were more orders, too, for the B-52s. For the first time Allen saw some "blue sky." The new military business, dollar-wise, would cushion the costs of improving the Model 707 commercial transport to come out of the *"Dash Eighty"* prototype, a slightly larger, modified design keyed to passenger comfort and airline economics.

The 707 passenger jet came out with a longer, wider fuselage and slightly more wing, quieter engines and more thrust-power, a 600-mile-an-hour speed, wider cabin capable of carrying up to 179 passengers, non-stop, coast-to-coast.

Airline people came and went through the mock-up. But they still weren't committing themselves. That kind of money would buy ten of the biggest propeller-driven airliners. Where the Hell could they get it, still deep in debt for their piston-engined fleets? Moreover, would the traveling public accept this new kind of power? It was a helluva leap from 300 miles an hour to ten-mile-a-minute transportation. They'd have to sell a lot of tickets, and some people were still afraid to fly 150-miles-an-hour in the DC-3.

As always somebody had to try it.

Pan American broke the ice when President Juan Trippe on October 13, 1955 ordered twenty of the 707s. Less than a month later American Airlines signed up for thirty more. Other airlines followed.

The Boeing family of jetliners went into production.

Meanwhile, *"Dash-Eighty"* is still flying, fifteen years old as I write this, but in the air almost every day, a flying testbed for some new electronic gadgetry, or some other device or operational technique to further jet transportation. On the flight line at Seattle, parked near the

Out of the jet-powered tanker/transport prototype came the first Boeing 707 commercial airliner. In the years ahead, the 707 in many versions would roam world's skies in U.S. airline fleets.

giant 747 *Superjet,* she looks so small. But it must be remembered, she started it all, and through the years she pioneered just about every new development which would go into the whole family of Boeing jetliners.

She was the "flying wind tunnel" to prove new wing flaps that would go into the ultimate wing design of the 747. They rigged her up with a test engine mounted on the side of her fuselage in the tail to try out the engine configuration for the 727 trijet. She was the first to test fly engine noise suppressors developed by Boeing, and a new reverse thrust device, "jet brakes" which afforded greater safety for the largest jetliners to use conventional length runways in heavy-load landings. Here and there, what she did, is seen in every jetliner built by Boeing.

The first time I saw her, back in 1955, she came roaring out of the western sky and landed at Friendship Airport serving Baltimore and Washington, D.C. after a record-breaking non-stop flight (less than four hours) from Seattle. The last time I saw her (September, 1969) she took off with a roar on another test flight.

"They're testing something, that has to do with the SST, a mechanic on the line said. "I don't know what the Hell it is."

Strangely, her wings above the Duwamish were the sound of yesterday when it was tomorrow, and still the sound of tomorrow when it is today.

"Dash-Eighty," as flying test laboratory tries out fuselage engine pod mounting later used in 727 trijet.

Perhaps, more than any other design feature, the sweptback wing, so evident in this photograph of 707 jetliner prototype, led us successfully into jet Age. After 15 years plane is still flying.

CHAPTER TEN

The Jet Age Evolution

THE summer of 1958, a 707 Jetliner glistening silver with blue trim, Pan American colors, and with Old Glory stenciled on her towering vertical tail to signify she was a U.S. Flag Carrier, was rolled out of the hangar at Boeing Field and readied for its delivery flight. With a Pan-Am crew aboard she took off for Miami, Florida, the airline's big maintenance base. There, after an uneventful shakedown flight, she underwent a last minute inspection and leaped off again, this time for New York's Idlewild Airport (now Kennedy International) where she was refuelled, took on new cargo and her first load of ticket-paying passengers. There was appropriate pomp and ceremony, and then, "Jet Clipper America," license number N707PA, roared into the sky inaugurating Pan American's trans-Atlantic jet service.

It was October 26, 1958 The Jet Age had begun for U.S. commercial air transportation. The advent started a revolution and an evolution on the ground and in the air. Overnight, jet transportation was a sensation.

The seasoned air traveler took to the jetliners with a passion. Why shouldn't he? Inside, the 707 was roomier than the biggest of the commercial propeller airliners. Flight itself was smoother and quieter, practically vibrationless. Passengers, to wile away the time, used to play a game: See how many coins you could stand on edge on the window ridge. It worked. You could never do that in a propeller airplane. But the big thing was SPEED. At near ten-mile-a-minute speeds, New York was just under six hours from London. And when transcontinental jet-

Nation's First Lady, "Mamie" Eisenhower, christens America's first jetliner as Pan American World Airways' President Juan Trippe looks on. Plane is Boeing 707 and was named "Clipper America."

Interior of the 707, and the jetliner family to follow, was much more luxurious and roomier than in propeller-driven airliners. Here, passengers board in First-Class section with two abreast seating.

liner service was started, you could have breakfast in New York, fly to Los Angeles and put in almost a full business day, and be back in New York in time for dinner. The jet traveler even had to think about changing his diet, let alone, changing his business routine.

Similarly, the airline operators, although they were faced with early problems of fitting the jets into the operational scheme of things, felt the impact of the jet revolution. The jet engines, because there were so few moving parts, and once the "bugs" were flitted out, required less maintenance and simplified procedures. The jets burned more fuel, but jet fuel was cheaper, and the advantage in speed began to show up favorably on cost operation charts. But the most astonishing thing of all was the jetliners' capabilities.

Shuttling back and forth across the Atlantic — with a minimum of turn around time — Pan American concluded, that one of its 707s could carry as many passengers to Europe as the *Queen Mary* oceanliner could do in the same period of time. There were prophets who said in ten years, the "Queens" would be forced out of business.

That was over 10 years ago. But in the summer of 1969, I was talking with a Boeing engineer about the potential of the 747 *Super jet.* (See Chapter 18) and he inferred that with "extended versions" there was the potential of carrying "great amounts of bulk cargo" at astonishing low rates, in many cases, competitive with surface transport. Indeed, the 747 *Super jet* and its capabilities could start another revolution, as did the first 707 at the start of the *sixties.*

But that's getting ahead of our story. By 1960, the jet future in commercial air transport was pretty well assured. Virtually all of the world's airlines were in the process of, or making plans for re-equipping their fleets with jetliners. Their demands started a revolution within the aircraft manufacturing industry which had a decided effect on Boeing.

How Boeing met the challenge is pertinant to be told here, because it resulted in a whole new family of jetliners with the ultimate decision to build today's 747 *Superjet.* And each new model, as it came into being, made its contribution to state of the art which would make possible the 747. There were, however, many problems along the way.

It was true, the 707 for the passenger inside its luxury-appointed, sound-proofed cabin was much quieter than the piston-powered airliners, its predecessors, along the world's far-flung air routes. But for those who stood on the ramp that October Day and watched Pan Am's first 707 with 111 passengers aboard take off for the inaugural non-stop flight to Paris, there was a deafening sound.

Therein, was the crux of a problem that the Jet Age brought with it. The first jetliners were, indeed, noisy as Hell, emitted a lot of smoke and smells. Nobody really wanted to stop progress, but there was need to adjust to the jet's presence in our environment, and the pressure was on the aircraft manufacturer, the engine people, the airlines and concerned Government agencies, including the military, to minimize the jets' inherent unpleasantries.

Military jet aircraft had been flying in considerable numbers for more than ten years *before* the first commercial jetliner made its debut into the picture. But military air bases generally were located far out from populated areas, and their defense mission seemed of such top priority, that the jet fighters and bombers didn't evoke much public protest. With the commercial jets and the desire to locate airports closer to cities, the sound and the fury stirred up a hornet's nest.

There appeared grotesque-looking, grid-like fences at take-off positions on airports – to "fence in" the sound when it was loudest. The airlines and the FAA (Federal Aviation Agency) working together, set up new flight patterns for take-offs that took much of the sound away from complaining neighbors.

These things helped, and the sound and the fury of protests from people on the ground, in particular those living near airports, began to subside. As more and more jetliners began to make their appearance, and the new form of transportation showed increasing signs of profit and pleasure in virtually every walk of life, public acceptance assured the jets of a permanent place in the transportation family.

The roar of the jets was a way of life. Like the roar of a Greyhound bus when it moves out from the terminal, or the rumble of a big semi-truck and trailer along city streets, or the ear-splitting horn of the railroad Diesels on the streamliner approaching a crossing.

Boeing, meanwhile, had approached the problem from a different angle, and the result brought great improvements in the jetliners, themselves.

II

THE first 707s sold to the airlines cost in the neighborhood of $5,500,000 apiece. Boeing spent three times that amount to eliminate some of the noise from the early jet engines. What finally emerged was a sound supressor, a cluster of tubes that became the tailpipe of the jet engine. In effect it "scattered the sound," dissipating much of the roar. Now, the jetliner could take-off with little more disturbing sound than a big *"Stratocruiser."* At the same time, they devised a means to reverse the thrust after landing which helped stop the big jets in shorter distances on the runway, putting the jets into airports which at first could not accept them. The jetliner itself was growing up. The basic 707 appeared in several new versions.

Right from the start, Pan American and other trans-ocean carriers who had bought the first 707s, wanted more range and more

Cluster-type tail-pipe was devised as "sound suppressor," and jets matched prop jobs for quietness.

passenger capacity. The Douglas DC-8 jetliner was in the air and promising this added performance. Recalling this period, a Boeing engineering vice-president confided: "Some of us old timers, who had worked on the Model 247 remembered how the DC-2 and DC-3 had come along and stolen our thunder. We didn't want it to happen again. This time Boeing had taken the lead in introducing the most popular jetliner, and we intended to maintain that leadership."

To make sure it stayed in the race, Boeing developed a "stretched" version of the original 707 design, which before it was through, came out almost fifty per cent new airplane. They called it the *"Intercontinental"* (Model 707-300 series) a longer fuselage, more wing area, increased fuel load, bigger engines which, of course, incorporated the new sound suppressors and the reverse thrust features.

About the same time the first *"Intercontinental"* made its maiden flight, a new type engine came along which permitted "stretching" the design once more Model (707-320B) giving it a 6000-mile range with the kind of payload the airlines desired. But let us digress a moment to talk about the jet engine development.

First generation jetliners (707s) were equipped with turbojet engines developed by Pratt & Whitney Aircraft, Boeing's long-time partner in the powerplant field. The turbojet principle is almost too simple. Started by a small auxiliary power unit, the big engine's compressor wheel powered by jet-driven gas turbines sucks in air through a frontal duct, compresses it, heats it and expels hot air past the gas turbines and through a small jet exhaust to produce forward thrust. That's all there is to it.

P&W and other jet engine manufacturers soon found a way to improve on this with a big fan at the front of the engine (in addition to the compressors) thus increasing the volume of air intake. Most of this increased volume of air, accelerated by the new fan section, is discharged around the turbine engine proper without going through the burner section, adding a new thrust force to the already escaping hot gases. Hence the name TURBOFAN engine which produces more push than a turbojet and has greater operating efficiency.

Such was the bonus in thrustpower available which enabled Boeing engineers to get even more performance out of the *"Intercontinental 707."*

Compared to the original 707 commer-

Introduction of Turbofan engines enabled designers to "stretch" the basic 707 design resulting in the bigger 707-320 "Intercontinental." It could fly farther and carry much greater payloads.

Addition of large fan in front of conventional turbine, increased airflow and rated thrustpower.

cial jetliner, the "*Intercontinental*" (707-320B) had fifteen feet more wing span, eight feet more main cabin length, almost fifteen per cent more fuel capacity. Translated into more meaningful terms: It could carry a maximum of 189 passengers in a tourist configuration (depending upon the customer airline's preference) at a cruising speed of 600-miles-an-hour, non-stop New York to Paris with plenty of fuel reserve.

Before it was three years old, the commercial Jet Age had the vehicle which permitted the air traveler to fly around the world, virtually at the globe's equatorial beltline in 40 hours with a minimum number of stops. More realistically, perhaps, anybody with the price of a ticket could fly from San Francisco to Sydney, Australia – 6800 miles – over the vastness of the Pacific with only two stops in Honolulu and the Fiji Islands. The "Land Down Under" was less than 15 hours flying time from the "City Of The Golden Gate."

But what about the person who could afford the price of a ticket, but wanted to take a jetliner New York to Chicago or from San Francisco to Seattle? The airlines, and justifiably so, didn't like the idea of using their 707s on anything but transcontinental through flights. It simply wasn't good economics.

There was in prospect the Lockheed "*Electra*" turboprop airliner for this kind of medium-haul operation. American Airlines had already ordered some of the "*Electras,*" and Capital Airlines was introducing the British-built "*Viscount*" turboprop airliner. It was generally conceded inside the air transport industry, however, that the turboprop airliners were considered merely as "interim equipment." What the airlines really wanted was a jetliner, but not as large as the 707 or the coming DC-8, yet capable of jet speeds over the shorter routes, and more economical. Granted, the turboprop airliners could do the job; but the turbojets were a hundred miles an hour faster.

Indeed, there was a market for a jetliner

Boeing 707-320B "Intercontinental," until the "Stretched" Douglas DC-8 came along, was world's largest jetliner. Built for transocean flights, the big plane could carry up to 189 passengers.

Engineers "shrunk" basic 707 fuselage and redesigned wing to come up with "intermediate" 720B jetliner for medium-range operations. Plane was more economical and proved faster for shorter flights.

in this new category. Boeing accepted the challenge and engineers took another look at the 707 as a starter. Only this time, as one engineer explained it – "We looked through the other end of the telescope."

If they could "stretch" the basic 707 design, why couldn't they "shrink" it? The outcome was a "new" jetliner, the Model 720. With a fuselage nine feet shorter than the original 707, it had the same wing span, but with a different sweepback and flap arrangements. Powerplants were the same as the latest 707 models, but fuel capacity was considerably reduced, a factor easily translated into more payload. Passenger-wise the 720 could accommodate 131 in a first-class configuration or 165 as a tourist flight. It proved to be about five miles an hour faster than the bigger jetliners. This advantage was increased in later models equipped with turbofan engines.

Operationally, the 720 served its purpose. It permitted the bigger jetliners to fly

"Intermediate" 720B jetliner in fuselage profile could easily be taken for larger 707. Window count, however, is dead giveaway. Also noticeable is different wing root, start of double sweepback.

Underbelly view shows 720B's "new" wing planform. Trailing edge flaps were also different from 707.

the intercontinental and the transcontinental routes, while it took over much of the medium-range operations, linking together the major cities at home and abroad.

III

"THERE'S only one thing wrong with the 720," one airline executive sounded off. "The trouble is, you people didn't go far enough. It's still too damn big and too damn expensive."

"What the airlines need," he went on, "is a more versatile and more economical jetliner. The optimum would be a 600-mile-an-hour airliner which could operate from any airport served by the DC-6 or the *"Constellations"* at about the same cost per seat mile. It should be capable of carrying 125 to 150 passengers. There should also be an all-cargo version . . . "

There was more, but that was quite enough.

It was a big order for any manufacturer to meet at this stage of the game, when the Jet Age, as far as airline operations were concerned, was less than three months old.

Still, it was pretty certain the customer, both at home and abroad, was waiting for just such a plane.

A survey Boeing had conducted in the spring of 1958 before the first 707 went into scheduled service, had indicated there was a potential world market for about 500 medium-range jetliners which could provide this kind of performance. On the strength of this report, Boeing Management decided to take a closer look at the possibility of a wholly new, medium-range jet transport design. They even assigned a Project designation – Model 727.

Jack Steiner, a capable young aerodynamicist, who had worked on the basic 707 project, was named to head a special

Jack Steiner, now a Boeing Company Vice-President, is credited with design of revolutionary 727 trijet.

committee to look into the matter. Steiner's job, which he tackled with enthusiasm, was to come up with some original design studies. Then, the powers that be would take another appraisal of the whole picture.

"There were times," Steiner would confide to close associates, "when I felt like they had put me out in endsville. Interest would run hot, then turn cold. It was frustrating to keep fired-up with the idea, but always it seemed to me, to be a category that the company couldn't just write off."

Steiner came up with several different presentations: A four-engined plane, basically another drastically scaled-down 707. "Hell, we'll be in competition with ourselves and the 720," he was rebuffed. He tried a two-engined configuration, engines in the tail in pods, mounted, one on each side of the fuselage. "Only two engines!" somebody scoffed. "The airlines are still skeptical of jet engine reliability, most of them want four engines." He tried a compromise, a trijet, three engines in the tail like the British were trying in their new DeHavilland *"Trident."* Nobody seemed to "buy" that, either – "too damn radical!"

It seemed, no matter what Steiner and

Steiner (left) with associate study wind tunnel model of new high-tail 727.

his staff came up with, there wasn't much encouragement. The "727" was stuck on paper and dying in the wind tunnel.

Then, suddenly, the picture cleared up a little. One year in the Jet Age, the airlines started talking more seriously about the need for a short to medium-range turbojet airliner. It was evident the jet transports were going to be money-makers. The possibility of equipment financing looked brighter. The right plane could sell. Sell big.

Other aircraft manufacturers saw the potential and were going after the business full blast. Douglas announced it was building a DC-9, a smaller version of the Big Eight. The French came out with the *"Caravelle,"* a jet with two engines in the tail, and the European market was going for it. In England the *"DH-Trident"* was exciting a great deal of interest. There was going to be a smaller jetliner, and if Boeing wanted "in," it was time for a decision.

The word came down from topside – "Let's take another look at what Steiner's been doing. Maybe, he's got something there."

Steiner had teamed up with a close friend a fellow aerodynamist with fresh ideas, Joe Sutter, who had also worked on the 707 and other jet transport designs. Together they had "on paper" and backed up with wind tunnel data a revolutionary new aircraft in their latest "727" configuration.

It had three engines, two mounted in the tail, in individual pods one on each side of the fuselage. The third engine, cowl-enclosed, was suspended from a beam at the rear of the fuselage, with an air duct leading to it from the base of the vertical fin. Thrust spewed out a big nozzle in the extreme tail. All three engines were isolated from the primary structure of the aircraft. The engines were the very latest Pratt & Whitney turbofan powerplants.

The fuselage was 11 feet shorter than the first 707, but it was the same width, providing the same cross-sectional space and the same degree of luxury on short-haul service as was found on transcontinental and intercontinental flights. There was room for 131 passengers in six abreast seating arrangement.

The wing was the "thing," however, shorter than the bigger jets in span and with less sweepback angle, but offering revolutionary new high-lift devices and "air brakes." These included triple-slotted trailing-edge flaps and leading-edge flaps and slats. (Later, when the "727" went into service it would become known as "the plane whose wing comes apart when it lands.") Mechanically operated, "the wing that came apart" was the "727's" secret of success. The leading edge flaps and slats, slowed it down sufficiently to permit landings on extremely short runways – in 2,000 feet or less. But for cruising, when the wing "went back together again," the wing provided excellent high-speed characteristics.

This was the proposed short-to-medium range jetliner design that Steiner presented to the Board of Directors in February of 1960. Everybody was very impressed. But the answer was – "wait and see."

Bill Allen, who ultimately would have to

The 727's high-lift wing devices gave design superb operating characteristics from small fields.

make the decision was keeping his "cool." If they went ahead with the "727" program, he had to face the facts. It would be the biggest gamble the company ever had considered in the commercial field; bigger dollar-wise than the 707 venture and with more risk involved because of the growing competition. The tooling, alone, would cost upwards of $100,000,000!

"We'll have to sell a hundred or more airplanes to get started," Allen admonished. *One hundred* that was the magic number. If the Sales People could show him that kind of business was there, then he'd go ahead and put the blue chips into the pot. He set a deadline, December 1, about nine months away.

On November 30, 1960 – one day before the time limit would expire – United Air Lines and Eastern Airlines signed up for eighty "727s," and some of those were "on option." The dollar figure involved totaled $420,000,000.

With this near *half-billion dollar* pot at the end of the rainbow, Allen turned on the green.

Boeing was committed to build the *727 Trijet*.

Twenty-four months later, almost to the day, November 27, 1962, the first "727" emerged from the Renton Plant. The high tail with the horizontal stabilizer and elevators on top, and the third engine scoop in the base of the vertical stabilizer, a very unconventional design, drew various comments from the observers. Somebody gave it a nickname – "The T-Bird."

The hope was that this winged "T-Bird" would become as popular along the skyways as did Ford Motor Company's revolutionary "T-Bird" capture the market along the highways.

Time would soon tell.

On February 9, 1963, the bird with the "T" tail swooshed into the sky with Test Pilots Dix Loesch and Lew Wallick at its controls. "She lifted off so quick, and climbed at such a steep angle, I thought Somebody up there had yanked her off the ground," one observer described the take-off. It was a characteristic that made Bill Allen, who was watching, very pleased. That was what everybody wanted, a plane

T-Bird of the airways, the Boeing 727 with three engines in the tail would become most popular jetliner.

that could get up and away without eating up to much runway.

It was the same way when Loesch and Wallick, after two hours of initial flight test procedures to check handling and component functions, landed at Paine Field, near Everett, Washington, a new Flight Test facility Boeing had leased, about forty miles north of Seattle. The "727" used very little runway in landing. Her "gimmicked-up" wing for slow speeds was just the ticket.

Test pilot Lew Wallick at controls of first 727 on maiden flight. Plane was "too good to be true!"

Basic 727 design was so popular that airlines wanted more of the same. With same wing and engines in the tail configuration, engineers "stretched" the fuselage to produce 727-200, a bigger model.

There followed an accelerated test program, cramming four to six months of flying into four to six days. The "727" was an eager eagle born to the sky and nothing seemed to go wrong with it. It permitted a tremendous amount of flying and a minimum ground time, another virtue that everyone was certain, the airline operations people would love.

During some of the high-speed runs, part of the test program, the "T-Bird" showed her thunder, hitting 670-mph, almost the speed of sound!

Later, on November 3, 1963, the "727" took off on a globe-circling demonstration tour, which before it was over covered more than 76,000 miles, and let people in 44 different cities and 26 different countries get a good look at her. Six months later, she was off again, this time for a 14,000-mile tour of Latin American countries, and everywhere she went she created a sensation. Her performance was spectacular.

She climbed out of small fields like she was shot from a catapult. And she landed on short runways – stopping, sometimes, in 1500 feet or less. At La Paz, Bolivia, where the airport was 13,358 feet above sea-level, she performed like a mountain goat, the first jet to operate in this region. She was quiet and swift and sure.

Jack Steiner said it best: "It appears that we've got a lot more airplane than we bargained for!"

The airlines of the world felt the same way about it. The "727" was not only the fastest jetliner flying, but she became the fastest selling jet transport. There was little doubt they would sell 500 or more, and they did. Sales of the "727" would push the whole commercial jet program over to the profit side of the ledger.

It was a thing that Bill Boeing would have loved to live to see. The day when The Boeing Airplane Company would be the leader in producing commercial airliners, and the planes they were producing would be a leader in making money for the company.

IV

"SINCE October 26, 1958, when Pan American World Airways introduced the 707, the Boeing family of jetliners has been connecting cities, countries and continents," said a Company press release. That family of jetliners included, with the new "727" going into service, four different sized jetliners, each designed specifically to fill a need. And more commercial jets built by Boeing were flying than any others. Sales hit the 1,000 mark in September of 1965. These figures did not include jet transports (and tankers) sold to the military. Looking at this picture,

At Renton, Washington facility, the T-Bird (727s) went into mass production. Scene shows aft fuselage sections with center engines being installed. Note the curved "stovepipe" for big air scoops.

there was an interesting point of note: Counting the B-52s and the B-47s, the company had built jets with eight engines, six engines, four engines and three engines. There were some who wondered why there never was a twin-engined jet to "round out the family."

This "new addition" was just around the corner. The popularity of the jetliners had generated a decided upswing in the number of passengers carried by the world's scheduled airlines. There was no doubt the swiftness and comfort of jet transportation was responsible for this growth factor. As rapidly as possible, the airlines were replacing their piston-engined fleets with the jets. The air traveling public demanded it.

The increase in the use of air transportation was evident in the so-called Local Service Carriers, as well as the major trunklines. These small airlines were busier than ever "feeding" the bigger major terminals. But the passenger in Kankakee or Kokomo, or Muskegon or Manistique, couldn't board a jetliner. He was still being offered DC-3 service in many cases.

Here, indeed, was an untapped market. There was need for a smaller jetliner to serve the smaller communities.

In February of 1965 Boeing decided to enter this field and announced that it was building a twin-engined jetliner, the 737, specifically designed for short-haul operations. Two months later, United Air Lines ordered 40 of the 737s supplementing a previous Lufthansa order for 21, and the 737 program was off and running. The first aircraft flew April 9, 1967.

The 737 was different from any other short-haul jetliners on the market and offered a wide range of capabilities. It could take-off from and land, under favorable temperature conditions, at virtually any airport that could accommodate the DC-3. Paradoxically, the 737 wing span was shorter than that of the DC-3, its fuselage 30 feet longer, indicative of more than three decades of aerodynamic change.

Demand for "short-haul" jetliner produced this twin-engined 737. Performance of plane made it virtually a "DC-3" of the Jet Age. Fuselage being so close to ground simplified loading and maintenance.

Advancements in the state of the art, permitted the 737 to carry six times as many passengers as the standard 21-passenger DC-3 configuration at almost four times the speed. Still, it was (and is) a specifically designed "short-haul" jetliner and, in many instances, has replaced the DC-3 on inter-city hops of 250 miles or less.

Typical, for instance, is United Air Lines' 737 service operating between Muskegon,

Cabin of 737 is as wide as the larger 707 and 720 Boeing jetliners, and can be easily converted into various seating arrangements. Above is posh-posh interior of latest 737E made up as Corporate Jet.

Production line at Renton plant shows 737 in final assembly. The fuselage greatly resembles original "Dash-Eighty." Plane has capability of being converted into all-cargo version in minutes.

Michigan and Chicago (170 miles) or Muskegon to Grand Rapids (30 miles) and slashing flying times by more than half over piston-powered airliners. And passengers ride in wide cabin comfort, the same as in a 707 or the bigger jetliners.

The Boeing family of jetliners, with the addition of the 737, could now serve the smaller towns as well as the big cities, countries and continents.

Recently, the author experienced what that means.

I had a six o'clock breakfast at home in Ludington, Michigan, drove the 59 miles to the Muskegon County Airport (the closest field which can handle the smaller jets) and boarded a 737 for Chicago, flying time about 21 minutes. At O'Hare International Airport, I boarded a Boeing 707 and arrived in Los Angeles in a total lapsed time of under eight hours. Because of the time difference, the business day in Los Angeles was just starting.

Before the jet service was introduced to Muskegon (population, about 90,000) such connections were impossible.

The Jet Age is like that.

On this particular trip, I was enroute to Seattle to visit the Boeing Company doing research for this book.

It was the summer of 1968, and at the massive Everett, Washington facility, I got my first glimpse of the 747 *Superjet* moving down the production line, the first plane about three-fourths completed.

There, I saw the birth of another era of flight – The Spacious Age.

Boeing had come a long way since the first "B&W" was rolled out of the Ed Heath Shipyard building on the Duwamish River.

In flight, the 737 has smooth lines. "Like a porpoise," it has been described. Note extreme thickness of wing at root where it joins fuselage. Wing and pod arrangement were entirely new concepts.

CHAPTER ELEVEN

A Plane To Carry Gulliver

THEY called it, "the big plane exercise." It all started in the summer of 1962 when Maynard Pennell and others, who had brought the KC-135 jet tanker and the C-135 military jet transport into reality, took a look at some possible "growth versions" with the idea of a super-sized military jet transport in mind. After a computerized study of the military airlift situation, a special analysis group concluded that a much larger plane would be needed in the future. One of the paper studies evolved around a plane that might weigh as much as 700,000 pounds; longer than a basketball court, as wide as a moving van; capable of airlifting hundreds of soldiers and their equipment at jet speeds anywhere in the world to help stamp out the so-called "brush-fire" wars, which seemed to be the trend of our potential enemies. Moreover, a study of existing military cargo planes showed many areas where the efficiency of the logistics transport operation could be vastly improved.

Maynard Pennell. He initiated studies for super-sized military logistics transport that became C-5A.

Definitely, there was need for greater volume to accommodate the newest military equipment, which would mean a plane almost double the size of the present types with beefed-up structures, improved cargo loading techniques, the application of the latest high-lift wing devices and new type undercarriage to permit take-offs and landings from small fields. The concept Pennell's group came up with incorporated all these innovations, and Boeing had the production know-how gleaned from experience in fabrication techniques with the B-52, two thirds the size they were talking about.

There was also every indication from the engine people that vastly improved and more powerful jet powerplants would be available. In short, there was no reason, technologically, why a plane weighing 350-tons or more couldn't be built. It seemed to be a logical next step for the military and very possible, the big jetliner of tomorrow.

Excited over the way things "looked on paper", Pennell took the giant transport concept to the Pentagon to see if he could stir up Air Force interest in the project.

"Fascinating," he was told by one of the Pentagon planners. "But, truthfully, we've never dreamed of such a big plane at this time . . ."

So, the big military logistics transport, for the time being at least, had to be shelved.

But what about a commercial version?

A survey of the potential growth of air transportation produced some astonishing statistics. By 1970, the forecast predicted, passenger volume would more than double itself. The future of air freight operations loomed astronomical – an anticipated 300 to 400 per cent increase in volume. The future was bright, but the picture was frightening.

High-density traffic, the growing number of planes in the scheduled airline fleets, thousands of corporation-owned aircraft, military bombers, fighters and transports, and the thousands of smaller, private planes were devouring up all available airspace at an alarming rate. The highways in the sky were jammed to the danger point. The potential growth factor fed into this congested environment, could throw all aviation into a tailspin from which it would be almost impossible to recover.

The numbers game was out of the question, according to the air traffic planners and analysts. Increasing the number of planes to handle the growing volume, they warned, would make things get worse, not better.

It would be like inviting the air traveler of the 1970s to a game of Russian Roulette in the skies.

But there might be another answer — *build bigger airliners!*

"Looking into the crystal ball," a Boeing engineer confided, "we saw our largest jetliner then in production — the stretched version of the 707 series — fast becoming a Lilliputian in a Gulliver's World. It was time to start thinking about a second generation jetliner, a sky giant to carry Gulliver."

Overnight, the picture changed.

II

IN Washington and in Dayton at Wright Field, there was suddenly new interest in the super-sized military logistics transport. The "seed" Pennell had planted seemed to be budding. The Air Force, perhaps because of the growing situation in Southeast Asia (Viet Nam) and the obvious need for a long logistics supply line for any forces that might be sent there, had become intensely interested in the super-size logistics transport. They even had a name for the project — CX-4. The Pentagon meant business.

Before long, the project evolved into a program, and the plane in question got an official AF designation — C-5A. Boeing, Douglas and Lockheed each got AF contracts to go ahead with detailed design studies for a big jet transport.

In Seattle, a 500-man engineering team went to work on Boeing's proposal. The C-5A got top priority.

That was in June, 1964. The paper proproposal, twice the size of a New York phone book, went to the Air Force in September of that year. In Seattle hopes ran high that Boeing would get the contract. Certainly, it seemed, they had the inside track because of the company's proven performance building the B-52, KC-135, C-135 aircraft and the whole family of big commercial jetliners. No other airframe manufacturer had had so much experience building big jet aircraft.

"Maybe, that was what went wrong," a top Boeing executive confided later. "Maybe, we had too damn much experience. Maybe, we knew too damn well the cost of things . . ."

The word came in September, 1965. Boeing's bid was too high. Lockheed was awarded the contract to build the C-5A.

Ironically, it would be built in the big Marietta, Georgia plant originally activated for the B-29 *"Superfortress"* program.

In a way, perhaps, and in the light of future developments, it was the best thing that ever happened. One thing seems true, the loss of the C-5A contract put a lot of pressure on the development of a big capacity commercial jetliner. It can be said that the 747 *"Superjet"* — today's largest in-production commercial jetliner — became more than a "dream" with the demise of the C-5A proposal.

"We had done a tremendous amount of paper work, and actually were well into the design of an airplane which would have been called the C-5A, except it would have been built by Boeing," Joe Sutter, who was to be Chief Project Engineer on the 747 explained. "I think this, more than anything else, influenced management to take a more positive approach in the development of a super-sized commercial jet transport."

Recalling how he got directly involved in the project, Joe Sutter told the author — "It was in August, 1965 and I was up at my summer cabin, alone, getting away from it all for a week or so. There wasn't any telephone, and I remember, I was asleep on the beach, when a neighbor lady shook me awake and said Dick Rouzie, the Director of Engineering for the Transport Division, was calling. Something very important . . .

Joe Sutter, Chief Project Engineer on the 747 project, which grew out of BIG military transport.

"When I called back and talked with Dick, he told me that management had decided to go ahead with a more serious study of the commercial plane derivative of the C-5A. Would I like to head the project? He said for me to think about it.

"I told him I didn't have to think about it . . . I'd like the job. It looked to me like a real challenge.

"When I got back to work on the next Monday, there was a series of meetings all day long, and before we quit, a Preliminary Design Group had been established. Our job was to come up with a design proposal for a big commercial jet to take to the airline people. I think, that was really the beginning, in earnest, of the 747 project.

"Within a month or two after that we did a lot of work on three specific airplanes. They all looked alike, but there were three different sizes. We wanted to test the market to find out what capacity (size) the airline people were most interested in, to give us a more specific target. In each category we did a lot of wind tunnel work and basic design studies before we took it to the airlines.

"Then, we made a whirlwind tour of all the major airlines. We went to London, the mainland of Europe, Japan, Australia and we talked to the airline people here at home. The airplane we finally settled on was closest to the largest concept we had in our studies . . . a plane that would weigh 700,000 pounds or more, capable of carrying double the payload of existing airline-type aircraft then in use.

"The impression we got from the airlines' people and based on our own conclusions was that a plane whose mid-life would be in 1975 – ten years hence – would have to be in this size category to absorb the growing rate of the passenger business and anticipated growth of air cargo.

"From that moment on the Boeing effort was concentrated on the design and development of the super-sized jet transport that would ultimately become the 747."

Joe Sutter was a good choice to head that effort. Born and reared in Seattle, he was graduated with a BS-degree in Aeronautical Engineering from the University of Washington, class of 1943. He joined Boeing in February of 1946 as an aerodynamicist, and subsequently held a number of Technical Staff positions in analysis and design of turbojet aircraft. He had worked on every Boeing commercial airliner since the *"Stratocruiser"* – Model 377 – and was credited with Jack Steiner as co-inventor of the twin-engine 737, latest jetliner to go into production before the 747. Officially he was named Chief Engineer, 747 Project in October of 1965.

The task ahead, he soon found out, was a big challenge and also a big headache. The competition was charging in from all sides. Lockheed, in a splendid position with the juicy C-5A contract in its fold had made it known that it was considering a commercial version of the C-5A and a somewhat smaller, so-called "Air Bus", Model 1011. Douglas, which had been in on the C-5A competition, had its own "Air Bus" version in the DC-10. Sutter's "task force" had run into Lockheed and Douglas representatives – also trying to sell the airlines their respective designs – everywhere they went on that whirlwind tour. There was a lot of interest, on the part of the airlines in both the Lockheed and Douglas proposals.

Boeing would have to come up with

something really spectacular. Because the 747 concept was much bigger than the others — a big leap ahead — it was, naturally, in a higher cost bracket. The big question was — *Could the airlines, even with their anticipated traffic growth, afford an airplane that would cost upwards of $20,000,000 per unit?*

Right from the start, Joe Sutter's group had a two-front war to fight. (1). They had to come up with a design that would convince Boeing Management it should go ahead with the program in the face of skyrocketing costs for materials, tooling and projected facilities that would be needed for the 747 project. (2) They had to come up with a design that would satisfy the airline crowd, always very demanding technologically and performance-wise, always cash cautious, and, heretofore, known not to be over wealthy.

"We had one thing going for us," Joe Sutter commented. "We were sure that this airplane, or one like it, *just had to happen!*

In the fall of 1965 things started to happen.

III

NOW that they were shooting for the really big plane concept, Sutter's group gave some serious consideration to a double-decked, over-grown version of the Boeing 707 *Intercontinental.* But they soon abandoned the idea. A bigger 707 wasn't the answer. It was "backward thinking." Besides, Douglas already had jumped the gun with the "Big Eight", an elongated version of the DC-8, and they already had sold a considerable number to the airlines.

The next approach was a much wider fuselage, a double lobe body, not unlike that of the "*Stratocruiser*" only with a mid-wing configuration, upper and lower cabin areas with double aisles on both levels offering 7-8 abreast seating. The airline people weren't very impressed. They didn't like the mid-wing idea.

One airline executive commented: "How would you like to ditch in the Atlantic in that thing, and be riding in the lower cabin?"

It was "back to the drawing board, again." This time, they came up with a low-wing airplane (considered safest for ditching) but they still maintained the double-lobe fuselage, upper and lower level passenger compartments. Airline acceptance was lukewarm. They still didn't like the double-decker configuration. There were two principal objections: Airline people wanted a plane that was compatible for both cargo and passengers. They wanted "convertibility", an airliner and an air-freighter. In this area the double-deck had its limitations. The lower fuselage lobe could accommodate loading big 8 x 8 ft. cargo containers, side by side, but the upper deck would require redesigned, specially tailored containers. The airlines wanted standardization for maximum use. It was also pointed out that the towering fuselage design in passenger configuration, with the floor of the upper deck twenty-five feet above the ground, posed serious problems during emergency evacuation.

Boeing tried about fifty different variations of its double-deck concept, but finally gave up. There emerged from Sutter's group a wholly new design.

It had a long fuselage (225 feet, 2 inches, nose to tail) with a circular cross-section (19 feet, 5 inches wide, and a height of 8 feet, 4 inches) for the main cabin. Below the main cabin floor there was still plenty of room for the big cargo containers, and the passenger cabin could, if desired, be converted for all-cargo. There was, however, still a "second story", an upper deck for the crew compartment and a forward lounge section, a spiral staircase (like the

Early 747 design was this double-decked, mid-wing model. Engine pods were farther inboard than on 707.

Models show several different versions of 747 in preliminary design stages. The girl is holding the first low-wing double-decker. At left, bottom, is "droop snooper," next to it, is ultimate configuration.

old "*Stratocruiser*") leading to this area. In profile, they had created a parabolic nose whose upper arc gradually slanted downward to the main cabin tubular section and tapered off in a conical tail. The effect was a beautifully streamlined body.

This fuselage configuration, aside from advantageous aerodynamic considerations, offered a wide, spacious cabin with two aisles and 9 and 10 abreast seating for maximum capacity. And for cargo convertibility, using a hinged nose arrange-

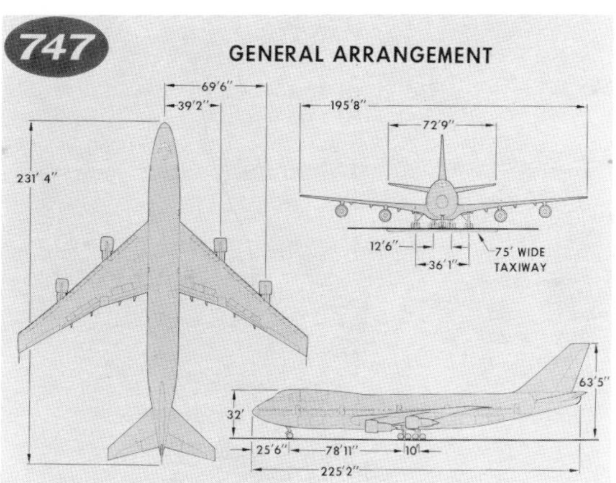

Three-view sketches show wing and fuselage profile of 747 and dimensions.

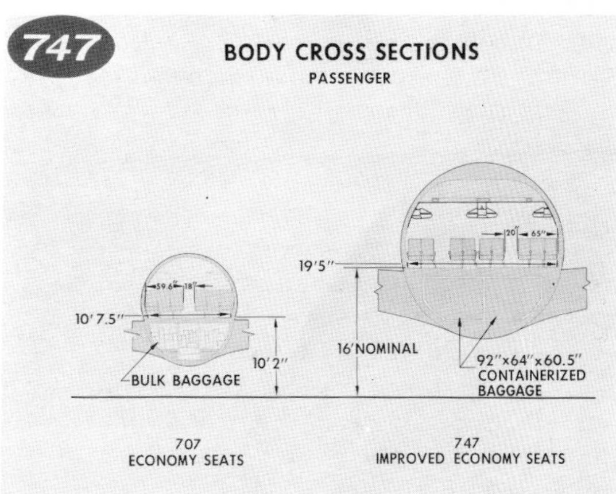

At left is cross-section view of 707 fuselage as compared with wide-bodied 747 fuselage cross-section.

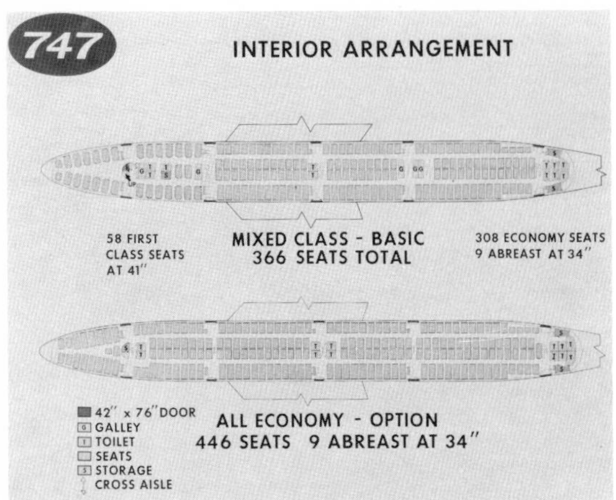

Planform of fuselage shows mixed-class seating and high-density arrangement for interior of 747.

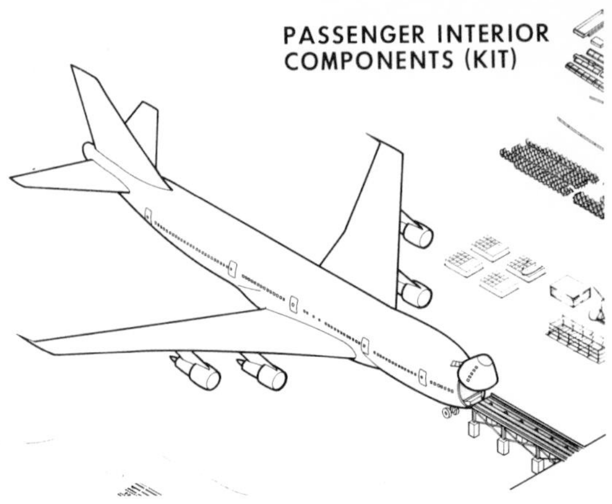

Drawing shows how lower nose section can be raised to permit forward loading and off-loading of cargo.

ment (like the jaws of a whale) it provided faster loading and unloading and maximum use of space.

It was a low-wing monoplane, this version of the 747. The sweptback wing, much like that of the 707, had a 195-foot, 8 inch span with four engines, two on each wing mounted in streamlined nacelles. the en-

747

LANDING GEAR

In this artist's sketch one can get an idea of the multi-wheeled main landing gear of the 747. Arrangement was designed to spread weight of plane over larger area. "Trucks" retract into wing and body.

gines, each developing in excess of 43,000 thrustpower were being developed by Pratt & Whitney (see Chapter 13) would give the plane superior performance over any present day jetliner. It would be faster and quieter than the present jets and twice as big.

Based on computerized studies gleaned from wind tunnel testing, the design Boeing proposed would have a comfortable cruising altitude at 35,000, a cruising speed of more than 600 miles per hour, a range up to 6000 miles. Its wide, long cabin could accommodate 400 to 450 persons or more, depending upon the seating arrangement, affording a spaciousness never before offered to the air traveler.

There was more, much more in its favor. They had incorporated the high-lift wing devices of the 727 to get its 350-tons off the ground in a hurry. Plus new wing features which would "increase the area" and slow the plane down to acceptable landing speeds. It could readily use the present airports which could accept the biggest jetliners then in service. A unique landing gear arrangement "spread the weight" to permit use of existing runway surfaces.

Such was the design proposal for its Model 747 that Boeing engineers and Sales people took to the airlines in January of 1966, about six months after Joe Sutter and his Preliminary Design Group had started work on the project.

This time, it was a different story. Maybe, it was because the airlines had had a good year. Their growth factor was maintaining a steady pace, about 15 per cent increase, annually. Every sign was that this growth would continue. Or, maybe, it was because everytime somebody tried to shoot holes in the proposed design, somebody had the right answer. At any rate, on the part of some of the big air carriers, the Boeing design seemed to be picking up momentum. There were favorable indications that potential customers were getting ready to buy.

At a meeting of Boeing's Board of Directors in March, 1966 the decision to go ahead, or not go ahead, with the 747 was tops on the agenda. "This program (the 747) involves financial risks many times greater than any of our previous ventures into the commercial aircraft field," Bill Allen would say. "It will have to be wholly privately financed . . . but, at the same time, the prospects of reward can be equally, many times greater than any of our previous efforts."

He recommended they build the 747.

And the Board approved the program on a tentative basis reserving firm committment for a later date. But the 747 had achieved formal project status. They would set up a full-scale engineering group. They would start looking for a suitable site and make plans for construction of a plant facility to build the big plane. With orders for present in-production planes – the 707 series, 720, 727 and 737 models – increasing at an unbelievably astonishing rate, it would mean doubling present manufacturing facilities. The 747, alone, would require the largest single final assembly building Boeing had ever contemplated. In view of the rising costs of everything, that plant could cost upwards of $250,000,000. Research, design and engineering costs, tooling up, materials and production costs for the whole 747 program put cost estimates *over* the *billion dollar* mark.

And at this stage, even though the Board had given a temporary flashing green light for the 747, there were no firm orders for the plane from the airline family.

But about a month later, April 13, 1966, Pan American World Airways, which all along had been the customer most interested in the 747 design proposal, announced it was buying 25 of the mammoth planes, two of them all-cargo versions.

The initial Pan-Am order totaled $525,000,000. It was the largest single order for one type aircraft in the history of commercial aviation. Still, that was only *half* the estimated cost Boeing would have to come up with to put the 747 into production. It would take orders for at least fifty airplanes to reach a break-even point.

But the Pan-Am order had really stirred up things. In its announcement, Pan-Am had said that it was "pioneering a whole new era in air transportation, introducing the *spacious age!*" Moreover, there was the possibility of cutting operating costs with the bigger planes; the more seats, the less cost per seat mile. There was even the suggestion that this might mean lower

In spring of 1966, Pan American's Juan Trippe announced $525,000,000 order for 25 of the 747s.

airline fares and cargo rates, at the same time offering faster, service and more luxurious accommodations. There could be little doubt, when it ordered the 747, Pan-Am was flaunting a challenge to its competition.

Other airlines got the message. As one Boeing executive put it – "After all the Pan-Am publicity, they started coming to us. And when they saw our 747 presentation their eyes bugged out. There was a rush to get in line for delivery position. By mid-August we had orders for 56 of the '*Super jets*' and more orders were coming in each week."

Now, Boeing was fully committed. There was no turning back. They were going to build – *"the plane to carry Gulliver."*

Paradoxically, the plane was so large that Gulliver would be a Lilliputian in the 747's world!

IV

THE company purchased 780 acres of land adjacent to Paine Field in Everett, Washington about 30 miles north of Seattle. This was to be the manufacturing site for the new jet. There was established the Everett Branch of the Commercial Airplane Division headed by Vice President Malcom T. Stamper, directly responsible for designing, developing and manufacturing the 747. Named the Director of Engineering, Everett Branch, was Joe Sutter, who was given

Exact 1/100th scale models show comparative sizes of Boeing jetliners. "Super jet" dwarfs 707 and 727.

some 2500 key engineering personnel to – "turn the paper proposal and wooden mock-up we had sold to the airlines into a practical, workable design ready for the production line."

"The biggest challenge was tying it all

Boeing Vice-President, Malcom T. Stamper became over-all "boss" of gigantic 747 program at Everett.

together," Joe Sutter declared. *"You have to watch this very carefully to insure getting a well-balanced airline-type airplane. The customer is very demanding. If you examine an airline's specification, they cover every nook and corner, and they want perfection. If you miss your drag by as little as five per cent, you've hurt the airplane very hard. If you miss any major structural item, you can hurt the production line. If you end up with systems that are unreliable, you've wrecked the whole program. The thing is, you have to design the airplane so as not to make it superlative in one area and a dog in another."*

In an exclusive taped interview, Sutter takes us behind the scenes to tell some of the problems that confronted his group in the design and development of the 747 and how they solved them. Let's listen . . .

Here are some excerpts:

"In designing an airplane of this size, there were structural problems which became a major design limitation. There are things you can do 'on paper' that you can't do physically, and we had to work around them. And all the while, you have to keep in mind that what you do has to, at one point, fit just right into the production line.

"It was true, we had a lot of experience in this area with the design and fabrication of the B-52, the largest jet aircraft then flying, but the 747 posed a different problem. The magnitude in dealing with structures was similar, but the design limitations are almost completely different in the commercial jetliner from the military jet bomber.

"The body of the B-52, for instance, was a heavy longeron-type, and only portions of the fuselage were pressurized. In contrast, the body of the 747 was a combination of stringers and skin and frame, and the entire fuselage, where the payload is, had to be pressurized for passenger comfort.

"Again, Boeing had the know-how gleaned from building its whole family of pressurized-cabin jetliners. But with the 747 we were dealing with a plane that was two-and-a-half times the size of our biggest commercial jet. Consequently, there were many unknowns in this area that had to be unscrambled.

"At Boeing, I think one of the things we stress is that when you build an airplane, you should not just engineer it from the drawing board. You have to spend large amounts of money in the laboratories and in the wind tunnels testing everything. I think this helped us more than anything else to be alert to the structural problems and tailor the 747 design to fit into the framework of their rigid limitation.

"We laid out a program that cost millions of dollars for testing the 747 design in the wind tunnels. There were two exact scale, nine-foot models which were very detailed, for example, and each cost as much as a DC-6 airliner. With these and many smaller models, each testing specific components, we ran up an unprecedented number of hours in the wind tunnels – five times as much wind-tunnel testing as we had done on any previous design. Only after this great expenditure of time and money, did the 747 begin to shape up as a well balanced airplane.

"As a result, the original basic design proposal that we had 'sold' to the airlines was changed many times.

"There are several examples: The engines were moved farther outboard on the wings, and the engine-to-wing mounting arrangement was changed, for better streamlining. We redesigned the flap system using one similar to the triple-slotted arrangment on the 727 which had proved highly efficient. The 747 got a new set of 'tail feathers', a new system of rudder and

Early wind tunnel model which was used to test various engine pod shapes and arrangement on wing.

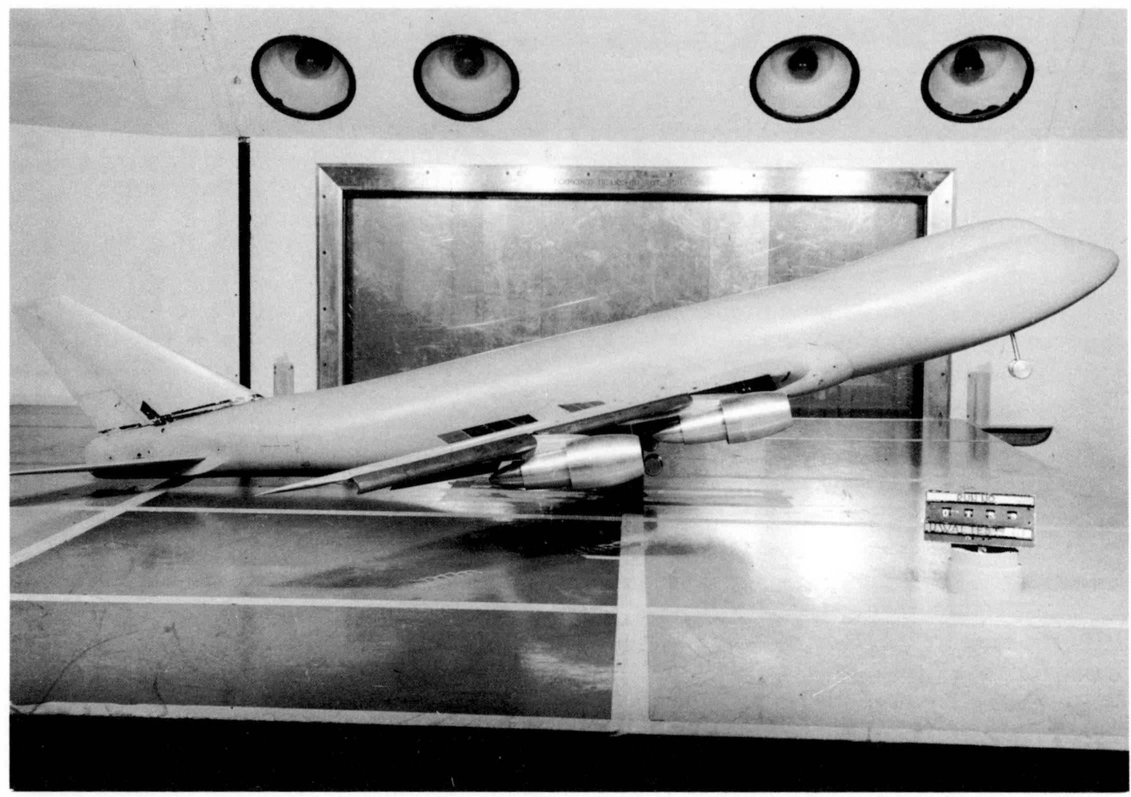

One of wind tunnel models that cost as much as DC-6 airliner in "rotation" test attitude. Note detail of engine nacelle design. Also model had workable leading edge flaps, new feature with 747.

elevator controls, and a thinned out tail cone which improved drag characteristics. We also went to a four-legged, dolly-type landing gear which let us spread the weight around more and gave us good growth potential. Each change, made the 747 a better airplane.

"All the while, to effect these changes we had something going for us that is, I think, the real success of Boeing. Just about all the top project guys on the 747 were 25-year Boeing men, representing an aggregate total of millions of hours of design and engineering experience. Some of them had never worked on anything but commercial aircraft designs from the 247 to the 747. And I think, this is what really made the 747 move along as rapidly as it did. And it was a helluva short time for a project of this magnitude, which really didn't get off the ground until the Fall of 1966 with a delivery date for the first airplane to Pan American scheduled for the fall of 1969. It taxed everybody's nerves.

"The real crisis came early in 1967, when there was a time the whole project went into a tail-spin. It was a time when we were really getting to understand the 747 design, things were looking pretty good in all areas. We were getting ready to say, 'this is it', but suddenly, we discovered that the weight of the airplane was getting way the Hell above our specifications.

"Naturally, we acquainted our Manage-

This model in tunnel was used to test different wing "root" and nacelle mounting arrangements.

ment people with the situation. What happened was that, instead of throwing in the towel and saying – 'Hell, you guys have done a lousy job' – they said, with understanding – 'We know you've got a good airplane, and we know you've got problems, but you'd better start hitting it a little harder.' And they gave us the support to do something about it.

"As a result we increased our development testing program. We put more people on the project, and this gave us a better handle on the problem. We also took a closer look at the state of the art and pursued it with more diligence to see if improved methods and new materials would help us come up with a solution to the weight problem.

"At the same time Management took another approach. Maynard Pennell and Jack Steiner, who were now both Corporate Vice Presidents, were named to head a Task Force of about 100 excellent engineers to take a new look at the whole picture. The top-side thinking was that, maybe, we guys who had been working so close to the project, were running a little scared. Maybe, we were doing something all wrong, tightening up, paying too much attention to the urgency of the scheduling program, any number of things. Maybe, what was needed was a fresh start with guys who could hit the thing with less inhibitions.

"Anyway, the Task Force moved in and set up shop in the basement of the building where we original Project guys had been working. We gave them all our data, and they started out to come up with some of their own ideas. The 747, at this stage, became a kind of competition between the two groups.

"When their studies were all done, a month or so later, there were two presentations made to Management, theirs and ours. We Project guys stood up and said – 'Well, here's where we are now, and here's what we think we can do.' Then, the other crowd made their presentation, which had tossed out part of our thinking and was a somewhat different approach.

"After careful consideration of both proposals, it was Management's decision to stick with the basic Project group's definition of things. It was a really a courageous decision on the part of Management, because at that point, we Project guys couldn't really give any assurance that we were heading for success. But we did have the go-ahead.

"The Task Force went back to its normal duties, and the original Project guys started in like a bunch of hungry beavers chewing away at the problem. Management's decision to back them, I think, sparked them to new heights, and the 747 came out of it all like a gal who had gone on a reducing diet. We actually drove most of the excess weight out of the airplane to come close to our original goals.

"We did this in several ways. Before all of this started, we had felt that the wings, aerodynamically and structurally were pretty good. The wing had already been through about four iterations, but we redefined it again, and in the process, we shaved off about a thousand pounds of weight.

"In another slimming exercise we used more Nomex, a highly flameproof chemically impregnated paper developed by Boeing and the DuPont people which, heretofore, had been used chiefly for internal structures. Then, somebody came up with the idea to use this for some external parts. It worked beautifully, and practically all of the big fairings, where the big wing joins the body, for example, are made of Nomex. This, too, saved quite a few pounds.

"We also used a lot more Titanium for some of the really big stuff. The main landing gear beams, nine foot arms, for example, are solid titanium and, I believe, the biggest structures of their kind made of this metal.

"In addition, we took a whole new look at the external loads imposed on the airplane and we redistributed the structural stress on some areas to get maximum efficiency for minimum weight.

"After all of this, plus some other lesser changes, we were convinced that we had greatly improved the airplane aerodynamically, as well as having learned to live within the weight limitations of the specifications.

"At this point, we were pretty sure we were heading for success.

"The 747 started to move rapidly out of

its design and engineering phase toward the manufacturing stage."

Meanwhile, things had been moving along at terrific pace in other directions. The place to assemble the plane was under construction at Everett, and another new multi-million dollar facility, a gigantic machine shop and warehouses complex, was going up at Auburn, Washington south of Seattle. The Boeing subsidiary at Wichita was also gearing up to manufacture certain component parts. And all over the United States and in some foreign countries, major sub-contractors were tooling up to do their part in the 747 program.

What was happening 2,000 miles east of Seattle at Pratt & Whitney, a division of the big United Aircraft Corporation was probably the most important of all. P&W, the engine people, Boeing's long-time partner in progress, was building the most powerful jet engine in the world to power the 747 into the sky and thrust its 350-tons through the air at near sonic speeds.

"Without a successful marriage of the airplane and its powerplant," somebody said, "this leviathan of the skies would be as lifeless as a dead whale."

Artist's drawing shows finalized version of 747 that came out of Joe Sutter's "mill." In all, there were hundreds of changes made in design from time of Pan Am order until production "go ahead" signal.

CHAPTER TWELVE

Struggle For Power

ORVILLE WRIGHT, in the autumn of 1896, lay ill in the bedroom of the white frame house on Hawthorne Street in Dayton, Ohio where he was born. His brother, Wilbur, was at the bedside reading an item to the patient from a newspaper. The story was about Otto Lilienthal, the great German glider enthusiast, who had plunged to his death a few days before while trying out one of his new winged machines. The Wright Brothers, who owned and operated a bicycle shop and did a lot of bike racing, for sometime now had been intensely interested in this fascinating "sport of wings," and were building a large man-carrying glider. And they had followed Lilienthal's experiments very closely. Only recently, they had written him for more data, and were anxiously awaiting an answer. They took his sudden death as a great loss to the science of flight, because they believed he was the foremost authority.

They were discussing the accident.

"You know, Orv, a flying machine to be practical, should not be at the mercy of the air currents," Wilbur expressed himself. "That's probably what killed Lilienthal. He, likely, got caught in a powerful downdraft and lost control."

"Control is the important thing," Orville agreed. "But there should be a power source of some kind other than the wind currents, an airscrew driven by a motor, maybe, producing a man-made mass of air to support the wings. Like putting a motor on a sailboat..."

These may not have been the exact words used, but years later, recalling the conversation of that day in an interview with the author, Orville Wright said – *"I'm sure that Lilienthal's death made us turn our thoughts, more and more, toward powered flight. We became intensely interested in reading everything we could find, not only about the principles of flight such as were known at that time, but also about the methods of motivation for gliders, and the experiments others had tried with steam-driven propeller models and full-sized vehicles of the air."*

Otto Lilienthal, the German glider enthusiast whom the Wright Brothers believed to be ahead of his time.

Later, as the Wrights achieved great success with their gliders at Kitty Hawk, and felt confident they had mastered the control problem, the idea of turning the glider into a power-driven machine became the next logical challenge. They wrote to the automobile manufacturers in 1902 – even though the motor car was very much in its infancy – and asked them to build a lightweight gasoline engine for the Wright glider. It is interesting to note that the auto builders, even Henry Ford, who later would do so much for aviation, answered that they didn't want any association with such a "hare-brained idea as a flying machine."

The Wrights decided to build their own engine. The project wasn't altogether strange to them, because they already had built a small, one-cylinder gasoline engine for their workshop to run the fan of the first wind tunnel. With the help of their chief mechanic, Charley Taylor, they succeeded in building a four cylinder engine which developed up to 17 horsepower and weighed about 170 pounds with all accessories. Admittedly, that wasn't a very good pound per horsepower ratio, but the Wrights were more than pleased. They didn't know any better at that time, being novices in the engine business. But it was more horsepower for less weight than they had figured on for their glider, and it per-

This was engine the Wright Brothers built themselves for first powered flyer. It weighed about 170 pounds.

First Wright Brothers' powered flying machine. The single engine drove two identical "pusher" propellers.

mitted them to use the saving in weight to make a lot of refinements which, undoubtedly, contributed to their success, where others had failed so many times.

The engine they built, was taken to Kitty Hawk, North Carolina where they had been doing their gliding experiments, and mounted on their modified 1902 glider to make it a power machine. The engine drove two pusher propellers which they also had designed and fabricated themselves.

The moment had arrived for their flight into history.

On December 17, 1903, at about 10 o'clock in the morning, with Orville Wright lying belly flat on the wing right next to the engine, and manipulating the controls with both hands, shoulders and feet, the engine roared, and the frail craft of wooden frame and cloth and glue came to life. It moved slowly at first over the mono-rail track on a small dolly, an arrangement they had devised to keep it heading into the wind, and with Wilbur running alongside holding onto a wing tip.

The next instant, it rose by its own power to an altitude of about three feet, before it came down again at a point higher in elevation than where it had started.

The flight lasted only 12 seconds, but in that fleeting fraction of a minute, history recorded the first successful flight of a man-carrying, power-driven, heavier, than-air flying machine. The airplane was born, and with it the genesis of the Boeing 747, although it was more than a half a century in the future.

The fact remains, however, that with their first airplane and the data they had accumulated in a crude, but efficient wind tunnel and their gliding experiments, the Wright Brothers gave us a high heritage. They were much more than just "early birdmen;" they were the Einsteins of the Air Age. The basic aerodynamic formulae for the design of a practical, controllable flying machine which they gave us, apply just as much to the 710,000-pound 747 as they did to the first Kitty Hawk flyer.

The 747, as it emerged in its finalized design concept out of "Sutter's Mill" late in 1967, would one day fly or fail, depending upon how well man had applied the Wrights' basic formula for flight, and used his advanced technology in the state of the art of aerostation. Its size and the magnitude of the problems was all that really had changed.

Paradoxically, the 747's fuselage was more than twice as long as the distance covered by the 1903 Wright machine on its first flight. The tip of its towering rudder, sixty-three feet above the ground, was more than twenty times the height the first flyer had achieved. Man had, indeed, built himself a big thing with wings.

It also might qualify as one of the world's biggest anachronisms. The plane that would become the world's biggest commercial jetliner in its then state – *without engines* – was nothing more than a super-sized, sophisticated Wright Brothers' glider.

Boeing turned to Pratt & Whitney Aircraft which had produced the powerplants for virtually all Boeing-built aircraft for more than 40 years, to design and develop and produce the engines for the 747. And Pratt & Whitney accepted the challenge.

II

THE kind of powerplant they were talking

about was a jet engine capable of producing more than 40,000 pounds of thrustpower which translated into horsepower, would be about equal to that of twenty Union Pacific Railroad diesel locomotives. Pratt & Whitney Aircraft had been working on the design concept for just such an engine as a result of the C-5A competition. They called it a "high bypass ratio" engine, bypass ratio being the ratio of the airflow through a fan at the front of the engine to the airflow through the main, basic part of the engine. Increasing the bypass ratio was the next step in fan-jet engine design beyond the fan-jets which had so greatly improved the performance of the 707, 720 and 727 Boeing jetliners. Only it was a king size engine and incorporated many refinements, new materials and new ideas.

"What we really did when we first designed a fan-jet," one P&WA engineer explained, "was to combine the best features of a turbojet and a 'prop-jet'. In principle, the fan-jet version of a jet engine is the same as the prop-jet, the geared propeller being replaced by a duct enclosed fan driven at engine speed. One fundamental difference between the fan-jet and the prop-jet is that fan-jets are unaffected by airspeed and can even fly supersonically.

"This means that fan-jets can fly much higher and faster than engines with propellers. Yet, unlike turbojet aircraft, fan-jet aircraft have almost the same superior takeoff characteristics of airplanes powered by prop-jets without the added complexity and weight common to propjets. The higher the bypass ratio, the closer the takeoff performance of a fan-jet will be to that of a prop-jet."

It was this kind of a new jet engine concept Pratt & Whitney Aircraft worked out for the heavy logistics military transport, the C-5A, when the Air Force was looking for a powerplant for its proposed new sky giant. The truth is, both Pratt & Whitney

The Pratt & Whitney Aircraft revolutionary 747 "high by-pass ratio" engine, the JT9D (at left) had frontal fan twice the diameter of the smaller JT8D engines (right) which powered biggest previous jets.

and General Electric had been working on *"high bypass ratio"* engines about the same time that the Air Force began thinking seriously about the big cargo plane. Some say, the fact that the two biggest manufacturers of jet engines in the U.S. were so close to the bigger engine concept, gave the real impetus to the whole C-5A program. We do know, that at a certain time, the Air Force suddenly completely reversed itself, and pushed for the big logistics transport.

While Boeing, Douglas and Lockheed were in competition for the C-5A contract, Pratt & Whitney and General Electric were in the race to get the engine contract.

We have seen in the previous chapter what happened when Boeing lost the C-5A competition to Lockheed; how they immediately turned to the development of a commercial derivative of their C-5A proposal which would become the 747.

And so it was, when General Electric won the engine competition for the C-5A, Pratt & Whitney Aircraft turned their know-how into the development of a bigger engine for a bigger commercial jetliner which, they believed must come along.

It was inevitable that the airframe people and engine people should get together. Boeing was shopping around for a large engine for its 747. Pratt & Whitney Aircraft was looking around for a big plane that needed a big engine.

III

"WE really threw the P&WA crowd a curve with our specifications for the 747 engine," Joe Sutter recalled. "The engine we wanted was bigger than the one they were talking about for the C-5A, and we wanted a lot of refinements. It had to be a lot quieter to meet the noise restrictions around commercial airports. And we demanded that it not throw out so much smoke, an air pollution problem that was starting to bug everybody. We were also asking for 43,000 lbs. of thrust power, minimum, with a good growth potential."

Could P&WA produce such an engine?

The whole situation was remindful of that day in 1926 when Bill Boeing had picked up the phone, called Fred Rentschler, and asked if it were possible to get the P&W *Wasp* for the Model-40A mailplane. But Fred Rentschler, the man who *"ran so fast in the right direction"* was dead. So was Bill Boeing.

Fortunately, a similar close relationship had sprung up between Boeing's Bill Allen and United Aircraft Corporation's Board Chairman, H. Mansfield Horner. United Aircraft was Pratt & Whitney Aircraft's parent organization, and "Jack" Horner made the decisions. He was "Boeing people," too, part of the breed, anyway.

Big Jack had joined P&WA as a stock chaser and messenger, the same year, 1926, that Boeing and Pratt & Whitney joined each other to put the first "Wasp" into the air in a Boeing-built Navy fighter. Now, in 1966, he was riding high, wide and handsome as a result of the big gamble he had authorized when the new *turbofan* JT8D engines were built, making possible the highly successful Boeing 727. He hadn't hesitated to make that decision in the face of strong competition from General Electric and Rolls-Royce. P&WA had spent $75,000,000 to give the 727 its muscle, and the competition ran hotter than the engine's own exhaust, right down to the line.

When the question of developing the engines for the 747 came up, Jack Horner didn't hesitate to turn the corner into the *Spacious Age.* Even though it looked like they might have to spend over a quarter of a million in development costs.

United Aircraft Corporation's H. Mansfield "Jack" Horner, who gave P&WA go ahead to build JT9D engines.

Huge eight-foot diameter fan at front of engine was one of "secrets" of increased thrustpower for JT9D. "We had a 46-bladed propeller up front," an engineer remarked, "which gave us a lot of air to play with!"

When he gave Boeing his answer, Jack Horner had written into the contract that Pratt & Whitney Aircraft would *guarantee* the required thrustpower. The engine would be quieter than any of the present types. It would also be virtually smokeless.

Work started immediately at the P&WA main plant in East Hartford, Conn. (where, incidentally, the first *Wasp* went into production forty years before) on the prototype engine.

It was called the JT9D, and although there had been a lot of paper-work done and a lot of preliminary test data accumulated, they were really starting from scratch.

The challenge was a whole new concept in power.

To begin with, the size of the thing introduced a whole new set of problems. The JT9D would have an eight-foot diameter inlet, twice that of the 18,000-pound-thrust turbofan engines in the long-range 707 and the Douglas "stretched" DC-8 jetliners.

The advent of such large-diameter na-

Special jig borer tool developed by P&WA for JT9D. Workman inside ring gives idea of engine's size.

Hamilton Standard electron beam welder. Used for welding titanium parts. It helped reduce engine costs.

celles and fan, necessitated a new family of machines for fabrication of such big components. It required special-purpose machinery in almost every area. Pratt & Whitney Aircraft scoured domestic and foreign markets to find such machines. Some, they couldn't find and they had to design their own, and build them. New highly sophisticated and highly expensive machines came into being to perform non-conventional

Grotesque fixture with plastic arms and rubber gloves permitted welding titanium under "controlled" conditions.

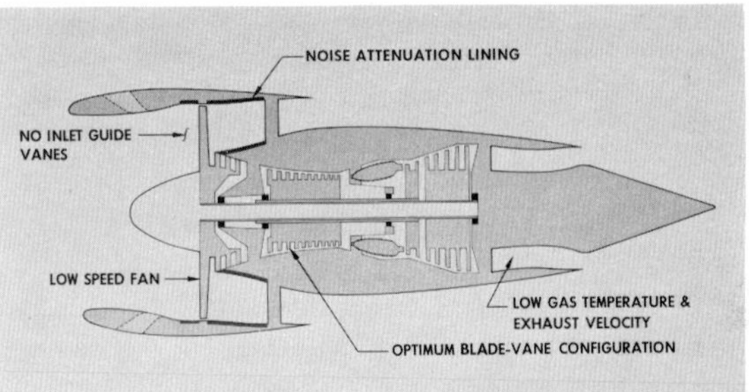

Cut-a-way drawing of JT9D points out features that made engine quieter, more smoke-free than previous jets.

machining of parts which, themselves, were new and revolutionary.

Describing a special problem and how they solved it, one P&WA engineer explained: "With existing tools, we initially machined a large, complex titanium ring, but it was an expensive and time consuming process. At that rate we could almost go broke on the drawing board.

"We tossed the problem to our sister company (The Hamilton Standard Division of United Aircraft Corporation) and they developed two large, numerically-controlled electron beam welders for us. We found that by varying the focus of the beam we could weld both thick and thin titanium parts simultaneously, giving us a ring with varying cross sections. The process reduced the cost by about 40 per cent."

In another area, the problem of getting double the amount of thrustpower over previous engines, was solved in the basic design of the new engine. The size of the engine, shortened the combustion and compressor section in proportion to the big di-

Actual engine "cut-a-way" shows inner structure as related to new features explained in above drawing.

ameter of the fan, making individual compressor stages produce higher pressure — a total airflow of 1,532 pounds per second (19,000 cubic feet) and a *by-pass* ratio of five to one. Use of a rotary spinner also improved the airflow conditions.

In short, they "whipped up a tornado" to make the fan *by-pass* airflow produce better than 70 per cent of the thrust.

More extensive use of titanium and high-alloy nickel steel, both high-heat resistant metals, helped solve the problem of withstanding the extreme high temperatures of the combustion chambers and the ambient heat of supersonic airflow.

The design also called for a lower jet-exhaust velocity to lessen the "roar," and a reduction in the speed of the fan at the front of the engine (compensated for by the large diameter of the frontal fan) to minimize the "siren" type sound so characteristic of previous turbofan engines. They also employed a sound-absorbent lining installed in the engine cowling ahead of and behind the fan, which cut down on noise decibels.

These were some of the major *breakthroughs.*

What finally emerged, the result of six years of research according to P&WA engineers, was a twin-rotor engine with 15 compressor stages, three low-speed compressor sections plus eleven high-speed compressors, and the big eight-foot fan section. In spite of its huge diameter, the engine was only 128 inches in length, a highly volatile, compact package of power. It weighed only 8,470 pounds.

With 43,500-pound thrustpower rating, equal to about 87,000 horsepower, it could produce about ten horsepower per pound of weight.

It had taken half a century to reverse things. At maximum power, although it could run only about a minute, the Wright Brothers' first engine produced about 17 horsepower, one horsepower for every 10 pounds of its weight!

The JT9D, prototype of the world's most powerful *by-pass* engine was run for the first time on the test stand at East Hartford in December, 1966, almost fifty-three years to the day that the Wrights made their historic first flight at Kitty Hawk.

The struggle for power was never ending.

"Anatomy" of the JT9D in this exploded view shows numerous ring sections. "It stretches out like dissecting a huge serpent," some one described the scene. Brought together, engine was shorter than predecessors.

First 747 engine is moved into test stand at East Hartford P&WA plant. JT9D took six years to develop.

One of the most dramatic moments in the development of the prototype JT9D engine came in the late spring of 1968 when the engine was ready for flight testing. It had been through many hours of initial running time in the big test cells on the ground.

But how do you flight test an engine of this size, when the airframe for which it was designed isn't built yet?

To answer that question, Pratt & Whitney Aircraft engineers leased a B-52 bomber from the Air Force and modified the aircraft for installation of the big engine. Two of the bomber's P&WA J57 engines were removed and the single JT9D was positioned in their place, the inboard nacelle of the right wing. More than four months were required to modify and reinforce the wing of the B-52, to build the special nacelle housing the test engine, and to install sophisticated instrumentation.

The aluminum nacelle housing for the JT9D was manufactured by the Rohr Corporation of Chula Vista, California, and the tail cone extending from the rear of the engine was made by Aeronca, Inc. of Middletown, Ohio. Design work on the test bed was done by engineers at Boeing's Wichita, Kansas facility where the B-52 bombers were manufactured.

When the work was completed, the B-52 "flying testbed" enabled the engine people to run the engine at altitudes of 45,000 feet and above, far exceeding any simulated

"Flying testbed" was this modified Air Force B-52 bomber. In this low-altitude fly-by of test plane, note smoke pouring from J-57 engines, lack of it from huge diameter JT9D on right wing.

Close-up of JT9D mounted on wing of B-52 shows good comparison of size of 747 engine next to smaller J-57 engines mounted in twin-pod arrangement. Single engine developed more thrust than pair of J-57s.

conditions that might have been created in special altitude test chambers on the ground.

In its flight test program, the engine was given a clean bill of health.

With certain modifications and refinements, the prototype engine for the 747 was ready to go into production.

Pratt & Whitney Aircraft had built a whole new jet plant to accept the outsized machinery, sophisticated techniques and specialized procedures to mass produce the JT9D for the 747. This effort and expenditure paralleled what Boeing itself was doing in building a new plant at Everett, Washington to build the big plane. The new facility had been moving along at the same time that the engine, itself, was being developed.

IV

IN United Aircraft Corporation's splendid quarterly publication, "THE BEE-HIVE" (Spring, 1969) John A. Cox describes the world's biggest jet engine plant.

"*Five miles east of the center of Middletown, Connecticut, on a wooded tract of land over-looking the Connecticut River as it flows on its way to Long Island Sound,*" he writes, "*the romantic past is being mixed with the present to provide for the future. . . For more than a year, Pratt & Whitney Aircraft has been converting the former Connecticut Aircraft Nuclear Engineering Laboratory (CANAL) which it also operated, into a sprawling complex to produce the JT9D turbofan engine for the Boeing 747 . . .*

"*The Middletown plant has now become the production center for the huge JT9D turbofan . . . In cases where buildings could not be renovated economically, new structures were erected. These include a new heat treat center where parts up to 108 inches in diameter can be conditioned in furnaces, de-scaled in molten salt baths, and processed in cleaning and anodizing lines. Close by is a chiller plant for air conditioning the manufacturing building to prevent wide temperature swings which could make the large JT9D parts contract or expand during machining.*

"*The new manufacturing building (itself) contains more than 500,000 square feet of manufacturing and assembly space, and it was specifically designed with JT9D manufacturing in mind. Because the engine's inlet is more than eight feet in diameter, more space than ordinary is required to move the parts from machine to machine. Thus the spacing of machinery, aisle widths, overhead clearance and the orderly flow of materials dictated the building's design . . .*

Aerial view of Pratt & Whitney Aircraft's facility, Middletown, Connecticut, built especially for manufacturing of 747 engines. Main building represents half a million square feet of manufacturing and assembly space.

Final assembly of JT9D in vertical position (to save space) gave "new look" to Middletown plant's production line.

In this factory scene, we can see how numerous parts of JT9D come together into compact package of power.

Lone worker, at right, operates control panel to guide huge special "tool" in machining process for JT9D ring. Giant machines required, changed whole complexion of P&WA engine production line.

Special welding techniques and jigs had to be developed to permit work on specific JT9D engine parts.

Intricate "pattern" of this JT9D ring gives an idea of complex tooling that the design necessitated.

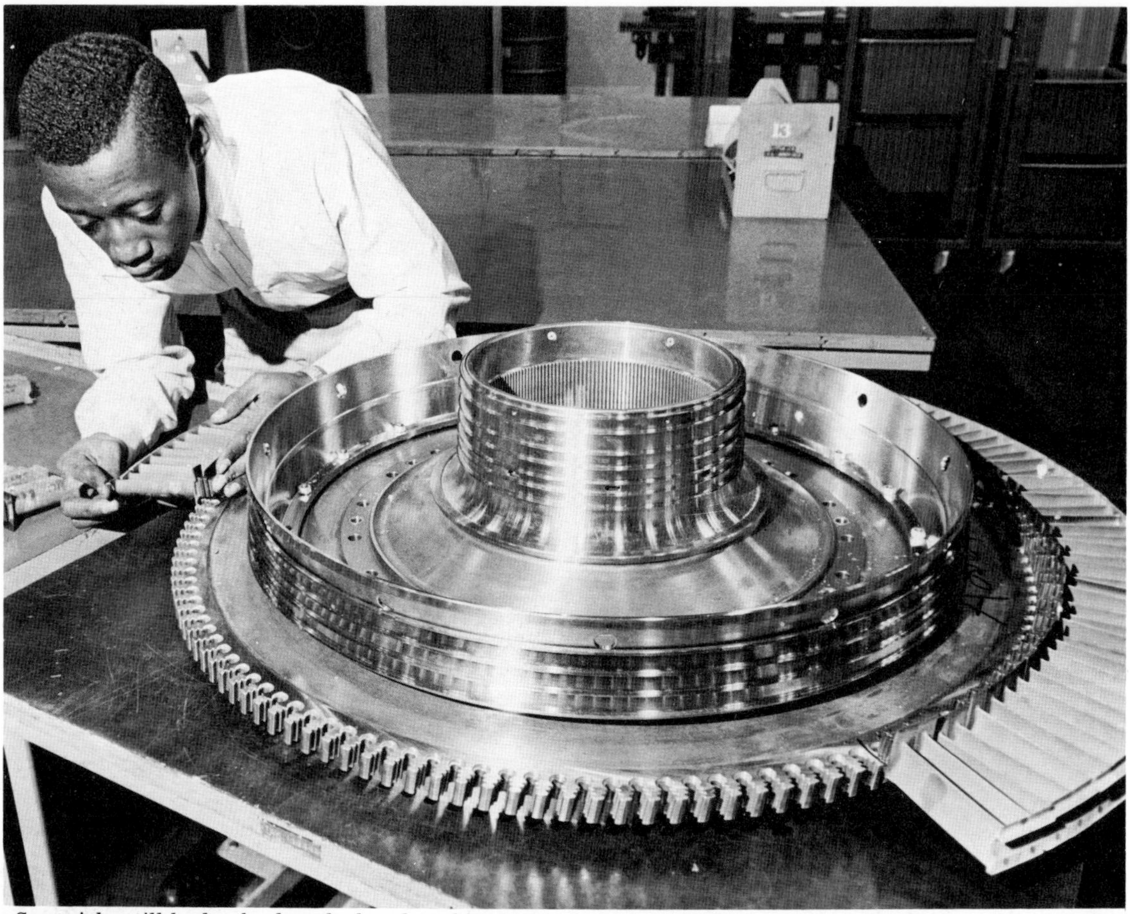

Some jobs still had to be done by hand as this worker illustrates, fitting small vanes into compressor wheel. Blades, themselves, required special machines and delicate touch in assembly process.

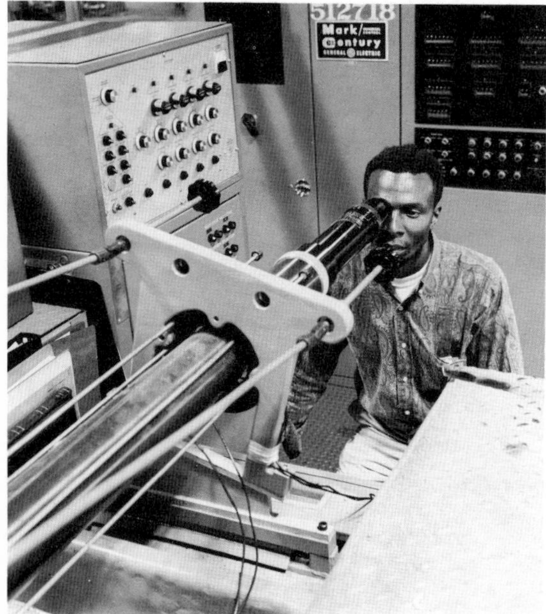

Electronic measuring devices and special optics were required in checking for minute tolerances.

Like "game wheel" at a Carnival, the small turbine blades on special mount pass inspection.

A near completed JT9D moves along production line hanging from overhead hoists and gets last-minute adjustments. The big rotary "spinner" on front of fan helped to improve the airflow.

Another view of huge engine in final assembly process shows detail of carefully machined frontal fan section. Diameter of rear ring is almost size of J-57 engine. Note polished exteriors.

Loading JT9D engine aboard huge jet freighter for shipment to Boeing at Everett, Washington where 747 was being manufactured. Ironically, 747 would dwarf skyfreighter that delivered its engines.

"For the present, Middletown has a single assembly line with five elevators, which enable assemblers to work on the large engines positioned vertically." John Cox concludes, *"A second assembly line and five additional elevators will be installed by the end of this year (1969) when a production schedule of 34 engines a month is planned."*

By mid-summer of 1968, however, the first production engines were being delivered to Boeing's Everett plant where major assembly of the first 747 was coming together. As fast as the engines were completed they were shipped by air to Rohr Co. in Chula Vista and thence to Everett.

Horsepower, a million times that which pulled the Conastoga Wagons in the great Westward Movement from sea to shining sea was on the move to help launch a new era in transportation.

In the near future, this horsepower would pull great fleets of the 747s through the Wild Blue Yonder.

The plane that *just had to happen,* was about to happen!

CHAPTER THIRTEEN

The Incredible Happening

ONCE the decision had been reached to go ahead with the 747 program, the place to build such a giant became a colossal problem. Boeing people looked at several sites, and finally decided on Everett, Washington about 30 miles north of Seattle. Located on Port Gardner Bay, a natural landlocked harbor at the mouth of the Snohomish River. Everett, before the 747 came along, was famed for its lumbering industry, neighboring winter ski resorts, excellent steelhead and salmon fishing. All of a sudden, in the spring of 1966 on a 780-acre site adjacent to Snohomish County Airport (Paine Field) near the outskirts of the 40,000-plus populated city, construction workers moved in with bulldozers, and started making room for the largest factory in the world to build the world's largest commercial jetliner. *"It's a project,"* one of the construction engineers explained, *"that's comparable in magnitude to building Grand Coulee Dam and the Panama Canal!* And so it turned out to be.

They moved 4½-million cubic yards of earth to clear the Everett site whose perimeter is 9.3 miles. This grading and surfacing caused such a change in the natural drainage of the terrain that the whole project was threatened with inundation before any building construction could begin. They had to build a holding pond with a capacity of 15 million gallons – enough to float the liner "*S.S. United States*" – to handle the

This was artist's concept of Boeing Everett, Washington complex, where 747 was to be built. Main assembly building, center, would become world's largest volume building, ten stories high, covering 63 acres.

Specially-built railroad cars are used to haul 747 assemblies up spur line, standard-gauge track constructed for rail access to Everett, Washington facility. Railway is second steepest in U.S.

runoff. Then, they black-topped 200 acres to get solid footing to start work on the factory foundation.

To bring in the necessary 34,000 tons of structural steel for the main building, they had to lay three miles of railroad track up a 5.6 per cent grade, the second steepest standard-gauge railroad in the United States. The spur joins the site with the mainline tracks 540 feet below. Chugging up the steep grade the front end of a locomotive is three feet higher than the rear coupling.

The railroad was first used to bring in building materials. The structural steel for the plant, alone, had it been shipped all at one time, would have required a train 12½ miles long. Today, many of the assemblies and components used in fabricating the 747 move over the rail spur which dead-ends at the top of its climb right inside the main plant itself.

You have to see this structure to believe it. One building, ten stories high, a single roof covering 63 acres, it is the largest volume structure — 205,000,000 cubic feet — in the world. Under its roof are housed the major portions of manufacturing, subassembly and final assembly functions for the huge 747.

The main section of the 115-foot-high building for major and final assembly consists of three large bays with 1,365,000 square feet of covered work area. Part of this area, for wing panel riveting, alone, is as large as a football field.

Jutting from a corner of the manufacturing and assembly building is a 165,000-square-foot structure for cleaning, sealing and painting airplane sections before they go into final assembly. A 150,000-square-foot building beside the main structure houses full-scale manufacturing mockups. This area is connected to the assembly building by a low bay sub-assembly area.

Also on the site are two warehouses, a plant services building, three office buildings and a large cafeteria.

All of these facilities are separated from the pre-flight area, a large concrete ramp apron adjacent to the Paine Field runway, by an access highway. Connecting the main manufacturing plant with the pre-flight area is a 60-foot wide bridge over the highway. In this area is a 60,000-square-foot paint hangar, whose great doors weigh 250 tons apiece.

Such was the $200,000,000-plus Everett Complex, the birthplace of the 747, when we visited the site in mid-summer of 1968 about the time that the first prototype airplane was moving down the assembly line towards completion.

But come along, let's see what happens in this eagle's nest where the big metallic birds are born.

II

INSIDE, the sprawling assembly plant is a maze of scaffolding, jigs, benches, elevated platforms, and grotesque-shaped machines each designed for a special purpose and mission. It is a world of color; red, green, blue, yellow, assembly tools, so color-coded to designate their function in the production process. A world of brilliance; tens of thousands of lights, enough candle-power to illuminate 32,000 average American homes. A world of sounds, the *rat-a-tat-tat* of rivet guns, the crackle of welding torches, the hissing of air guns, and the shouts of workers. A world of smells, of exhaust fumes from vehicles moving to and fro over roadways where the speed limit is 5-mph inside the building. The color, the "sunlight," the sounds, the smells are everywhere, and mixed together they are the "magic formula" that will turn the 747 from fantasy into fact. Standing there in their midst, is like watching a miracle happen.

Look there! The giant overhead crane on a track a hundred feet above your head has just picked up a complete 747 tail section, and is moving it slowly into position to join the fuselage and wings. The tail section, a sub-assembly consisting of the horizontal

No. 1 Boeing 747 "Super jet" at this stage was just getting her engines installed. Scaffolding and platform in foreground is three stories in height. Scene shows one bay of main assembly building.

A thing this big on an assembly line seemed almost incredible, but there it was right before our eyes. One bay in main building had three of "Super jet's" wings, fuselage and tail assemblies all joined.

stabilizer and part of the aft section of the fuselage, has a wing span almost as great as that of the old DC-3 airliner. And you remember, that the DC-3 just before World War II was the biggest commercial airliner flying.

The 747 you are watching, as the pieces come together, will be 40 times the weight of the first DC-3!

Now, let's take a ride in the cab of one of those giant overhead cranes. From this lofty perch, high above the factory floor, you get a bird's-eye view of the production line flow pattern. The anatomy of a 747 is spread out below — the rounded nose sections, the tapered wings (right and left) seven-feet thick at butt end where they will join the fuselage and a third as long as a football field, the six-story high rudders and vertical fins, the DC-3 wing length horizontal stabilizers and elevators, the huge tubular fuselage sections of the main cabin, the tapering tail cones, (all sub-assemblies) grouped together, each in its own little corner of the world. Each is like the headwaters of a tributary that feeds into the mainstream of a great river.

For that's the way it works. The movement of the mainstream is indescernable, because actually the line stays still for days as each of the sub-assemblies comes together fed from smaller "headwaters," stockpiles of the smaller parts, engine nacelles, landing gear trucks, fuel tanks, cables, ducts and other accessories.

But from our position high above, gliding the full length of one of the big fabricating bays, the huge plane comes together quickly — the nose, the fuselage, the wings, the empennage (tail assembly), the landing gear, the nacelles and finally the engines themselves.

Right before your eyes a winged giant is born!

The *Incredible Happening.*

But let's take a closer look.

It marked "Incredible Milestone" as banner proclaims, when body and wings of first "Super jet" were joined.

Overhead crane swings forward fuselage into place. At left, note thickness of wing where it joins body.

Center cabin section with wings joined (left) and forward body section move closer together on rollered cradles.

Crane operator high above, jockeys forward body section into position to mate with center fuselage and wings.

Aft fuselage section of No. 1 "Super jet" moves high above factory floor to join wings and rest of body.

From different angle, crane operator lowers aft fuselage section into position.

The long fuselage of first "Super jet" begins to show its profile. Note two-story profile of forward section.

Horizontal stabilizer, almost as big as DC-3 wing, is moved forward on rollers to join with tail.

Towering rudder and vertical fin are moved by overhead crane to be joined with horizontal stabilizer.

For first time, fuselage, wings, and tail assembly of No. 1 "Super jet" are one. Note the five cabin doors.

First production JT9D engines for 747, shipped by air from Middletown, Conn., arrive at Everett.

First four JT9D engines, tail cones looking like ballistic missiles, are wheeled into installation area.

The "marriage" of powerplant with airframe marked another milestone in birth of No. 1 "Super jet." Here, inboard portside JT9D is being moved into place. Note leading edge flaps in extended position.

Ready to go to the paint hangar, No. 1 "Super jet" poses for her picture amid myriad of lights inside final assembly hangar at Everett. Protective covers have been placed over engine frontal areas.

Back on the floor level again, a train horn sounds; you look behind to see three flat cars rumbling to a stop inside the plant. On the flat cars are some of the nose sections just arriving after a 1600-mile journey from the Boeing plant in Wichita, Kansas where they were fabricated.

Our guide, Bob Montgomery from Everett 747 Public Relations further explains: "About 65 per cent of the weight and 50 per cent of the dollar value of each 747 is subcontracted to firms other than Boeing. Estimates are that in 1971 at peak production, there will be approximately 1500 prime suppliers of Model 747 components, and an additional 15,000 secondary suppliers located in 49 states and six foreign countries. These subcontracted units, built to Boeing engineering specifications and quality standards, are shipped to the Everett plant for assembly into completed airplanes."

In the scene we are watching – workmen starting to unload the nose sections – there is a bit of irony. The sky giant for which these nose sections were built, in the next ten years, will probably write *finis* for the proud, luxurious transcontinental *super trains* that once carried the bulk of the railroads' passenger business. But the Aircraft Industry, whose end product generated the exodus from train to plane, with such vast needs for heavy machinery, construction materials and the materials that go into the building of planes like the 747 and other sky giants to come, has increased railroad carloadings many times fold.

The 747 couldn't be built without the Iron Horse!

Moving to another section of the plant, we stop before a huge machine that looks like the world's largest "waffle-iron" – a half-block long maze of grids and honeycombs. It shapes and forms one-inch thick, one hundred-foot-long wing skin panels of solid aluminum to fit the contours of the

"It looks like the world's biggest waffle iron," someone remarked. But the long gridded structure was really another of the grotesque machines used in forming the wing skin of the 747.

Each of the body sections of the "Super jet" was fabricated in special jigs. Series of pre-fab panels go together to form the circular fuselage. Note large cross-beam that squares off cabin ceiling.

patented Boeing airfoil, one of the 747's secrets. Not far away, is a battery of rivet guns that does the work of ten "Rosie the riveters."

At another station, it appears, they are fabricating large diameter furnace boilers. But the elongated, tube-like sections actually are part of the 747's main cabin. Some jokester has hung a sign on the cave-like opening of one of these sections – "BEWARE OF BATS." Indeed, you walk inside Kentucky's Mammoth Cave.

In another area you'd swear you were at the world's biggest quilting bee. Here, they are making "blankets," – hundreds of square yards of aluminum-foil covered,

Forward section of main cabin and second-story lounge is being sound-proofed and insulated with aluminum foil "blankets." Note how skeleton frame is series of rings, stringers and cross beams.

paper-thin plastic (Dupont's Tedlar) and Dacron sandwiched together that looks like quilting, to be used for sound-proofing.

You can walk for miles, stopping here and there at various assembly points, each a fascinating operation; man and the machines he built, working as a team to create a new titan of the skies.

At the time of our visit there was a 747 community of about 10,000 persons working at Everett, another 5,000 were expected to join them by the end of 1968. Altogether across the nation, engaged in building the 747, we were told, there would ultimately be a work force of about 50,000 persons, half of them employed by Boeing, the rest by subcontractors and suppliers. Everett expects to turn out seven or eight planes a month at peak production.

That's some goal considering there are 4½-million parts including fasteners in one 747. The plane requires over 100 miles of wiring and over 2,000 pieces of tubing. Seventy-five thousand engineering drawings were used in production of the Number One airplane.

"Nothing like this ever happened before," said Malcom Stamper, Vice-President and Manager at Everett. "The whole 747 program is the shining example of the free enterprise system of American business in its finest hour."

Stamper, who came to Boeing in 1962 after 14 years in management skills at General Motors, pointed with pride to the fact that Boeing, without any assurance of government orders for a military cargo version of its 747 design took the big gamble. "Now, we're building the prime mover of the world's trade and commerce in the skies for the next decade," he explained.

There is a great deal of feeling about this fact among the men and women who work on the 747. Many of them worked on the B-17 *Flying Fortresses* that knocked out Hitler, and the B-29 *Superforts* that finished off Japan with the A-bombs. But now, workers can see this "big plane know-how" culminating in the creation of a great ocean liner of the skies. In this, there is a lot of pride.

Everywhere, throughout the huge plant, we saw signs that reflected the spirit of these Boeing people. "WE CAN DO IT", referring to the deadline for roll-out of the first plane by the end of September, 1968. "THE INCREDIBLES" stenciled on workers' plastic helmets.

This was Everett, at a time when five of the 747s were moving down the production line. An "incredible thing" when one was well aware that no aircraft of this size ever had flown before.

III

EVERETT is the plant from which the finished 747s in their glistening airline colors will roll out and first meet the big sky. But Boeing built another new $150,000,000 facility at Auburn, Washington, about twenty miles south of Seattle where the raw stock is turned into the biggest component structures that make up the 747, and where many of the giant jigs, huge specialized machines and precision tools for building the plane are fabricated. "Auburn is the big machine shop," our host told us. "It had to be because we had to design special tools for the 747, and fabricate them, ourselves. The policy is to "make or buy", but in a thing of this magnitude and unknowns, you can't buy certain necessary tools, you have to make them."

"Some wing assembly jigs for the 747," he pointed out, "are as large as railroad bridges, yet they must be precisely engineered. We built the jigs, dies, fixtures, templates and gauges used for the fabrication and assembly work to be done at Everett. It requires probably the most highly skilled technicians in the industry. And a helluva lot of non-conventional tools to build the tools themselves."

Auburn is where the 747's skin, spars, stringers, ducts and other machined parts with extremely close tolerances are produced by specialized machinery.

Typical was a huge skin mill we saw, on whose 130-foot long bed, raw stock for the 747 wing panel is milled down from a gross weight of over 9,000 pounds to 2,380 pounds. In this case, the raw material was a solid sheet of aluminum 104 feet long, over an inch thick and about five feet in width.

As we watched, the massive cutting tool moving slowly back and forth over the aluminum slab, spewed thin metallic shavings on the floor, building huge piles of the stuff,

Aerial view of Boeing's "machine shop" for 747 at Auburn, Washington. Here, special tools to build the "Superjet" were fabricated. Long buildings are huge warehouses for storage of needed raw materials.

like saw-dust in a planing mill. These shavings go back to the mills to be melted down, and come back again, another aluminum slab, to be cut into another wing panel at some future date.

The cutting tool operator said with a grin – "Plane No. 20 might well be built from the shavings Plane No. 10 left behind."

This 747 wing closure panel they were machining, incidentally, is such a compli-

Worker checks long slabs of aluminum which will be machined and shaped to become wing panels for 747.

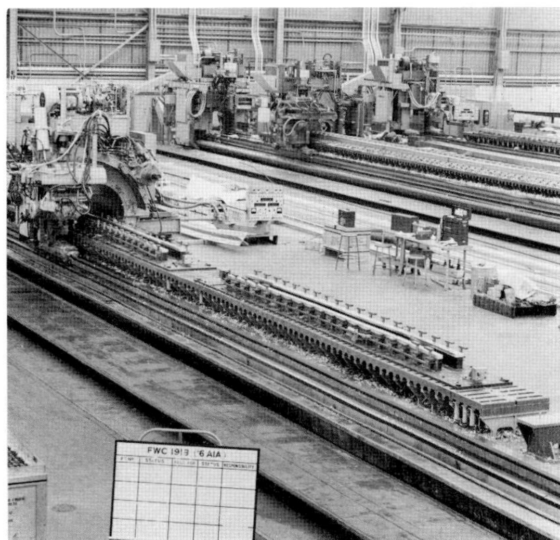

Huge planing mill, with specially-designed cutting tools, shaves down aluminum wing panel that is 104 feet long.

After planing mill gets through, 747 wing panel looks like this. It is then picked up by crane and moved for transport to Everett. The solid aluminum slab is "machined" to save weight and maintain strength.

cated operation that it requires more than two-and-a-half miles of numerical control tape to program it for 21 hours of continuous cutting time in the skin mill.

Just about everything in the whole 747 fabrication process is computerized. At both Auburn and Everett there are Central Control rooms where batteries of computers are clicking and clacking and making whirring sounds 24 hours a day. The computers, it is estimated, have stored up over 200 *billion* bits of information pertinent to the program. Data pertinent to the design and fabrication of specific parts is put on tape and fed into the tooling and fabricating machines, themselves.

In some cases, workers don't even have to select their own tools. They drop a coded card in a slot, a "lazy-daisy" round table turns slowly, and up pops the right sized wrench or screw driver, or drill bit. They pick up a telephone and call the dispatcher wanting a two-ton structural member; a computer finds it, and sends it on its way to the proper station. One man presses a button and a battery of drilling machines, positioned by taped instructions (electronic templates) makes a hundred holes.

"The 747," one shop foreman said, "is an electronic revolution."

Engineering Director of the 747 Project at Everett, Joe Sutter, whom we met in a previous chapter, puts it this way – "One of the greatest breakthroughs on the tooling and construction of the 747 was the use of computerized lofting. Even though this airplane is built all over the U.S. and in some parts of Europe, it fits together like a glove. All of these parts come in and they mate beautifully. Much better than with any previous airplane, and the reason is that we lofted the airplane on computer machines . . .

"You can take a cut any way through the 747 that you want, and you can get an exact definition of any part," Sutter adds. "Since everybody uses the same tape you eliminate little human eccentricities which often occur. This, I think has really made the program so successful. If we had not used computerized lofting plus tape-controlled machinery the 747 might be in a helluva lot of trouble."

The skin mill working on the huge wing panel at Auburn was one example of what Sutter was talking about.

Another machine we saw at Auburn, was a one-of-its-kind *Froriep* spheromill. They call it the "*Fantastic Froriep!*" The machine was built on special order in Germany's Industrial Ruhr Valley, and shipped halfway around the world. The secret is, this five-axis milling machine enables a cutter to approach a workpiece at virtually any compound angle in a single set-up. One of the first pieces milled on this machine weighed in excess of 56 tons.

It was an endplate for one of Auburn's five large autoclaves, giant "heat curing" ovens essential for new metal bonding operations which, in many instances, have replaced conventional riveting and welding of certain 747 parts. In Auburn's Sheet Metal Shop, we saw huge stretch presses forming these components which later would be bonded together. Once this "shaping process" was completed, the individual parts moved by overhead conveyors to a special environmental dust-free area. There, workers apply the special "metal glues" and join the pieces together. Later these pieces are moved on huge trays into the ovens. The whole place looks more like a bakery than an airplane fabricating shop.

The metal bonding process, incidentally, provides a greater strength-to-weight ratio and smoother surfaces to reduce drag. It helped Sutter's gang when they had to cut down on the weight during that "crisis" which we talked about earlier.

There were many other interesting sights to behold at Auburn, each playing an important role in the fabricating of the 747. The scene, for instance, where so many women workers are covering large mandrels like dressmakers' dummies of all

The "fantastic Froriep" spheromill which was shipped half-way round the world to Auburn. Huge circular ring is endplate for autoclave. Machine operates on five axis, permits cutting from almost any angle.

shapes and sizes, with yards of pre-impregnated resin cloth. Only the "arms, legs and torsos" are unusual-shaped parts for the big plane, mostly tubes and ducting used for fuel, water, oil and air-conditioning. There are, for example, over 2,000 separate tubular parts and over two miles of ducting in the 747. These plastic and plaster forms, from what could be called the world's largest "ceramics shop" also go into the big ovens.

Or, let's stop for a minute by the big "swimming pools", huge vats where they "dip" the different shaped tubing and ducting now formed in metal (mostly titanium) from the plastic and plaster molds, into specially prepared chemicals. Before titanium can be welded – the parts joined to make grotesque-looking assemblies – all foreign substances must be removed.

The welding process, too, is unique. For the welding of titanium is done in chambers where an inert atmosphere protects against contamination which would weaken the seams. There, men in strange costumes, face masks and special gloves, operating metallic arms inside a vacuum chamber to handle the pieces of titanium, looked like Space Age creatures in a different world. A world the fabricating process needed to build the 747, brought into our midst.

IV

LEAVING Auburn, we visited another part of the Boeing complex, the plant at Renton, Washington where they are building the 707s, the 727s and the 737s. There, recalling the scenes at Everett, you get the idea of how really BIG the 747 is. By comparison, the fabrication and assembly process is like doubling the size of everything. There, too, in a large auditorium they have constructed a full-scale wooden mock-up of the 747's passenger cabin, the Flight Deck and other components to give the visitor a sneak preview of what air travel will be for the next decade. For the first time, you see the 747 as the passenger will see it when he or she walks aboard. Take a deep breath – this is the Waldorf Astoria with wings!

This mock-up of the passenger cabin, alone, cost more than a million dollars, enough to buy the largest airliner of the 1940s. In great detail it duplicates the long, wide cabin of the 747 with all the posh-posh and frills for luxurious living aloft.

"It's purpose," explained our escort, "is to permit designers and specialists to study various seating arrangements, lighting, accoustics, color schemes and entertainment systems, to meet the high standards of passenger comfort that modern air transportation demands. Because of the fierce competition, the inside, sometimes can give us more headaches than the outside."

He pointed out that the interior configuration changes frequently to satisfy the whims of various airline customers who come to inspect it. Each airline has its own arrangement based on its particular requirements. The day we were there, representatives from four different airlines toured the mock-up.

The arrangement we saw had a 58-passenger, first-class section at the front of the fuselage with three long, economy-class sections having seating arrangements for 308 more passengers. In the first-class section seats were two and three abreast with a wide center aisle, a parlor-like atmosphere. In the economy-class sections, the seats were closer together, arranged in rows two abreast on the left-hand side, a big aisle, four abreast, another large aisle, and then three abreast on the right side of the cabin. The individual economy seats were each wider and more comfortable than the first-class accommodations on the 707 in which we had flown to Seattle.

The color scheme, as well as dividing partitions, help alleviate the feeling you get, that this is a long, narrow theater. At the entrances – five double-width doors on each side of the cabin – there is a color dividing line; different colored seats in each section. The impression is that you are walking from one railroad parlor car into another only, the cabin width is much wider. High, squared-off ceilings, the wide aisles and big windows, completely eliminate the feeling of "being inside a tube", common to most airliners.

In the extreme nose of the mock-up, we entered a special lounge-like section which is separated from the main first-class cabin. It's like being in a cocktail lounge with a small bar and galley.

Walk through the double-width door, turn left, and this is the scene one beholds in the forward section of the 747 mock-up at Renton. The distinctive feature, of course, is "spiral staircase."

In the extreme nose of the 747 mock-up, the decor and arrangement was like that of a small lounge. This section, incidentally, is ahead of "Flight Deck" which is above and behind. Note large windows.

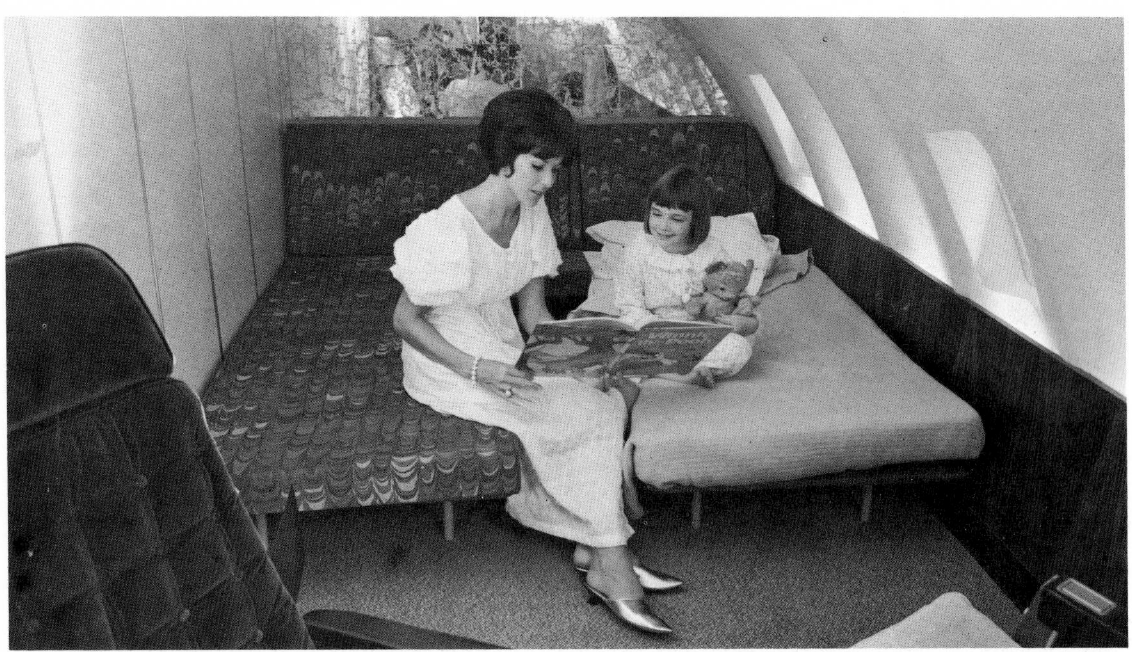

"Upstairs" in the 747 mock-up. In this configuration, half of the normal "First-Class Lounge" was made-up as stateroom. Partition divides area. Forward wall is reflection showing other lounge chairs.

Remindful of the old *"Stratocruiser"*, there was a spiral staircase leading upstairs to another ultra swank and exclusive lounge section. It can also be used as a business office, or made up into two staterooms with full-sized beds. The upper level also has its own bar and galley.

The mock-ups also included a preview of the 747s galleys, two in the first-class section and three in the economy-class sections. And below the cabin level, in the belly of the main cabin, we saw the compact "kitchens" and food storage cabinets, with the small elevators to bring the food trays upstairs.

There were also fifteen lavatories — two in the upper-level serving the lounge or staterooms, three in the lower level first-class section and ten in the economy sections. Lavatories were complete with vanity tables in the powder rooms for the ladies, wash-basins with modern design fixtures, electric shavers for the men — and flush toilets.

"They've really fixed the plumbing," we were told. "One of these lavatories because of weight and size limitations can cost as much as $60,000, a damned high priced Chic Sale!"

The mock-ups also gave us an idea of what they planned for entertainment on board. Big (28 by 76-inch screens) were mounted at the forward end of the first-class section and on the walls of the center galleys and lavatories in the economy sections, for showing of wide-screen movies.

Projectors suspended from the ceiling can show up to four and one-half hours of films — two full-length features. Or, passengers can tune in on eight channels of stereo tapes, anything from classical music to children's stories. Individual selector panels were located between the seats. In sight and sound they had planned everything for the 747's spacious wings.

But the most impressive reaction of all that we got from this preview of the Spacious Age, as we walked through the 747 cabin mock-up, was that we weren't inside an airplane at all.

One of the men who helped design the 747 put it this way: "There's a saying that millions of people would love to fly, but they want to keep one foot on the ground. Well, the 747 is big enough to take a hunk of the earthly environment right along with it. You will be able to walk out of the terminal lounge through a covered corridor and step into another room that is almost as large and as luxurious as the one you left. Only this room's got wings."

Three rearward sections of mock-up make up the "Economy Class" seating configuration. Partitions are "gallies." Flat ceiling, wide-aisle, give idea of spaciousness. Note overhead storage bins. The only three-abreast seating is on left-side of main cabin. The whole atmosphere makes one feel to be inside a small auditorium.

Entertainment systems aboard 747 mock-up featured wide movie screens. (1) In Economy Class section screen is located on wall of forward galley. (2) Another arrangement is smaller overhead screen. (3) In First Class Section screen pulls down from ceiling covering front bulkhead. Different arrangements are illustrative of purpose of mock-up.

That day was close at hand. Our tour of the 747 complex ended on a high note. They told us the first plane would be rolling out of the big factory at Everett in four or five weeks. It was scheduled to make its maiden flight on December 17, 1968 – 65 years to the day after the historic flight of the first Wright airplane at Kitty Hawk.

CHAPTER FOURTEEN

The Spacious Age Begins

THE first 747 parts built at the Auburn fabrication facility began to arrive at the Everett assembly plant in August, 1967. On September 12, the first stringers were loaded into the wing panel jigs, marking the actual start of assembly of the first airplane. Late in the year, components for the first nose section arrived from Boeing's Wichita Division. They went into assembly jigs also built at Wichita and shipped earlier. Concurrently, the first components manufactured by the major subcontractors began arriving at Everett.

From East, West, North and South, by air, train and motor freight they came; the big ailerons and flaps from Fairchild-Hiller Corporation, Hagerstown, Maryland; sections of the main passenger cabin from Northrop Corporation, Norair Division, Hawthorne, California; the 16-wheel main landing gear from Cleveland Pneumatic Tool Company, Cleveland, Ohio, and the tail surfaces and rear body section from LTV Vought Aeronautics Division, Dallas, Texas. And with the flow of materials came the flow of manpower until by the end of 1967 there were 10,000 Boeing employees, alone, working on the 747 program; 5,000 of "The Incredibles" at Everett.

There, in January, 1968 they had completed a detailed, full-scale manufacturing mockup, and all non-structural items tested in it were ordered into production.

Three months later, the largest wing ever built by Boeing was removed from its Everett assembly fixture. This first 747 wing weighed approximately 28,000 pounds.

Boeing designed and had built special truck to transport 747 components from Auburn facility to Everett. Shown here on its first trip the "double-cab" truck was used to carry 95-foot long wing stringers.

Some parts for 747 were so large that standard-sized freight cars could not be used for transport. Special over-sized railroad cars like these were made to do the job. Spur line ran right inside the factory. Tolerances in loading cars was so delicate that laser beams were used to insure long parts went in straight.

Full-scale engineering mock-up of 747 cost several million dollars. Mock-up was used by engineering and manufacturing departments to develop installations, components and manufacturing methods with which production airplanes would be built.

Every major component part of the 747 went through mock-up stages. Here we see wood and paper engine nacelle installed on inboard wing section. Mock-ups were built to exact scale and were used to see that various components fitted properly into the over-all structure. When everything was perfect, parts were ordered into production.

Another mock-up installation featured 747's unique trailing edge flap system. In this close-up, we can see how the big wing literally "comes apart." Mock-up was fully operable to enable testing flap mechanism before sending individual components to be manufactured.

Largest wing ever built by Boeing. Inspection holes make it look like long super airliner's fuselage.

On May 2, the wings and fuselage stub of the first airplane were joined together. By the end of the month the two forward body sections, and the two aft body sections were united.

Mid-June saw the wings and body come together, and for the first time the Number One "*Super jet*" began to look like an airplane.

It was not until early September, however, that the first engines were installed in their nacelles. Late in the same month the jillion-and-one other things were completed to give the giant its brain and brawn, and bring it to life.

We see her now in the huge paint hangar getting a beauty treatment, and being made ready for her debut. She is not very pretty; raw skin and blemishes, like a gal in curlers and mudpacks.

But there, they scrub her and rub her, and give her a bath in special cleansing liquid.

Then, painters in face masks and white coveralls and gloves, looking like a group of surgeons in a hospital room, start their own operation with spray guns and brushes. They swarm all over her on special platforms that hang down from the ceiling and

No. 1 "Super jet" in gigantic paint hangar is surrounded by special scaffolding, huge paint spray guns and overhead heat lamps for "quick drying." Some surfaces are "masked" to permit color scheme markings.

from atop other grotesque-shaped scaffolding. She is splotched, here and there, with masking tape to allow for the different color patterns of various insignia and lettering. Indeed, she is a winged witch in transformation!

One can almost hear her saying:

> *"Mirror, mirror upon the wall,*
> *Who's the fairest of them all!"*

And suddenly, *she* is! A red-white-and-blue American beauty. Proud new member of the Boeing family.

Glistening white, with a wide red stripe running the length of her fuselage at window level; another red stripe on her towering vertical tail fin, Along with dark blue lettering proudly proclaiming BOEING 747. And a rainbow of colors, the insignia of the various airlines around the world who will put her into service, stenciled on her fuselage forward section. All of her skin so highly polished you can see yourself walking around beneath her expansive wing.

She is ready, a debutante about to take her bow into a world which her very presence will change in many ways. A new day of elegance for the air traveler.

And Mal Stamper, Vice-President and General Manager of the entire 747 project, has arranged for a gala coming out party.

II

IT is a Monday, September 30, 1968, and since early light, there has been a lot of activity around the big hangar; photographers getting their motion picture cameras and still cameras in position to record the event from every angle; workmen putting the finishing touches on the special platform built for the christening ceremony, the dedication speakers and VIPs. All morning long a crowd has been gathering. Mostly, it is comprised of Boeing people, of men and women, who themselves, or whose relatives have helped build the 747 that is waiting behind the big hangar doors to make her appearance. But there are hundreds of others, too, who have come from far and wide to see the launching of this new sky queen. It is unlike other "roll-outs" because this is the biggest

One year, almost to the day after start of assembly at Everett, the No. 1 "Super jet," a glistening beauty, proudly displaying the insignia of the various airlines she will serve, is rolled out of the hangar. The "Incredibles" had done job right on schedule.

thing Boeing has ever attempted. There is nothing secret about it, like when they rolled the XB-52 out of its hangar nest. "The Incredibles" and Management, too, want the world to see how they got their name and why. Now, the moment has arrived.

It is 11:10 AM, and a crack appears in the giant curtain as the hangar doors separate. The 747's nose appears, her cockpit windows, three stories high, looking like a pair of huge sunglasses on a bulbous nose. Head-on she looks like a giant pear-shaped gondola for some monstrous balloon. Then, you see her wing roots, seven-feet thick where they join the fuselage, and the inboard nacelles, eight-feet in diameter. Wider and wider, the picture frame expands until all of her wing and four engines are exposed along with her many-wheeled undercarriage.

The low-slung, specially-designed tug is starting to pull her out. Ever so slowly she moves from the cavernous hangar with its beamed superstructure and myriad of lights, a "Moby Dick" coming out for air.

Now, she is out in the open for everybody to see. The crowd cheers, but mostly it is a cheer of *"oohs"* and *"aahs"*. Her size is an awesome sight to remember. A band salutes her, playing *"Pomp and Circumstance"*. She is all of that and more.

When she is in position near the speakers' platform, Mal Stamper proudly introduces the "Queen" to the ladies of her court — 26 pretty stewardesses, representing the airlines who have ordered 747s, whom he has had flown in from all over the world. He has supplied each with a bottle of champagne for the christening.

"The 747," remarked an observer, "entered her world with a big splash!"

Significantly, the first 747 and all those that would follow, would have tremendous impact on that world of which they soon would become a part.

Size of the world's largest commercial jetliner is evident as she towers high above persons on the ground who came to her debut. After ceremony, thousands climbed aboard to view sky leviathan's interior.

Listen to these words of the then Secretary of Commerce, the Hon. C. R. Smith, who was principal speaker at the dedication ceremonies – *"The sales of the 747 will contribute to our international balance of trade and strengthen our balance of payments. Already Model 747 airplanes to a value of $1.5 billion have been contracted to foreign airlines, alone.*

"Your aviation companies represent the shining stars in our world export trade, and Boeing stands out in this colorful assembly. During the last ten years our aerospace exports have averaged $1.65 billion each year. A high percentage of that represents commercial aircraft. For the past ten years the annual export of commercial aircraft has averaged more than $300 million. In the first six months of 1968, you averaged more than $100 million each month.

"These figures take on new importance because our traditional margin of U. S. exports over imports have been sharply reduced during the past two quarters – even going over to the negative side in some months. For the past several years, we have relied on this favorable balance of trade to help reduce our country's large balance of payment deficity. Therefore, the strong contribution of the aircraft industry means a great deal.

"The 747 is a national asset . . . It will provide a standard of comfort and convenience never equalled before. It will make a new contribution to the prestige of United States aviation!"

For many in the vast crowd, the speaker's words may have sounded a bit dry and unmeaningful there in the awesome shadow of the 747 technological accomplishment. But for a few, like Bill Allen and T. A. Wilson, who only six months before had been promoted to be President of Boeing, and others in Boeing Management, who had made the decision to build the 747, "CR's" remarks were most encouraging.

The 747 was not just a big airplane. They had backed the development of a new national resource, a transportation giant that would seem destined to help build a smaller and better world.

It was up to man now, to put the machine to work.

The next milestone was her maiden flight.

III

"THIRTY years ago, in 1938, the market value of the airlines in the United States was on the order of $10 million," C. R. Smith had said at the 747 dedication. *"Today the market value of this single plane is twice that much!"*

Immediately following the roll-out, the $22,000,000 airplane – Boeing 747 No. 1 *"Superjet"* – was turned over to Connie Smith (no relation), Preflight and Delivery Superintendent at Everett. Smith was initially responsible for helping plan and coordinate equipment and facilities necessary to insure the plane was ready for its first flight. Before she could spread her wings, the 747 had to be put through a whole series of engineering ground checks. These tests covered every aspect of the plane's functional systems: control surfaces, landing gear, fuel, electrical and fire control systems.

Outside hangar, numerous tests were run with the 747's various systems. Head-on view shows height of cockpit.

Outside the big hangar, for instance, they filled the plane's fuel tanks to *overflow* capacity – more than 48,000 gallons. The idea was to check the fuel system for leaks, and test the vent system function.

There, too, out in the open, they tested again and again and again, the plane's elevators, rudder, ailerons, leading edge and trailing edge flaps. It wasn't enough that these control surfaces had been cycled a million times on the control system mock-up. This time it was the real thing.

Inside the hangar, they lifted the 747 up on jackstands and tested its multi-wheeled undercarriage. Gear up! Gear down! Re-

In pre-flight testing, the 747's fuel tanks were pumped to over-flow to test for leakage and ventilation.

tract! Extend! A giant doing "push-up exercises" to get into A-1 condition.

These and other functional tests completed, they installed on board the most extensive and expensive flight recording and monitoring equipment available in this electronic age. In all, this equipment could take approximately 1300 different measurements; the temperature of the jet-stream exhaust gases or the vibration of a minute skin wrinkle on an aileron's surface; the distance a pilot's hand moves on the throttle quadrant to get another 1000-pounds of thrust, or the slightest movement of a needle on a rotor fan r.p.m. gauge.

Nearly 100 miles of wiring went aboard for flight instrumentation alone, in addition to the plane's normal complement of more than 100 miles of wiring for its various electronics systems.

"Altogether the test equipment put aboard weighed approximately 60,000 pounds," explained Connie Smith. "That's nearly the weight equivalent of a fully-loaded B-17 *'Flying Fortress'* of World War II vintage."

With state-of-the-art advances, Boeing's flight test documentation capability had more than doubled since the 727 was first flown in 1963. Moreover, the size of the 747 and its great load-carrying potential, permitted putting on board instrumentation, some of it quite heavy equipment, that never before could be airborne.

Test instruments hang from landing gear during cycling on the ground, part of pre-flight tests.

Inside, the No. 1 "Super jet" was fitted with tons of specialized equipment for measuring performance.

"No aircraft ever was given a better opportunity to tell us about itself than this one," remarked one test engineer. "The audio/visual presentation we expected to get back from her first flight would fill ten volumes of the Encyclopedia Britanica!"

He cited the on-board camera equipment as one example. "There are motion picture cameras mounted in the cabin, cockpit and on the under side of the plane," he explained. "One camera in the cabin, its lens pointing out the window, is there to record movements of the variable camber leading edge wing flaps. Another camera just aft of the flight deck monitors the activities of the flight crew. Another takes pictures of the instrument panels, cameras record take-off, landing and autopilot performance.

"In addition, on board, we put tape-recorders, a pulse code modulation (PCM) system, oscillographs, accelerometers, computers and telemetrics that nobody ever had heard of before.

"Hell, the pilot couldn't cough, or the plane give a *squeak*, unless we got it on tape," he concluded. "And if a rivet popped, we had it on film. We could even photograph the jetstream in living color."

More than 175 ballast containers were installed to alter the airplane's center of gravity. These 55-gallon water barrels were mounted in the two lower deck cargo compartments and on the main deck aft of the wings. To compensate for fuel useage, or to maintain a specific center of gravity for specific flight tests, water could be transferred variously to determine the effects of weight and center of gravity changes on the jetliner's over-all flying stability.

On subsequent test flights engineers seated at consoles would measure and control the effects of the weight changes (by transferring the water ballast) and monitor the flight test instrumentation.

The main cabin, aft, was fitted with water barrels for ballast to permit changing center of gravity during various flight test maneuvers. Photo gives idea of "Super jet's" wide bodied interior.

But on her maiden trip, there would be only a three-man crew aboard the first 747.

IV

"*THE three men who will fly the first 710,000-pound Boeing 747 super jet on its maiden flight are Jack Waddell, Brien Wygle and Jess Wallick,*" said a Company press release in January of 1969. "*Waddell, senior experimental test pilot at Boeing was named to the 747 program in July, 1966 and will be at the controls of the big plane when it takes off from Paine Field sometime early next month. Wygle, assistant director of flight operations for Boeing's Commercial Airplane Division, will be in the co-pilot's seat. And Wallick, a senior instructor flight engineer, will be flight engineer.*"

Born in Forsyth, Montana, February 25, 1923, Jack Waddell earned a bachelor of science degree in engineering physics at Montana State College. He served as a Navy pilot flying a variety of airplane types during World War II in the South Pacific. In 1952, he received a master's degree in aeronautical engineering from Cornell University. Before joining Boeing five years later, he served as engineering test pilot at North American Aviation on F-86 fighters. At Boeing his duties, until the 747 came along, included flight test work on the B-52 intercontinental bomber and the whole series of Boeing commercial jetliners. He was well qualified to head the flight test program for the 747.

"Jack's the kind of a test pilot, slide-rule/seat-of-the-pants, engineer/flyer breed that Eddie Allen once told Bill Boeing was the kind of a test pilot the advancing technology of this business demands," remarked one long-time Boeing employee who knew both men. "Hell, he even looks like Eddie, talks like him and acts like him."

Typical, perhaps, are some of Waddell's actions and observations regarding the whole 747 program.

"I was in on the 747 project from the very beginning, almost the initial conceptual stage of it." Jack told the author. "I'd been on the C-5A program as 'project pilot' and when this one came along, I told my boss, Dix Loesch, that I'd like the same job on the 747 . . ."

He got it. And right from the start Jack got very much involved. For one thing, he helped design and develop a very specialized taxiing trainer, a 747 cockpit mounted on a truck, to enable practicing ground-handling of the large aircraft.

"The thing before we got through with a lot of sophisticated modifications probably cost as much as three DC-3s (about $100,000) but it paid good dividends," Jack explained. "I think for one thing it led us to concentrate a lot on the development of '*body gear*' steering for the 747

In their hands, Boeing entrusted its "billion dollar" investment. Left to right, Jess Wallick, Jack Waddell and Brien Wygle ("the three W's") who were selected to fly the 747 on its maiden flight.

Chief 747 Test Pilot, Jack Waddell, standing in front of cockpit taxiing test rig which he helped to design.

which certainly gives the 747 more controllability on the ground. By making the back pair of landing gear 'trucks' steerable, we made the 747, despite its size, nominally easy to handle during taxiing."

"Waddell's Wagon on stilts", as somebody dubbed it, was also used to test various combinations of landing lights, a closed circuit TV for monitoring the position of the wheels at all times, (optional) a unique buried wire system for taxiing which guides the plane electronically (never adopted), and for practicing docking, and to familiarize pilots with the high elevation of the cockpit above the ground.

"We got so we could taxi the simulator up to a cargo dock with a plus or minus six inches tolerance," Waddell said. "But mainly, I think it proved to a lot of our customers that the size of the 747 wasn't going to be the bugaboo around airports that they had anticipated. Surprisingly, when we moved from the simulator into the real thing, it was remarkable how quickly one could adjust to a plane twice the size of anything we had taxied before."

"When we got into the first airplane for taxi runs," he added, "it took about ten minutes and you started to pick it up just like any other aircraft. I remember, in the early stages, we used the closed TV for watching the wheels, so there wouldn't be any surprises, but we found out, although the system did a good job, it wasn't really necessary."

"Waddell's Wagon," the simulated 747 cockpit mounted on truck, was used to familiarize crew with ground handling and taxiing of the 747. It's "Flight Deck" is three stories above the ground.

Both Waddell and Wygle spent many hours in the taxi simulator. And for about a year and a half they did a lot of "on paper" flying while the 747 itself was being built. Using analog and digital computers, they checked out every detail of the plane's predicted flying qualities and characteristics. There were also many hours spent in flight simulators which would result in a whole new simulator training program for the 747 (See Chapter 16). Perhaps, no flight crew was ever better prepared to step aboard. Wallick, too, went through gruelling hours of similar preparation.

At this stage while they were, themselves, learning about the 747, they were actually helping to write the textbook for all future training programs for the 747.

All three confessed that the toughest part was – "waiting for the plane to be made ready for its first flight."

It was an unexpected long wait. The previously announced date when the 747 would first fly – December 17, 1968 to commemorate the 65th anniversary of the Wright Brothers' first flight – came and passed. The weatherman did not smile kindly on the Seattle area in the weeks that followed the rollout, hampering preflight preparations. One of the most severe winters in years hit the area. The work dragged on. Not until late January, 1969 was the plane released from preflight preparations to Flight Operations.

For the first time Waddell, Wygle and Wallick could get the "feel" of their charge. There followed a series of ground handling tests, and more modifications *before* the 747 was ready for her most critical preflight moment – the high-speed taxi runs.

"The taxi tests were kind of a graduated exercise," Waddell described them. "For two days we taxied the airplane, checking the flight controls, steering and brake systems. Each time, we kept increasing the speed, until we finally got up to 168 miles per hour, and I could feel her wanting to break free."

"I'll never forget when I pulled the nose up to approximately take-off attitude for the first time," he continued. "That's what we call *rotating* the airplane and boy, it was quite a dramatic sensation. All of a sudden you're riding pretty high even though the main wheels are still on the ground. I remember, I told Brien (Wygle) that, maybe, we should go over to the Space Needle for some transition to get used to the cockpit height. But after we did it a couple of times, I didn't notice anything. In a very short time, it began to feel just like any other airplane. It just

No. 1 "Super jet," her eighteen-wheeled undercarriage kicking up a mist from wet runway surface, shows her tremendous size rolling down the runway during one of series of highly critical pre-flight, high-speed taxi runs.

handled better than most of them."

When they had finished the high-speed taxi tests, Waddell reported – "I think we've got a real airplane, here. She's as ready as she ever will be."

V

IN the rainy predawn darkness of February 9, 1969 Boeing *"Superjet"* No. 1 waited patiently on the ramp at Paine Field for her date with Lady Blue Sky. It was anything but an ideal day, the weather somewhere between bad and uncertain. But shortly after 11:00 A.M. the overcast thinned out and lifted. Here and there, were splotches of blue. The word passed quickly through the large crowd which had gathered – "They're going to fly it. Everything is GO!"

Waddell, Wygle and Wallick were already in the cockpit, had been for more than an hour, checking things, and waiting for the weather to clear. They hadn't really made much fuss about it. "I don't know how you can glamorize it," Waddell said later. "I had a good night's sleep at a motel near Everett the night before, got up and had a waffle and some sausages, my favorite, and went out to the airplane."

BOEING MAGAZINE, the official company publication, described it later with this prose – *"One of them wore rubbers against the damp underfoot. All three wore uniforms of the U.S. Pacific Northwest – raincoats flapped against their legs as they crossed the chill and windswept concrete, filed up passenger stairs to a large airplane. Ties knotted, shirts white, business suits pressed, three gentlemen were on their way to work in the morning. Their work: flight testing airplanes."*

Admittedly, for the trio it was pretty much like "going down to the office," but still, this was different from other days. It was different because they had never flown in anything so huge before. Perhaps, too, they were thinking about the fact that so much depended upon their expertise. In their hands rested the responsibility for a $22,000,000 piece of machinery. Everything possible had been done to make the machine perfect. Now, it was up to the human element.

On the Flight Deck everything was going along just as it should. But outside, there were things that caused some apprehension.

Waddell looked out the big view windows. What he saw was disturbing. There were hundreds of people lining the runway and they were much too close. "Can you get the people to stand back?" he requested of the Tower. "This thing could

Minutes before take-off on 747's maiden flight, its three-man crew posed for their picture on "Flight Deck." Waddell is in left-hand seat, Wygle to his right, and Wallick at Flight Engineer's console.

The moment arrives! Poised at the end of the runway, No. 1 "Super jet," engines roaring, starts her take-off run.

The moment of lift-off! After using up less than half the runway, the world's biggest jetliner is airborne!

Leading edge and trailing edge flaps extended for maximum lift, No. 1 "Super jet" leaps for the sky.

cause quite a blast in its wake and somebody might get hurt."

The people on the runway or near it, mostly photographers and special guests who wanted the vantage spot – where they thought the big plane would lift off – were moved back.

Waddell was concerned about something else, too. He noted the sky was filled with private planes flying about. He cracked to Wygle – "I hope everybody stays clear."

Wygle nodded. Affirmative. He was talking to the tower – "OK, we're starting the engines."

Minutes later the ground crew pulled the landing gear lock pins and the plane started taxiing out to the end of runway 16 and into position for take-off.

There was another delay, a warning from the Tower – "Somebody says there's a panel off the Number 4 engine strut . . ."

Those in the cockpit couldn't see it. Ground observers checked and the word came back, "You're OK. No panel off."

They were at the end of the runway now, and heading into the wind, ready for take-off.

"Cleared for take-off," said the Tower.

Jack Waddell eased forward on the throttles and the 747 started to roll. Wygle called out speeds as the giant moved faster and faster over the concrete ribbon. Flight Engineer Jess Wallick's eyes were glued to the gauges . . .

One thousand feet . . . 2,000 . . . 3,000 . . . she was eating up the ribbon. One hundred . . . 120 mph . . . 150 mph . . . faster and faster she began to move.

"*Rotation*," yelled Waddell.

And the nose lifted.

"Speed – one six four," shouted Wygle.

164-mph! At that speed at the 4300 foot marker on the runway – less than half its 9,000-foot length – the world's biggest commercial jetliner, was airborne.

It was 11:34 a.m.

At that moment, "*quietly and almost serenely*," BOEING Magazine recorded, "*the age of spacious jets began.*"

Observers on the ground could hardly believe their own eyes and ears. Minutes before they had seen the F-86 chase plane take off leaving a trail of dark smoke mixed with the rumble of thunder.

Above the clouds, on her maiden flight, Boeing's "billion dollar baby" poses proudly for her portrait. Chase plane pilot, Paul Bennett, described it as "fantastic sight!"

The wake of the huge 747 was virtually smokeless. "The engines," said one observer, "made no more noise than a stiff breeze through a forest."

Some excerpts from the taped record of the first flight best tell the story:

WYGLE (minutes after take-off) – *"The airplane's flying beautifully."*

After 1 hour and 16 minutes aloft, during which Waddell put the plane through various test maneuvers, the big plane using full flaps for "braking" slips down out of the sky for smooth landing.

WADDELL (to Chase plane) – *"Has this air got much bumpiness in it to you?"*

PAUL BENNETT (in Chase plane) – *"The air, I'd say, is light chop."*

WADDELL: *"Beautiful. OK, we're easing along here heading 240, 1500 feet, a little turbulance. The old girl soaks that turbulance up very nicely."*

WYGLE: *"VFR at 4600 feet now we're climbing slowly, gear and flaps down. Beautiful."*

WADDELL: *"I just got to do some minor rollercoasters here just to feel the pitch..."*

And later . . . *"That aileron action we put in this thing really does the job."*

WADDELL: *"We're now at 140 knots. 25-degree flaps. The flaps are very buffet free and it feels pretty good at these speeds. Let's go to 30-degrees..."*

WYGLE: *"OK. When we hit the stops on the 30 there was sort of a bump."*

PAUL BENNETT (in Chase plane) *"I saw the right hand inboard flap move a little bit, shake a little bit. What's normal?"*

WADDELL: *"Sharp bump in cockpit. We're going back to 25 degrees..."*

PAUL: *"Everything still looks normal as far as I can tell, Jack. The only thing I've seen abnormal during the whole flight is just that inboard flap..."*

WADDELL: *"Roger. What kind of a lookin' ship is this from out there, Paul?"*

PAUL: *"It's very good looking, Jack. Fantastic!"*

WADDELL: *"Rather majestic, you might say?"*

PAUL: *"Roger, that's the word, Jack. Majestic . . . One thing I've noticed throughout the whole flight, I've never seen any black smoke come out at all. You can't tell from the outside if the engines are running or not..."*

WADDELL: *"They're clean, all right."*

And so it went . . . voices in the sky as Waddell put the *"Super jet"* through various test maneuvers . . . performing sideslips . . . simulated loss of hydraulic systems . . . half power on the outboard engines . . . pitch and yaw . . . bank and turn.

He cut it short because of the "slight flap vibration", but not until the photo plane had come up to take some pictures. Then, he headed back home.

At 12:50 P.M. the *"Super jet"* touched down on the Paine Field runway.

"I just closed my eyes at 200 feet," Waddell confessed. "She landed herself!"

Moment of touchdown! Slipping down out of the sky after maiden flight, the plane's starboard wheels touched first to runway's still wet surface. That's mist kicking up cloud behind her.

Using thrust reversers, Waddell brought the big plane to a stop using only about half of runway. Even on slippery surface, the "Super jet" proved she had extremely stable handling characteristics.

Casting her shadow on the slick, wet surface of Paine Field at completion of her historic maiden flight, the new "Queen of the skies," Boeing 747 "Super jet," rolls to a stop at end of runway. It was a Day to Remember (February 9, 1969), the beginning of the "Spacious Age."

On the ground, he used light braking and thrust-reversers to bring the plane to a brief stop using about half the runway. The 747's landing speed was about 150-mph without full flaps.

The flight had lasted 1 hour and 16 minutes. Waddell reported that the 747 proved extremely stable in all flight regimes tested. Control forces and feel were near optimum, with good airplane response. Cockpit location provided excellent visibility for the flight crew during take-off, approach and landing. Approach was stable, with little effort required for flare and touchdown.

"The plane is a pilot's dream," he remarked. "Although there was some turbulence reported in the area we didn't feel it. The plane handles beautifully . . . I'd call it a two-finger airplane, you can fly it with the forefinger and thumb on the wheel!"

After congratulating Waddell and his crew, Boeing Chairman of the Board, Bill Allen commented: *"Today we have taken a major step in the opening of a new and significant era of aviation. The 747 launches the 'second generation' of commercial jets which will bring a new dimension to world travel and world commerce, and which will have a substantial impact upon the economy of our nation."*

Ahead for the 747 and four of her sister-ships as fast as they rolled out of the factory was the most extensive and comprehensive flight test program yet undertaken in commercial aviation history.

Could she take it?

CHAPTER FIFTEEN

Toughest Test On Wings

LONG before the first 747 lifted its revolutionary 18-wheeled landing gear off the runway at Paine Field on its maiden flight, the toughest test on wings was in progress. The planned program included laboratory testing of the plane's systems and components, pre-flight engineering tests on the ground, a five-plane flight test program, structures tests and FAA certification tests. Before it was over, the continuing program, expected to last four years (1967-1971) would involve more than ten million manhours, some 1400 hours of test flying, more than 1300 individual tests and costs upwards of $165,000,000. For the world's largest commercial airliner, Boeing had laid out the most extensive test program ever undertaken in the history of air travel. The goal – *to prove an airframe life of more than 60,000 hours for the 747, the equivalent of more than fifteen years of normal airline operation!*

It would fill volumes to describe all the tests, but some of the highlights of the program should be of interest to the passenger riding in this new $22,000,000 jetliner. He or she can be assured that every part, every system has been tested and tested again, far beyond the limits of normal operations. The "torture tests" which the 747 endured before the first paying passenger would take his or her seat in its commodious cabin, put far more stress and strain on its wings and frame and all of its various components and systems, than the individual parts of the whole airplane would experience in its lifetime of scheduled flying.

Consider, for example, the big plane's pressurization system which provides "sea-level" environment for crew and passengers at high-level operation, altitudes up to 35,000 to 40,000 feet. Based on normal airline operations, the air inside the cabin to permit normal breathing and moving around at such altitudes requires pressurization up to 9.4 pounds of pressure per square inch. But the tests didn't stop there. They pumped *twice* that amount of pressure, 18.4 pounds per square inch, into one 747 airframe. The "sealed-tight" pressure cabin of the 747 didn't even let out a hiss.

During early test, 747, comes in for landing with leading edge and trailing edge flaps fully extended. Flaps, which serve as "extra lift" devices helped make it possible for plane to land on same airports as 707.

They also ran numerous "decompression" tests, to see what would happen when the pressure cabin was punctured, and determine the effect on the various systems in the aircraft. There were other individual systems tests both on the ground and in the air.

The 747, for example, has a series of variable-camber leading edge flaps much different from those on previous Boeing jetliners. These fiberglass flaps are extended during take-off and landing to increase the wing area providing more lift. Without them, the 747 probably would require much longer runways than are now in existence. These flaps, because they were new and revolutionary, needed to be thoroughly tested and proven *before* they became an integral part of the 747's design.

To do this, engineers installed the 747's flaps on a 707 jetliner and flew the plane through all possible maneuvers including stalls, verifying design and wind tunnel predications.

Another 707 was used to test the Inertial Navigation System (INS) which provides primary attitude and heading information to the pilots' flight instruments, the automatic flight controls system and the navigation systems aboard the 747 "*Super jet.*" On a 10-hour, 5,000-mile flight from Seattle to Samoa with the test 707, the INS proved 80 per cent more accurate than its design specifications called for. Performance on similar flights for an aggregate of 70 hours flying and 25,000 miles pronounced the system "ready" for the 747.

In yet another phase of the test program, they built a full-scale operating replica of the airplane's flight controls system. This "iron bird" duplicated the operation and responses of the 747's controls, enabling engineers to refine the system well ahead of its installation in the first airplane.

Jack Waddell summed it up this way – "With this test rig we got the *feel* of the 747's controls long before the plane was ready for its first flight."

Leading edge flap mechanism is one of 747's "secrets." When expanded, it increases area, but keeps airfoil curvature.

Not until these tests and many others were completed was the first airplane released for the full flight test program which in the life of any new airplane is the most dramatic and most critical stage.

The Flight Test Program began with the 747's maiden flight which we described in the last chapter. After that, perhaps, no new aircraft design ever was put through a more rugged test of its performance capabilities.

"The first flight was really quite curtailed," Jack Waddell explained. "The slight trouble we felt with the flap functioning, made us decide to cut the flight time short to be certain nothing more serious developed. We didn't even pull the gear up on that first flight . . . "

Six days later, however, the No. 1 "*Super jet*" was back up in the skies again (February 15, 1969) and this time she performed perfectly, including full flap retraction and landing gear cycling. Then, during the next ten days, the plane made six more flights for an accumulative 12 hours and 28 minutes of flight test time.

During this period, the 747 achieved a maximum speed of 287 miles per hour and

On her second flight, the 747, her flaps and landing gear "tucked away" presents a sleek, streamlined profile of a sky leviathan. Note the huge fairings that join the sweptback wing to "Super jet's" fuselage.

flew to altitudes of 20,000 feet at various weights up to 520,000 pounds. Mostly, they were interested in learning the plane's general handling characteristics.

"If there was anything dramatic about these early tests," Waddell said later, "I think it was the fact that we were so pleased with the plane's performance, that after about eight hours flight time we took Mr. Allen, the Chairman of the Board, up for a ride. We were that confident we had a really beautiful airplane!"

On February 25, the plane was flown from Paine Field, Everett, to Boeing Field, Seattle, focal point of Boeing's FLIGHT OPERATIONS. For the first time, the 747 appeared in the skies over a heavily populated area. For the first time, residents of Seattle got a glimpse of the newest and biggest member of the Boeing family of jetliners.

It was there, inside the big maintenance hangar that the author saw the 747 for the first time since he had seen "the pieces come together" at Everett eighteen months before. The plane was in "lay-up" being modified for the next phase of its flight test program.

Specifically, workmen were rigging a mechanical device on the *"Super jet's"* wing tips to induce vibrations into the airframe. *Flutter testing*, they called it. The idea is they shake the airframe at various amplitudes and frequencies at high and low speeds in flight. Then they measure the airplane's inherent structural ability to dampen and smooth out the shimmying or *flutter*, hence the name.

Other testing would be carried on concurrently with the "flutter work," we

Mechanical devices on plane's wing tip were used to induce vibrations in airframe during "flutter" tests.

Test fleet of five airplanes valued at more than $150,000,000, including sophisticated test equipment, on flight line at Boeing Field, Seattle. "Needle nose" (foreground) is special electronic probe.

learned. It would include further evaluation of the airplane's stability and control characteristics, autopilot, inertial navigation and air-conditioning systems, engine performance and auxiliary power unit operation. No. 1 *"Super jet"* was going to be a very busy aircraft for the next several months.

She would soon be joined by the next four airplanes to come off the production line – all of which would be assigned to the Flight Test Program.

Essentially, all five of these test aircraft would be doing the same thing – *proving the 747 operationally.* Each of the aircraft, however, would be assigned to specific chores. One plane, for instance, would concentrate on engine performance, fuel consumption. Another, would be used for testing the landing gear, the flap mechanisms, on-board electrical systems, the pressurization, and so on. Planes No. 4 and No. 5 would be assigned to perform all the standard operational procedures of scheduled airline flying.

Brien Wygle, Assistant Director of Flight Operations and co-pilot on the 747's maiden flight, summed it up this way – "We fly these airplanes, and with millions of dollars worth of sophisticated test equipment on board we measure the plane's performance in every phase of operations. In short, we ask ourselves this question – *What is this airplane?* And then, we go looking for the answer. Where it is deficient, or not up to what we would like it to be, we make changes and we measure it again, until we are convinced *this is the situation we want, this is the kind of airplane we want to deliver to the customer.*

"That is the whole purpose and mission of the Flight Test Program."

Let's take a close look. Come fly with Boeing test pilots as they put the world's largest commercial jetliner through one of her most dangerous and dramatic trials.

II

"*SUPER JET*" No. 1 is poised on the run-

Poised at the end of the runway at Grant County Airport, No. 1 airplane is about to start critical VMU tests.

Engineer checks panel of electronic measuring instruments, part of equipment aboard "Super jet" during flight tests.

way at Grant County Airport, Moses Lake, about 130 miles east of Seattle beyond the Cascades. It is Sunday, March 29, 1969. They have flown the plane here from Boeing Field to run some special tests called VMU's – *Velocity Minimum Unstick* – in Flight Test jargon. Jack Waddell explains: *"We want to learn the slowest speed at which the plane will become 'unstuck' from the runway in take-off."*

The 747 has been especially modified for these tests. On its underbelly in the extreme tail is a ten foot long maple beam – like a keel on a boat – with a steel plate on the underside, the way they used to make the rails on the early railroads. We'll soon learn why it is there . . .

But, just imagine, for the moment, that we are riding in the jump seat up front on the 747's Flight Deck just behind Waddell and Lew Wallick, another Boeing Test Pilot who is in the co-pilot's seat. There is

Test pilot Waddell (right) inspects steel plate on "Super jet's" underbelly before start of VMU tests.

another observer in the cockpit with us, Boeing's President, T. A. Wilson. Like Bill Allen, T. Wilson is no arm chair executive; he likes to keep on top of things. And below us, in the main cabin of the plane which is filled with test equipment, are some twenty or more engineer-technicians manning the numerous cameras and other recording devices. We already have made several take-offs, and each time Waddell has lifted the nose at a sharper angle, presenting the massive wing area to the rushing airstream to lift the 350-ton plane up, up and away.

For the layman, Waddell explains – *"When we increase this angle of rotation, we present more wing area with a resultant increase in lift-off potential, while at the same time reducing the required speed of the forward movement of the aircraft . . . This time, we'll drag the tail right on the concrete and make the sparks fly . . ."*

He forgets to add, that this takes a helluva lot of pilot skill. It takes a lot of delicate handling. The maneuver could break the big plane's back!

Now, everything is set.

Waddell's hand pushes forward on the throttle quadrant; four knobs, a fistfull of power, the reins of a hundred thousand horses!

The 747 starts to roll, but the movement is barely descernable, she is so huge. And up here, it is so quiet you can hear the whirring of the movie camera monitoring the pilots' movements.

Then, suddenly, the horizon drops away. There is a jar, a tremor through the airframe, but that's all.

No. 1 "Super jet" (left) in extreme rotation attitude during the VMU tests. In close-up photo (right) tail with steel plate, can be seen scraping on surface of runway. Observers said "sparks flew."

The 747 is airborne. And below, there is still a lot of runway left.

They drive the Stock Cars faster at Daytona than the slowest speed at which the 710,000-pound 747 become *unstuck*.

T. Wilson is all smiles.

The VMU's came up to expectations. In meaningful terms the tests showed that the big plane could get off the ground in a hurry. Within certain weight limitations, she could probably operate from any jet airport in the world.

More important! From a safety standpoint, the VMU's proved that even with a loss of power during the critical take-off period, the giant plane could get airborne at a remarkably slow speed, and in an extreme attitude.

For observers on the ground, the test was even more spectacular. Said one eyewitness – "When she rocked back on her tail, it looked like the runway was on fire. A thousand Fourth of July sparklers touched off at once!"

The same day they ran some further tests; landing gear taxi tests with a gross load of 685,000 pounds, up to 195 knots per hour, and without a shimmy from the 16-wheeled main gear.

"She's as nimble as a 727 trijet," Jack Waddell reported. "Just like driving a Cadillac!"

Darkness settled over the Grant County Airport that day before the planned tests were completed. Then, the 747 made its first night take-off and its first night landing back at Boeing Field.

There, they removed the "steel keel" used for the VMU's, and prepared the aircraft for her next series of tests. These included some flyovers to test for noise levels.

On the ground, they set up "electronic ears" to record the big plane's PNdB – perceived noise decibels. Then, they flew the 747 across Boeing Field at altitudes ranging from 400 to 4,000 feet. They also made flyovers at the same altitudes with a 707-320B jetliner. The *"Super jet,"* although twice as large, with two-thirds again as much power, was less noisy than the 707. The engine people had done a good job with noise supression.

No. 1 *"Super jet"* also had another role. Because she was *Number One*, she served as a kind of "flying classroom" for Boeing test pilots until the other four airplanes

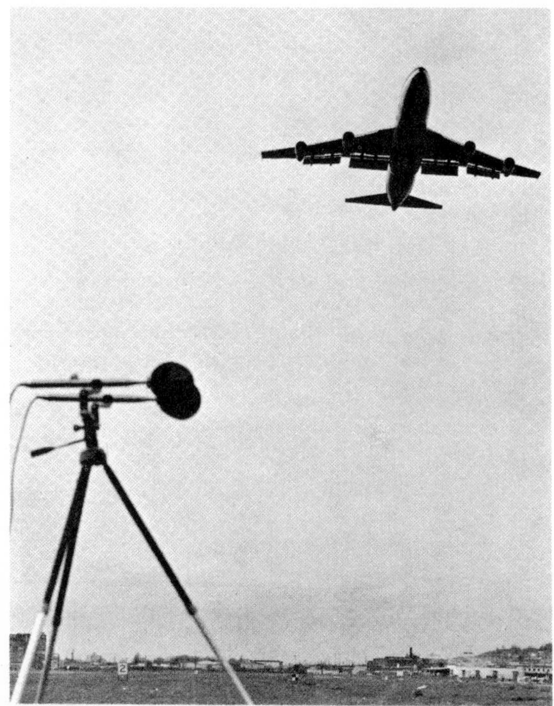

Electronic "ears" on tripod on ground, record the "Super jet's" noise level during low-altitude fly-by.

In Pan American colors, No. 2 "Super jet" poses with No. 1 during roll-out ceremonies. After flight tests were completed, planes with airline markings were completely refurbished before joining air carrier fleets.

were ready to join the test fleet. Brien Wygle, Don Knutson, Lew Wallick, Paul Bennett and other veteran test pilots got "checked out" in No. 1. Then, each in turn took over responsibilities for No. 2, No. 3, No. 4 and No. 5 "*Superjets*" to carry out each plane's specific assignment.

No. 2 "*Superjet*," all bright and shiny in her blue-and-white Pan-American World Airways' colors (after the flight test program, she would be refurbished and turned over to Pan-Am) was rolled out March 5, 1969. She made her first flight with Brien Wygle at the controls on April 11. After that, she began her test assignment: engine performance, fuel consumption, electromechanical systems and avionics, i.e., automatic flight systems and communications. Before her job was done, she would bring some disturbing news.

Meanwhile, No. 4 "*Superjet*" was making history. With pilot Don Knutson at the controls in the evening hours of June 2, 1969, the plane took off from Seattle on a non-stop flight to Paris. She carried a 41-man crew, including Boeing Board Chairman, Bill Allen, a number of other key top executives and some invited guests. Purpose of the flight was two-fold: (1) They would run many tests on an actual maximum range operation. (2) The 747 would be Boeing's "show-case" at the 28th Inter-

They flew No. 4 "Super jet" non-stop Seattle to Paris. P. J. DeRoberts (left) Don Knutson and S. L. Wallick.

In Paris, Britain's Prince Philip (left) was among VIP's who inspected 747. SST "Concorde" in background.

Spectacular angle shot of the "Super jet" at Paris show, makes her appear as some huge whale-like monster.

national Aeronautical and Space show at LeBourget Field, just outside Paris.

The big plane made the 5,160-mile flight from Seattle in nine-and-a-half hours landing right on schedule, breaking out of a 500-foot overcast precisely lined up with the center of the runway. At the show it was the center of attraction along with the British/French *"Concorde"* Supersonic transport. Many dignitaries got to see a preview of the

On U.S. soil again at Dulles International Airport serving Washington, D.C., large crowds streamed through the world's biggest jetliner. By time she arrived back in Seattle No. 4 "Super jet" had flown more than 11,000 miles.

Army Probe of My Lai

e Committee's investigation of
cident.
ers announced Friday he was
off his committee's investiga-
nd was creating a four-man
mittee to conduct an "in
inquiry into the incident.
ny and Defense Department of-
, sources said, were worried
some of the statements being
in connection with the Rivers
ittee's investigation last week
prejudice prosecution of sus-

'Injustice' Protested

ATLANTA — (UPI) — Former GIs protesting an "injustice to a fellow American" meet today to discuss their petition campaign for dismissal of the murder charges against 1st Lt. William A. Calley, Jr.

James A. Smith of nearby Kennesaw, Ga. said the meeting was to provide information for interested people as to "what we are trying to do and how far we have gone."

"We are just Americans protesting an injustice to a fellow American," Smith, who served in the Air Force from 1947 to 1949, said. "We are merely interested in the security of the American serviceman as to what he can be responsible for."

Smith said he had distributed 200 petitions asking that President Nixon dismiss the charges against Calley. The petitions, which Smith said have been copied by many others, will be sent to Georgia Senator Richard Russell.

★ The Seattle Times ★

Second Front Page

Published by The Seattle Times Co., Fairview Avenue North and John Street, Seattle, Wash. 98111. Second-class postage paid at Seattle. Vol. 92, No. 348 Monthly home-delivered subscriptions: Daily and Sunday—$3.00; Daily only- $2.25; Sunday only—25c per copy. Mail subscription rates are listed in classified section.

Seattle Times Telephones

All Departments MAin 2-0300

Classified-Want Ad Direct Lines MAin 4-8484

(Classified commercial accounts, please call MAin 2-0300)

Protest?

No, It's

Christmas

The Big Bird 'Blew It' Yesterday

A Boeing 747 superjet lay tilted on a Renton Airport runway after the right outboard section of its four-truck main landing gear partly collapsed when it touched down short of the runway yesterday. The right outboard engine touched the runway during the landing, the cowling was torn off and several tires blew out on the landing-gear truck. Pilot Ralph C. Cokeley who said he had miscalculated in his landing effort, was able to bring the plane to a controlled stop within 2,500 feet. Boeing officials described the damage as "superficial."—Times staff photo by Bruce McKim. (See Pages A3 for another photo and C1 for details.)

Spacious Age touring the 747 on static display.

After that, the plane was flown to Dulles International Airport, Washington, D.C. where it also attracted huge crowds.

It was back in Seattle at Boeing Field again on June 7, after completing an 11,495-mile journey.

"Some test," remarked Joe Sutter who had gone along on the flight to Paris, "for an aircraft that had only had about 18 hours flying time in its logbook!"

By the end of June, with all five test airplanes in the air, the Flight Test Program began to accelerate. *Phase One*, they called it – *developmental testing.* It involved the process of Boeing finding out what kind of an airplane the 747 *really was!* Would it come up to design expectations?

III

"*SUPER JET*" No. 5 was back up at Grant County Airport, Moses Lake. Boeing's senior engineering pilot, S. L. "Lew" Wallick was demonstrating the plane's stall characteristics. The Boeing test crew on board included: Ralph Cokely, senior experimental test pilot; flight engineers, Ken Stroms and Andy Johnson, with R. K. Frinell lead test engineer; and Fred Pittenger, operations manager. Also on board was Earl Chester, FAA Supervisory Test Pilot. Uncle Sam was "riding shotgun" to see that the tests were carried out to the letter of the law. The tests are among the most demanding in the Federal Air Regulations.

Stalls occur when the airplane's wing moves through the air at so steep an angle that the air flow seperates from the wing and no longer supports the airplane. The maneuver is never experienced in normal airline operations, but circumstances could develop that would put the airliner in such an attitude. In the interest of safety, the airplane – *before* it can be licensed to carry passengers – must demonstrate inherant design capabilities to live within certain stall and stall-recovery limitations. Hence, the stall test requirement.

In the skies above the Moses Lake area, No. 5 "*Super jet*" was "stalled" under more than 180 different conditions of configuration, weight and attitude. They stalled the airplane with its center of gravity fully forward and fully aft. Stalls were done with full power on, with the engines at idling power and with one engine inoperative. The maneuver was carried out from straight and level flight, with the airplane in 30-degree banking turns, with the flaps at various settings, during take-offs and climb-out, and during landings. Result: "*The 747 has better stall characteristics than any airplane I've ever flown,*" said Wallick, 18-year veteran of Boeing experimental and developmental test flying. "*She's so flyable throughout the stall, it's just amazing.*"

Meanwhile, No. 1 "*Super jet*" was also getting quite a workout. Jack Waddell had her up in the sky for some high speed runs and high altitude trials. Waddell explained the situation: "*The result of wind tunnel tests, computer analysis and on paper calculations, we had predicted the 747 had a design limit for maximum speed at 30,000 feet of .97 Mach Number . . . that's .97 per cent of the speed of sound at that altitude. Our job was to prove she could prove our predictions . . .*"

Result: "*We took the plane up to 30,000 feet and we let the horses run,*" Waddell

Testing for maneuverability, Waddell puts "Super jet" into a sharp bank. Note wing's "sweep-back."

During flight maneuvers, the plane demonstrates she can climb for the sky at a surprisingly sharp angle.

Test observer's view, looking out window at wing and nacelles during one phase of "flutter tests."

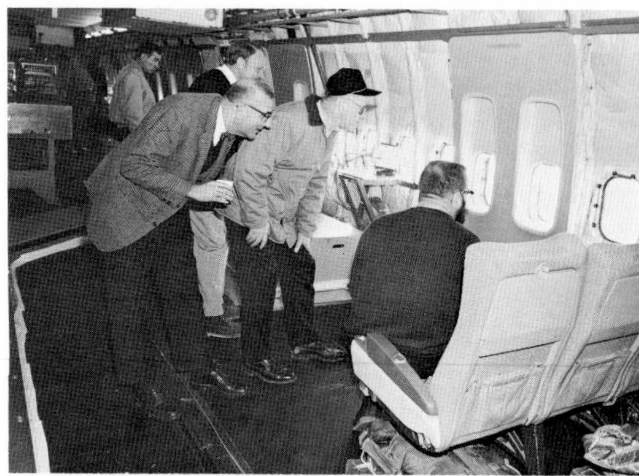

Inside cabin, observers watch wing during "flutter tests." Camera captured test on film.

explained. "*We clocked her at .98 Mach Number, 660 miles per hour true air-speed!*"

"That's 29,040 feet per second," he added with a grin. It is no secret his hobby is training thoroughbred race horses. He knows how to time with a stop watch and measure in feet as well as mph.

In the stretch, the big red-and-white "*Superjet*" was like Big Red, "Man-O-War."

They learned something else, too. In the paralance of horse trainers, the winged steed was a real "hay burner." The big engines had a ravenous appetite for fuel. They were performing, A-OK, but they weren't delivering the gas mileage promised. During a fuel consumption test, No. 2 "*Super jet*" indicated something amiss.

Mal Stamper, Manager of the 747 program at Everett, when he heard about it, told a NEWSWEEK reporter: "*It's 50/1000's of an inch that is screwing us up . . . The problem is ovalization: at full thrust, the present Pratt & Whitney engines tend to go out of round, ever so slightly – as a matter of fact, 50/1000ths of an inch . . .*"

"The result is increased fuel consumption and decreased efficiency for the 747," he explained. "We know that's wrong and we're looking at the most efficient way to fix it."

Back in Hartford at Pratt & Whitney Aircraft, the engine people came up with the answer to eliminate the 50/1000ths of an inch trouble spot. The problem delayed Boeing's deliveries of the 747 to the airlines by about two months. Even then, the first planes for Pan-Am would go into service with the less efficient engines; replacements would be made later.

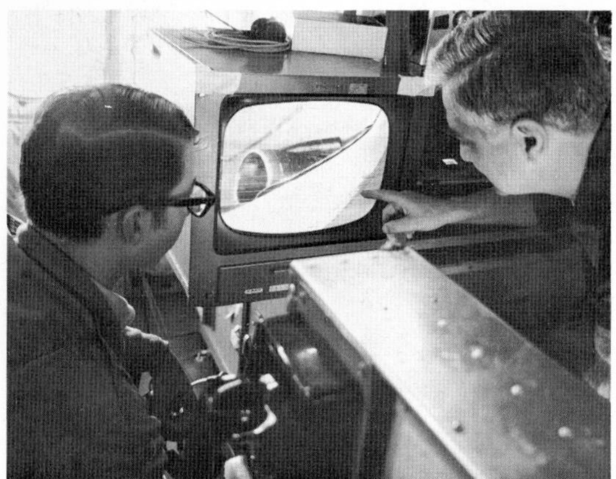

Via "closed circuit" television, these observers are monitoring air flow over leading edge flaps, nacelle and wing.

Test engineers, monitoring electronic measuring device, record instantaneous results on graph to check later.

The Flight Tests continued at an accelerated pace.

Night and day they were airborne at home and away. No. 1 *"Super jet"* was at Edwards Air Force Base taking advantage of the extra long runways, and "the Mojave Desert flatness" for the hazardous "engine out" take-offs. There, too, she lifted off with a gross load of 718,000 pounds – four tons more than her design gross weight!

"In the desert sky, we took her upstairs to find her ceiling, well above 45,000 feet," Jack Waddell explained. "And we put her through some high-speed maneuvers. It was the first time we wore crash helmets and parachutes, like Hollywood test pilots. We felt kinda silly; she was steady as a rock."

About the same time, No. 2 *"Superjet"* was at Roswell, New Mexico, doing a series of landing and braking tests on Roswell's 15,000-foot runway.

Meanwhile, the other three based at Boeing Field, Seattle roamed the western skies of the United States, including Alaska, performing a variety of tests: flying simulated airline flights touching down at Seattle's International Airport (seatac), at Oakland, California, Wichita, Kansas; shooting "blind" automatic landings; searching for icing conditions and adverse weather to prove the 747's mettle.

Test flying is like that.

By November 4, 1969 according to a Boeing Press Release, the five planes had flown 628 flights and logged more than 1,010 hours in the air. *Phase One:* Developmental Testing was nearing its completion.

Boeing was satisfied it had one helluva great airplane.

There was other evidence of proof. All the while the five Flight Test airplanes were performing their assignments, on the ground two complete 747 airframes were undergoing a different kind of test program.

They call it *"Structural Verification."*

The purpose: To prove the 747's structural soundness.

"Maybe it's not as glamorous as test flying," said one Structures Test engineer, "But when you see a million dollar wing or fuselage wrinkle, and crack, and literally break-up right before your eyes, it's a scene you can't call exactly boring. But that's our job, to torture the airframes to total destruction."

IV

AT Everett, near the 747 Final Assembly hangar, there looms a grotesque structure of pipes and steel girders and concrete that looks like – as one observer described it – "engineers ran amuck with a giant erector set." This is Boeing's Fatigue Test Tower, where complete 747 airframe, wings, fuselage and empennage ultimately will be worn down under simulated stress loads far in excess of those that the airplane ever would be subjected to in flight. The tests began in September of 1968 three months before No. 1 *Super jet* made its first flight.

The technological version of *"The Anatomy Of A Murder"* is being produced here; for the step by step break-up to ultimate destruction is recorded on film.

Let us digress for a moment to describe what goes on:

Boeing's 747 Structural Verification Testing involves three distinct but related pro-

Towering beams, cables and netting surround wing of 747, applying pressure loads in Static Test Rig.

Under tremendous tension and torsion, the wing of Static Test 747 starts to bend to breaking point.

Structures Verification Program involved fuselage and wing in this uncompleted Fatigue Test Tower.

grams – *static testing, fatigue testing* and *flight load survey.*

Static Testing is conducted in three phases: proof load, ultimate design strength loading and destruction.

Static testing is concentrated on the wings, flight control surfaces, high lift devices (trailing and leading edge flaps), engine support structures, total fuselage, vertical and horizontal stabilizers, and all other major structural components subject to loads while the airplane is in flight or on the ground. Tests are conducted to conform with guidelines established by the FAA. In effect, the FAA says the airframe must come up to certain load tests before the vehicle is safe for commercial service. Hence, the term *"proof load tests."*

It is interesting to watch how they apply these "loads" to the static test airplane. The 747 airframe rests in a maze of steel latticework. It looks not unlike a submarine in dry dock.

Our guide explains: "There is enough structural steel in this test rig to build a 150x300-foot building three stories high. It is anchored in an acre of concrete poured three feet deep."

Cradled in this superstructure, the 747 – raw aluminum skin and frame – appears pock-marked with thousands of small strain gauges to measure the simulated flight loads applied to her skin by hundreds of hydraulic jacks waging a kind of "tug-of-war" to try and tear her to pieces. You can see and almost feel the forces she is fighting off; torsion and tension, a skin wrinkle here, a rivet popping there. She is being subjected to the maximum stresses that she will ever experience in service operation.

There is recorded proof that she can take it. Part of this test phase also includes cabin pressurization, described earlier in this chapter.

FAA observers are satisfied.

But Boeing isn't. The entire airplane is designed to sustain loads 50 per cent greater than the maximum loads expected in service. Although physical testing is not required by the FAA, the men who designed the 747 want to know beyond any question of doubt that their creation is everything they predicted.

The "torture test" is stepped up; the "tug-of-war" escalated until the ultimate design loads are met.

Beyond this, there will come a day when they will build up the test loads to ultimate destruction of the airframe.

Then, and only then, will they know the maximum strength available in the various structural components.

Joe Sutter, whom we have already met as one of the designers of the 747, had this to say about the total destruction tests – "It isn't pleasant to think about destroying something you worked so hard to create. But these data are vital to know in planning for the future. When we know the breaking point of the airframe, it enables us to set guidelines for the airframe growth potential."

And all the while the Static Test airframe was meeting its requirements, another

In Fatigue Test Tower, fuselage and wings of 747 are subjected to repeated loads simulating those found in airline operation. Hydraulic devices and weights apply extreme stresses to all structural members.

Flight Load Survey test crew adjusts tail loading formers on flight test aircraft, No. 3 "Superjet."

complete airframe was being subjected to the *Fatigue Testing* phase of the Structures Verification Program.

The goal of *Fatigue Testing,* we learned, is to determine the effects of repeated operation of flight controls and loading on the airplane structure, similar to the loads and stresses found in airline service. Through a complex system of quick response hydraulic devices, engineers simulate flight conditions on the *Fatigue Test* airframe, producing all the stresses the aircraft experiences in flight – while the actual airframe remains on the ground.

Typical *Fatigue Test* "flights" include all the phases of airline operations: taxiing, take-off, climb to altitude (including cabin pressurization), final approach patterns, landing and taxiing to the ramp. The whole idea, of course, is to test for "wear and tear" – by repeated operations, the same thing over and over and over again – simulating the daily routine of the 747 in, let's say, its operational routine plying the New York to London route.

The difference is that with the sophisticated *Fatigue Test* equipment on the ground, under controlled conditions and monitored by hundreds of recording instruments, they can run a typical "flight" which with the real aircraft would last for several hours, in about *eight minutes.*

Before the *Fatigue Tests* are completed, the test vehicle 747 will have made more than 20,000 flights, far more than it is likely any 747 would make in 20 years of airline service.

The third Structures Verifieation Program tool which we mentioned above – *Flight Load Survey* – spans the gap between "flight" simulation in *Fatigue Testing* and the actual flight condition measurement.

No. 3. *"Super jet"* to come off the production line in the late spring of 1969 was subject for the ground test portion of the *Flight Load Survey* program. Then, at a later date, the plane was turned over to Flight Test Operations. Loaded with tons of specialized instrumentation specifically designed to measure actual flight loads, sheer, torsion, load magnitudes and pressure centers, No. 3 *"Super jet"* was put through a series of vigorous flight maneuvers, the most severe of any yet performed.

Data from these flights were used for reanalysis of the airframe strength margins, for re-adjustment of *Static Test* load applications and to insure accuracy in the *Fatigue Test* simulated flight load surveys.

As the Structures Verification Program progressed, the five Flight Test aircraft were flying a total of 35 to 50 hours a week to complete *Phase Two* of the Flight Test Program – *the FAA Certification Tests.*

V

"WHEN we are satisfied with our *Development Tests,"* explained Brien Wygle, "we say to ourselves – *'This is the kind of airplane we have. These are its performance characteristics and capabilities.'* Then, we set up certain standards, operational procedures, which we recommend for the airplane, as prescribed by the results of *Developmental Testing.*

"These standards which we set for the airplane, of course, are in line with the best of our know-how and capabilities to fulfill the requirements of the airlines who are customers. The standards we set for the airplane we have to *prove* to the FAA in a series of tests with their technical people of board. In addition to proving the plane is capable of meeting our own standards, we must also prove that the aircraft (in this case the 747) meets certain safety standards, both technical and legal, as prescribed by U.S. Federal Aviation Regulations. The FAA examiners, who participate in these flight tests, are in effect Judge and Jury during these trials.

"At the culmination of demonstration flights, provided the airplane meets all of the requirements, the FAA issues a *Certificate of Airworthiness* which essentially says – *'We have examined this airplane according to the laws of the country and we license it for the carriage of passengers for hire.'* "

The FAA tests involved more than just flight operational requirements. In compliance with Federal Aviation Safety Regulations, part of the test involved emergency evacuation procedures. For those readers who one day may be riding in the spacious cabin of the 747, mention of the results of these tests seems appropriate here.

These tests were conducted in the Boeing Flight Center hangar in Seattle. Test subjects, volunteers from clubs and service organizations, included oldsters in their 70s, pre-school youngsters, teenagers and parents. The tests were carried out in darkness using only the airplane's emergency lighting, battery-powered units available when all the aircraft's normal electric systems are inoperative. Several tests were run, and each time different persons participated.

Thirteen stewardesses, a normal cabin crew complement for the 747, were in the airplane to supervise passenger movement during the tests. The normal Flight Crew of three, pilot, co-pilot and flight engineer were on board. Of the "passengers" in the airplane, 412 were seated in the main passenger deck seats, first class and economy class sections, and eight were in the upper deck lounge. Remainder of the 499 persons were on platforms outside the emergency exits not in use for the tests. As the test proceeded, those on the platforms entered the cabin to join the emergency evacuation movement – to test for very-high density seating which has been considered by some airlines.

Many of the test "passengers" had never flown before. Few of them had even seen the interior of the 747. All were briefed by cabin attendants after being seated, just as airline passengers are briefed before a flight. Emergency instruction cards such as those in the airliner's seatbacks, were also provided. Cabin windows were blocked out, and the "passengers" did not know which exits would not be used – to give the tests realism.

Outside, in the illumination of the plane's emergency lights, FAA officials, airline representatives, Boeing test conductors and observers, watched the emergency evacuation slides inflate automatically as soon as the doors were popped open.

"It was like scooting down the fire chute in the old red school house," one test subject remarked.

Results of the tests showed they could evacuate 499 persons from the 747 in *90 seconds!*

The 747 had passed another FAA requirement.

The long ordeal of "The Toughest Test On Wings" was over, and the FAA pronounced the 747 design ready for airline operation. The First of the *"Super jets"* would soon be delivered to Pan American World Airways, whose $525-million order for 25 had launched the 747 program back in April of 1966.

VI

PAN-AMERICAN'S first 747, Serial Number 19640, FAA licence number N733PA was the No. 6 airplane which we had seen in its fabrication stage on the production line at Everett in 1968. It was completed on May 18, 1969, a day ahead of schedule, and finished in the paint shop bedecked in Pan-Am blue and white colors six days later. On October 24, 1969 the plane made its first flight.

On December 12, 1969 Pan American World Airways accepted N733PA as a provisionally certificated aircraft (for training and route familiarization for crews) and the following day the plane, was flown away from Seattle.

Pan-Am's Chief Pilot, Atlantic Division, Captain Robert M. Weeks was at the controls of the plane when it took off from Boeing Field at 12:37 p.m. for a five-hour flight to Nassau and thence to its home base, New York's Kennedy International Airport.

Spray from the wet runway rising from its wheels, the first Boeing 747 to be delivered to an airline, Pan American World Airways, "Clipper Young America," takes off from Boeing Field for Nassau, The Bahamas.

Distinguished "four" who played major role in decision to buy 747. They are: Harold E. Gray, PAA Chairman of the Board (right), Charles A. Lindbergh, member Board of Directors, Najeeb Halaby, PAA President and directly behind him, Juan Trippe, retired Board Chairman.

Also on board the aircraft were Captain Douglas M. Moody of Darien, Conn., Pan American check pilot, Bernard Reilly, Huntington, N.Y., and Rudolph F. Folts, East Islip, N.Y., Check Flight Engineers and two FAA observers. The flight – Seattle/Nassau/New York, in effect, was also a training mission before day-to-day training began.

The plane arrived at JFK (John F. Kennedy International Airport) at 9:30 p.m. on December 13, 1969, where it remained for two days for demonstration flights and on public exhibition. After that, it was flown to Roswell, New Mexico where the airline operates its Flight Training Center.

There, the plane was joined by other 747s as they completed their airworthiness tests and were turned over to Pan Am crews for similar shake-down flights – Seattle/Nassau/New York, a company policy. At Roswell, a former Air Force base in the isolated desert region of New Mexico, Pan Am crews began their last-minute familiarization training with their new equipment in preparation for the beginning of scheduled daily operations across the Atlantic. Only Pan Am's senior captains, with millions of miles of flying experience would get "first crack" at command of this newest, biggest and fastest member of the nation's transportation family which the airline was proud to introduce.

Next, on January 11, 1970, we find Pan American's 747, aircraft N735PA, the first fully certificated "*Super jet*" making the first Atlantic crossing with a commercial airline crew on its Flight Deck. Pan Am called it a "full dress rehearsal" for the beginning of New York to London daily operations.

The plane, piloted by Captain Jess Traner made the ocean crossing in six and a half hours, landing at London's Heathrow Airport. On board were 361 passengers, mostly Pan-Am employees, and 18 other flight crew members including sixteen stewardesses. The flight also served as a final proving demonstration for FAA personnel, who went along.

At Heathrow, there were two interesting sidelights to the trip, both pleasing to those far-sighted individuals who had brought the "plane to carry Gulliver" into reality. When the full complement of passengers (Pan-Am's 747's have a seating arrangement for 362 passengers) disembarked in 13 minutes which proved the big jet didn't disrupt things too much, a favorite claim of its critics. Moreover, at Heathrow, officials of the United Kingdom Federation on Aircraft Nuisance made a check of the noise level of the 747 as it flew over a field west of London Airport.

Considered opinion, as reported by one of the test officials. – "The 747, created less noise than a 707 which had flown over minutes before. The 747 is noisy, but not as much so as it was feared."

Back in New York, ten days later, Pan-Am readied its first 747, which had been christened by President Nixon's wife, Pat, as *"Clipper Young America,"* for the first scheduled New York to London flight. It was January 21, 1970, and for the first time, "The Spacious Age" belonged to anybody with the price of a ticket – $375.00 one-way, first-class; $210 one-way economy fare.

Unfortunately, it was an inauspicious beginning.

Flight Two, so designated on the Pan-Am timetable, was scheduled to depart at 7:00 p.m. (New York Time), and arrive in London at 7:30 a.m. (London time) but things

During special ceremonies at Dulles International Airport, the nation's First Lady, Pat Nixon, smashed champagne against plane's nose, christening Pan American's No. 1 747 – "Jet Clipper, Young America."

didn't work out that way.

Right on schedule, there was a small ceremony a few minutes before final loading time in which Kristen Miller, 10 years old, whose father Sam Miller flew Pan-Am's 707 first commercial jet across the Atlantic in 1958, cut an entry ribbon in the big jet's wide doorway. Then, 336 passengers filed aboard walking into the plane on a blue-carpeted and blue-domed ramp.

Then, the trouble started. A bulky door wouldn't close. There was a delay of 25 minutes loading 15 tons of cargo. Not until 7:25 p.m. did the plane move away from its docking position.

Captain Bob Weeks, a 26-year veteran who had flown the first 747 on its delivery flight, was at the controls as ***Flight Two*** taxied out to its take-off position. There, it was next in line for take-off when the No. 4 engine showed signs of overheating. And Weeks turned around and taxied back to the Pan-Am terminal. The passengers disembarked while they readied a stand-by 747 for the historic inaugural flight.

Not until 1:52 a.m., January 22, after a six hour and 52 minute delay did the reserve 747, *Clipper Victor* (re-christened *"Clipper Young America")* get airborne. It landed at Heathrow Airport at 8:05 a.m. which would be only 35 minutes behind schedule except for nature's clock which said it was 1:05 p.m., London time!

It was a flight to remember, never-the-less, for history was made that day and night when the world's largest commercial jetliner, the 350-ton, $22,000,000 Boeing 747 *"Super jet"* made her debut in scheduled airline service.

With it came great promises and many problems.

CHAPTER SIXTEEN

The 747's Changing World

ON the 747's "Flight Deck," pilots Jack Waddell in the left-hand seat, Brien Wygle in the co-pilot's seat and Jess Wallick at the flight engineer's station, were making a final approach. It was night-time, and the night was dark. There were low-hanging clouds that wrapped the whole area in a grey shroud. The ceiling was below 1,000 feet; ground visibility less than a mile. The air was turbulent as the big jet mushed down through the overcast. Waddell was using all the plane's automatic aids, and all his own pilotage to bring the plane in; flying "blind", using the ILS, instrument landing system.

Then, it happened. The red fire warning light flashed on the instrument panel. An alarm bell sounded.

Instinctively, Waddell's eyes spotted the trouble.

"FIRE!" he shouted. "Number Three engine . . ."

Wygle saw it, too.

"Number Three, OVERHEAT," he repeated the alarm. Then, he started calling off the emergency check list procedures for such a situation . . .

"Close throttle!"

"CLOSED"

"Start Lever."

"OFF"

They had ten seconds. If the red light didn't stop flashing, there was abnormal fire in the engine. That could mean trouble; lots of trouble under these adverse conditions.

The red light kept blinking.

Wygle kept reading on down the list . . .

"Fire control. Pull!"

"CHECK"

"Nacelle anti-ice . . ."

"OFF"

"Fire extinguisher . . ."

"DISCHARGE."

The red light went out. The bell was silent. No. 3 engine was inoperative; smothered to death by foamy chemical stuff released automatically inside the JT9D jet engine's nacelle.

The "*Superjet*" roared on, a little trickier to handle now, minus one-fourth of its thrust power. But Waddell had it manually; he had flipped off the auto-pilot system. And he had her climbing out of the approach pattern for another swing around and another try. The immediate danger was past. He could bring her down safely on the three remaining engines.

"Whew!" Waddell said, wiping his brow. "Let's face it. This thing's too damn real."

"I'm sweating, too," Wygle commented.

Wallick grinned. "Okay, you guys. Knock it off. Let's go get a '*Seven Four Seven*' sandwich at Milo's . . ."

The "*Seven Four Seven*" burger was real: two hamburger patties, mayonnaise, relish, lettuce, tomato, onions and pickle. Priced at 89 cents, a specialty of the house, served at Milo's Drive-in near Boeing headquarters in Seattle.

It was about a fifteen minute drive from where the "three Ws" – Waddell, Wallick and Wygle (The same test crew who had flown the No. 1 "*Superjet*" on it's maiden flight.) had just completed their engine-out exercise in a 747 Flight Simulator, a sophisticated new training tool.

The truth is, they had never left the ground. The 747 "Flight Deck" didn't even have wings. There never was any fire.

The "emergency situation" they were in, however, was *real* enough. The $3,000,000 747 Flight Simulator, located in a large room at the Boeing College of Jet Knowledge in Seattle, Washington, can be fed by computers, just about any problem that might confront the flight crews on the real airplane.

There is, perhaps, no better example of the impact of change introduced by the advent of the huge "*Superjet*" than is demonstrated in the simulator training program.

Boeing's Tom Layne, Chief Pilot Flight Crew Training, says, "There isn't anything in the 747 program as far as the training aspect is concerned, that hasn't produced a major change."

Because of the tremendous investment in the new equipment ($22 to $23-million

Flight Simulator, a $3,000,000 training "tool" is suspended on hydraulic arms to permit free movement.

per aircraft) the airline customers and Boeing, Layne points out, took a revolutionary approach to the 747 training program. "For the first time, the airlines pooled their best training experts and worked with the manufacturer in a joint effort to set up the most efficient training techniques," Layne explained. "Working with the Air Transport Association's Training Committee which correlated the airlines' ideas, we had the best brains in the world to set the guidelines for the 747 training program involving all phases of ground school and flight training. More important, for the first time, all of these data were documented, resulting in a 2,000-page 'Bible' describing the various tasks each 747 Flight Crew member has to perform and the background he must have to carry them out.

"All of these data based on 'specific behavioral objectives', the result of thousands of hours of research detailing everything that needs to be known about the 747 was then fed into computers . . . If you want to know, say, what a co-pilot needs to know for taxiing the 747, you can punch it out . . . If you have the responsibility of developing a Ground School for the 747 hydraulic system, you can punch it out . . . The computer will give you a baseline to develop the program . . .

"In this area," Layne concluded, "I believe, the advent of the 747 has made as great a contribution in future training programs as it has in introducing the *Spacious Age*."

Diagramatic electronic trainer (instructor pointing) uses light to show the "Superjet's" hydraulic system activity.

II

THE "Flight Simulator" just mentioned is, in itself, a revolutionary change. Built by Conductron Corporation, the simulator is a full-scale replica of the "*Superjet's*" Flight Crew compartment suspended amid a series of hydraulic actuators which permit duplicating the 747's various flight attitudes. In operation, the Simulator can duplicate *vertical, lateral, fore* and *aft, roll, pitch* and *yaw* attitudes of the 747 with the realism of actual flight. Previous Flight Simulators could only provide three movements – *roll, pitch* and *yaw*. By introducing the new six degree motion system, the 747 simulators portend many changes in pilot training programs which will apply to the whole spectrum of jet operations. "With these second generation Flight Simulators," Tom Layne explained, "we can duplicate virtually every movement the aircraft does on the ground and in the air."

Using the 747 Flight Simulator at Boeing's "College of Jet Knowledge", they manufacture their own weather; simulating icing conditions, rain, turbulence, lightning "strikes" and other conditions which Flight Crews may face in daily operations. They can cause engines to "overheat" and "Flame-out". They can hang a landing gear so that it won't come down, cause a malfunction in a critical wing flap mechanism, "blow-out" a pressurized cabin, or "bug" the 747's essential power system

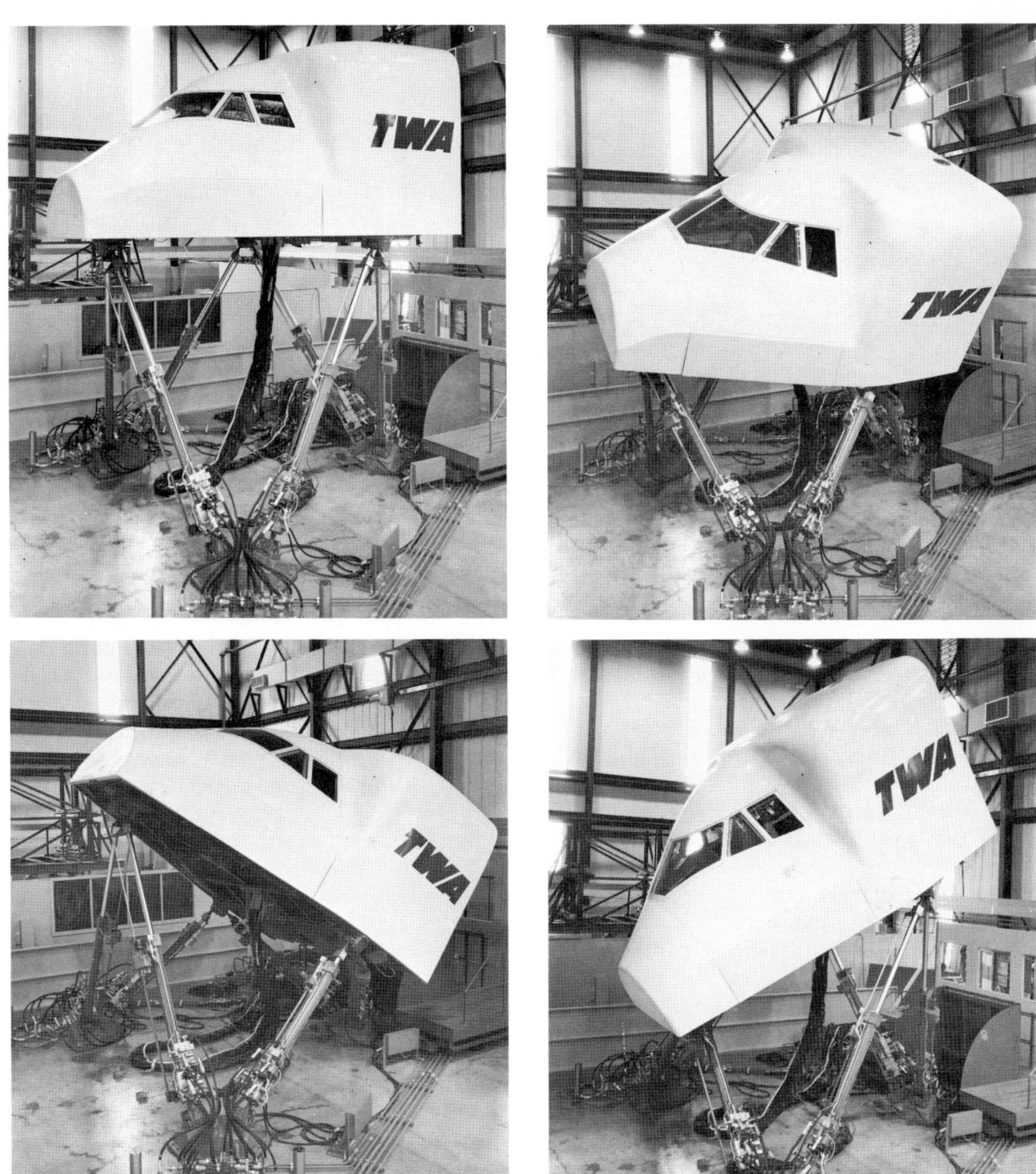

TWA 747 Flight Simulator at Kennedy International Airport demonstrates its range of flight attitudes: Flying level (upper left) Banking to port (upper right) Climbing (lower left) and Diving (lower right).

so the instruments will make like crazy. They can make it night-time, pitch dark, when it is still daylight and the sun is shining outside the building where the simulator is anchored.

The 747 Flight Simulator is an authentic facsimile of the aircraft's flight compartment and duplicates all portions of the external cockpit structure normally visible to the Captain and First Officer. It is also equipped with a station for the Flight Engineer. There is also a position for both pilot and flight engineer instructor there to observe and instruct trainees. On board,

Inside, the Flight Simulator is an exact replica of the 747's "Flight Deck," all instruments and systems.

during a typical training mission, the instructor at a special console can "push a button" and set up numerous problems and headaches for the trainees.

An instructor, for instance, can push a "freeze button" and stop the big 625-mile-an-hour *"Superjet"* at 35,000 feet dead in its own vapor trail, back it up, and "fly" the problem all over again. That, of course, is the beauty of flight simulation training. They can do things with the Flight Simulator that nobody in his right mind would think of doing with the actual aircraft. The cost would be too high, and the risk of human life prohibitive.

Consider, for example, the cost and risk involved in the scene we described at the beginning of this chapter with Waddell, Wygle and Wallick in the Flight Simulator. To perform an "engine out" mission of this nature with an actual 747 aircraft would mean *jeopardizing* the $22,000,000 plane; all such maneuvers are critical for both machine and personnel. In short, they are asking for trouble. Hazardous conditions prevail.

Aside from this risk, there is the economic factor. It costs about $2800 an hour to fly a 747 (depending upon the individual airline's bookkeeping procedures) while it costs only about $300 to $400 an hour to train in the Flight Simulator.

Moreover, with the Simulator, under controlled conditions on the ground (with no concern over loss of the aircraft, no risk of life and limb of flight crews, and much lower operational costs) the flight crew can come face to face with just about every conceivable situation which might occur in the air or during take-offs and landings. The obvious advantage of such a program to teach crew members the "dirty tricks" the jets can play, is easily translated into passenger safety and a higher degree of proficiency for pilots and flight engineers under adverse conditions.

The whole idea is based on the psychological belief that man, in the face of unknown dangers stands still, muscles tensed, skin tingling, heart pounding and tends to breed carelessness and confusion. On the other hand, if he knows what is happening, has come through it before, knows what to do and how to do it to alleviate the danger, then he is better prepared to combat the crisis with calm and confidence.

The Flight Simulator program makes the unusual and the unexpected, by repeated "conditioning" and practice, a matter of standard operational procedures with a minimum risk to personnel and equipment.

In particular, the coming of age of the 747 *"Superjet"* brought into being, the most advanced and sophisticated Flight Simulators that the state of the art could conceive and create.

At present two companies are building the 747 Flight Simulators. One is Conductron, a division of the McDonnell/Douglas Corporation. The other is the Link Group, owned by Singer-General Precision, Inc. Both 747 Flight Simulators are being used by the various airlines now already operating the 747 or soon to put the plane into scheduled operation.

The arrival of the 747 on the scene has resulted in the airlines and the aircraft manufacturers and the FAA taking a whole new look at training techniques.

According to Captain John A. Walker, Chief Training and Check Pilot for Pan American (first airline to put the 747s into service) and also chairman of the Air Transport Association Training Committee, "there will be many changes in pilot training and in Federal Air Regulations."

III

IN another area of change, the 747 has brought a "new look" to the whole environment at airports around the world which must fit it into their daily operations. Passengers, who boarded Pan-Am's New York-to-London inaugural flight at John F. Kennedy International Airport, had they chose to survey the surroundings would have seen the transformation taking place. "Spring remodeling for the bright summer of the Spacious Age," one airline official described it. "And for the most part the airlines — who are the tennants — will be footing the bill."

According to the Air Transport Association, "voice" of the Scheduled Air Transport Industry, by 1975 the airlines will have spent upwards of $2.5 BILLION for new and expanded terminal facilities.

For its 747 operations, and the "third generation" supersonic airliners, Pan American is building a $70-million passenger terminal at Kennedy International, scheduled to be completed in 1971. The new terminal will be six-and-a-half times the size of the existing terminal, which it will incorporate.

Some features include: A two-level roadway system penetrating the heart of the terminal with a 500-car rooftop, short-term parking area. Six gate positions for the Boeing 747 *"Super jets"* and ten other positions for the smaller jetliners. There will also be a Federal Clearance Center for Government Immigration, Health and Customs offices, and a baggage handling system capable of handling 6,500 pieces during the peak traffic hours.

At this writing, with a limited number of its on-order 33-plane 747 fleet in operation, the airline is already using two of the 747

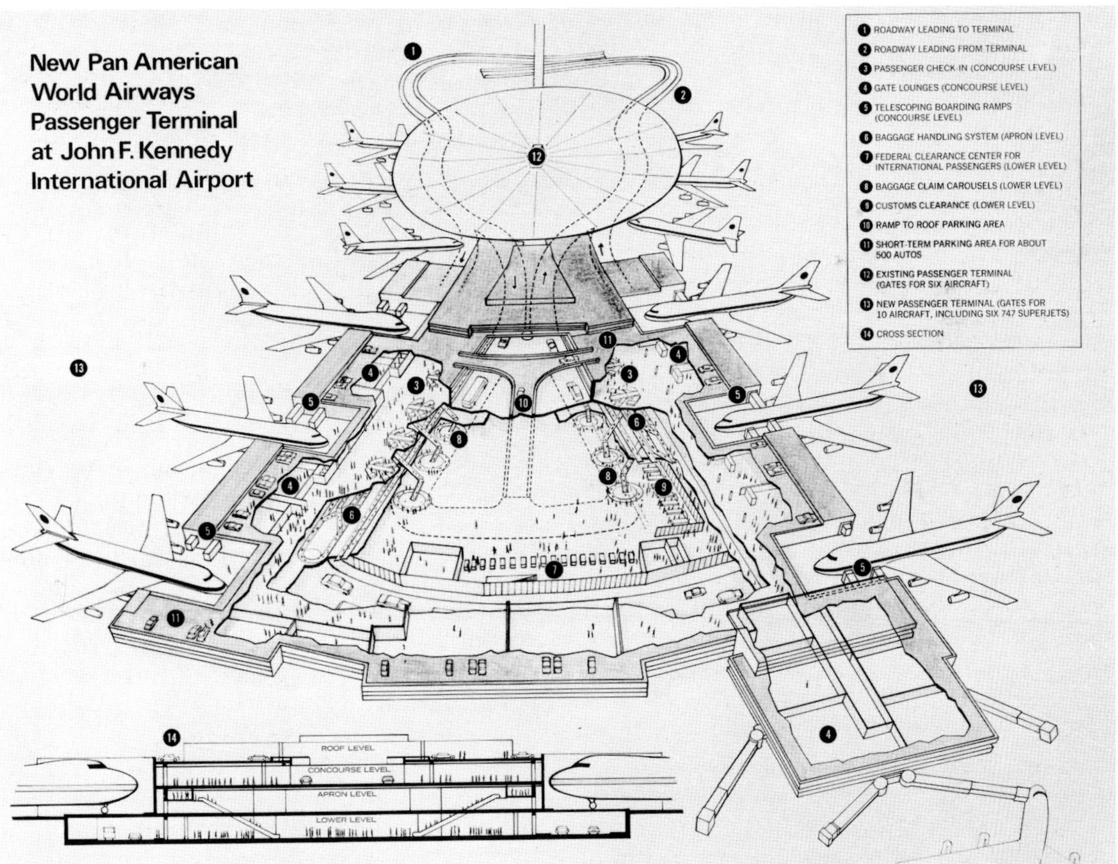

Artist's diagramatic drawing of Pan American World Airways' $70-million terminal complex at Kennedy International Airport. When completed in 1971 it will be capable of handling "Super jets" as well as "Supersonics."

Model of Pan Am terminal complex at JFK highlights 500 car roof-top parking and gate positions for aircraft.

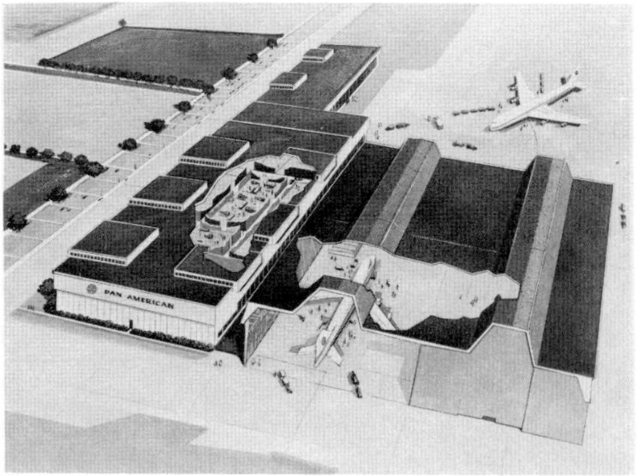

Artist's concept shows schematic view of Pan Am's maintenance base (Jet Center) at Kennedy International.

gate positions. The same docking facilities are also designed to accommodate the British/French *"Concorde"* and the U.S. Supersonic Transports expected to be flying late in this decade.

The new terminal will provide lounge space for more than 4,000 persons. It will house a 300-seat restaurant, two coffee shops, a helicopter check-in lounge (for those who select this mode of getting to the airport) and numerous concession stands.

Besides its new terminal facility at JFK, Pan-Am is spending another $57.7 MILLION for new hangars and maintenance shops. Nucleus of the new maintenance complex, located on a 195-acre site at the southwest corner of the airport, will be a sprawling jet aircraft component overhaul building, the size of 11 football fields in total area. This building, called the Jet Center, is designed to permit repairs and overhauls on virtually every type of aircraft component, such as engines, landing gears, hydraulic assemblies and electrical systems. The engine section will even be able to handle the 63,000-pound thrust General Electric GE4 engines which will power the Boeing 2707 Supersonic Transport.

In addition to the Jet Center, two huge hangars each capable of housing the 747 *"Super jets"*, the *"Concorde"* and the Boeing 2707 SST, will add their silhouettes to Kennedy's skyline. Each hangar will be 284 feet long, 263 feet wide, 90 feet high, twice the height of previous hangar structures.

Perhaps, of more import, by the fall of 1970, Pan-Am's maintenance complex will employ over 8,500 mechanics, electricians, instrument repairmen, machinists, supply specialists, administrators and other support personnel. By 1980, it is estimated there will be 12,500 workers with an annual payroll of over $100-million!

Trans World Airlines (TWA) which was first to put the 747 into domestic U.S. operation – New York-Chicago-Los Angeles – also built a multi-million dollar Passenger Terminal at Kennedy International that is capable of handling four 747s simultaneously.

TWA, second largest airline in the world, also is spending millions at its terminals around the world to accommodate the new generation of jets.

The same is true of all the 28 airlines who have ordered the 747. Individually and collectively, they are engaged in expansion programs to accept the Spacious Age.

In Chicago (with O'Hare International Airport, the busiest in the world) there is talk of building a new airport (possibly a man-made island in Lake Michigan) changing geography. Admittedly, the 747 did not generate this idea, alone, but as one planning expert put it – "fantasy-thinking, became fact-thinking in a helluva hurry!"

New terminal programs are also underway in Los Angeles, Seattle, Miami, Minneapolis and other U.S. cities. While at

Changing the face of things at Kennedy International Airport is this new Trans World Airlines' passenger terminal complex nearing completion. Loading positions can handle four "Super jets," three 707's simultaneously.

Montreal, a new $100,000,000 airport at Ste. Scholastique about 25 miles from the city (to be opened by 1974) already is dubbed – "the jumbo jet airport."

At Orly Field, outside of Paris, two new satellite terminals have increased capacity to permit handling better than 10,000,000 passengers a year.

And at Heathrow airport in London – first to accept the 747 on foreign soil – a $40,000,000 new terminal even has "moving sidewalks" for boarding passengers.

Thus, in these few examples, and there are many more, can we see the physical change that the new generation of jets has brought with it.

Trans World Airlines' new terminal at JFK, as one approaches front, is symbol of modern architecture.

Inside the TWA "Spacious Age" passenger terminal at JFK, everything is designed to expedite service.

IV

THE sheer size of "the plane with all the room in the world" as we know, has introduced a new dimension of luxury aloft for the airtraveler of the 70s. Something special in "spacial relations." At the same time, the 747's size brought with it some king-sized problems. We have already mentioned how it has necessitated new docking facilities, hangars, maintenance shops and related airport facilities. But these things, probably, would have come into being as more and more people and more and more cargo are carried by the airlines. There are, however, some areas peculiar to the 747, alone, which have made things different.

Such as: *What kind of equipment is needed to tow a 350-ton airplane out of its hangar or around the ramp? How do you load or unload 37-tons (74,000 pounds) of cargo, luggage, mail and express which a 747 can carry below deck? For that matter, how do you board 360-400 passengers through ten doors that are second-story high? Or, put aboard enough food and beverages for the same number? Or clean 400 ash trays? Or inspect the tip of the rudder which is 63 feet above the ground?*

These are typical of some of the problems the 747 brought with it, with the result, that a whole new family of so-called "Ground Support" equipment, on-loading and off-loading techniques have come into being.

Here are some of the solutions:

Low-slung Unit-Rig tow tractor has "locomotive" power to move 710,000-pound Pan Am 747 on ground.

The Unit Rig & Equipment Company of Tulsa, Oklahoma and International Harvester Company of Chicago, have come up with two vehicles that can move the 710,000-pound 747 in all kinds of weather. Push it, or pull it, depending upon different attachments. These jumbo tractors for the jumbo jets look like flat-top trucks (see accompanying photos) and are equipped with all kinds of gimmickery, radio communications, four-wheel drive and steering, and "ballast control" to give them "locomotive" pulling power. Cost is between $80,000 and $126,000 apiece.

New loading techniques: You'll never see that new matched set of luggage you bought especially for a trip on the 747 once you've "checked-in" at a Satellite or the main terminal. They've designed special aluminum baggage containers, each capable of holding about 50 pieces of passenger luggage, average size. There are shelves, so that your luggage is not "piled" in, but "placed-in" like you would, putting it in a rental baggage locker. And you can do it yourself at the check-in counter.

At the airport, the container is hauled out to the waiting 747 on specially-designed baggage cars, complete with elevated roller conveyors to reach the cargo hold. Similar containers, shaped to conform with the cross-section of the 747's underbelly compartment, are used for cargo.

Passenger loading also has changed. There's a three-level stairway rampway, mounted on a truck bed which Heathair Aircraft Equipment Wollard Corporation has produced. Essentially, you board the 747 like you'd board a DC-8, only you have to walk up a lot more steps!

United Air Lines has another approach to the problem at its New York, Los Angeles and San Francisco terminals. It features covered ramps or arms (much like those used in 707 and DC-8 loading) only these will be telescoping walkways that slide out over the wing of the 747 using the two forward doors. Another "tunnel" reaches to the rear door of the aircraft. Called "Skylanes", in operation it looks like an "Octopus" attacking the air leviathan. Each "Sky-Lane" can be positioned in about 30 seconds after the plane comes to a stop.

Special containers designed for 747's cargo hold have added a "new look" to loading techniques.

Tractor/trailers, equipped with roller beds and elevator lifts (rear) were built especially for 747.

According to a Pan-Am brochure, they've got a better way to get people on airplanes. "*Future plannings,*" says Pan-Am, "*includes a self-propelled passenger loading elevator which will roll right up to the aircraft. This unit will be in two sections – a forward compartment and a rear compartment – with an elevator for each. After the unit is positioned at the aircraft, the forward compartment is raised to the cabin level and remains there throughout the boarding process.*

"*Passengers will be brought to the aircraft by special bus and enter the rear compartment in groups of 35 to 40. Then, this will be raised and automatically levelled with the forward section. Passengers move from the rear compartment to the forward compartment, which will open directly into the cabin. Meanwhile, the rear elevator will have descended to pick up a second load of passengers.*"

All of this, without getting wet, if it happens to be raining. And with just a few steps from the terminal to board the boarding bus. Promises . . . promises . . . promises!

They've solved the ash-tray problem, too. A special high-powered vacuum unit, the size of a wheel-barrow has been designed to do the job. It can be wheeled out to the aircraft, connected to suction outlets, while the "ash tray" gang aboard the aircraft with suction hoses does the clean-up job. It's done in minutes.

There is also a truck called the "Z-Loda", an enclosed lift, or elevator, mounted on a van-like body designed especially for food service loading of the 747. The van is refrigerated and the foodstuffs and beverages goes aboard in special containers.

Imagine! A fully stocked 747, says Pan Am, will carry 1,450 coffee cups, 1,395 plates, 1,098 glasses, 400 pounds of food, 2,950 ice cubes, 186 bottles of wine and 25 gallons of liquor.

No wonder they need a special truck to load it aboard.

There are, of course, many other innovations representative of the 747's changing world. It has been estimated, for example, that something like 25,000 square feet of ramp space will be needed for the Ground Support equipment around the 747.

Altogether, an "Army" of trucks, baggage carts, mobile ramps, two tractors – most of them specialized equipment – will move in and around the big jet as it prepares for departure.

But, let's see for ourselves, and go where the action is at Kennedy International Airport, where we'll board a 747 for our first trip in the plane Joe Sutter said – "*just had to happen.*"

Mobile ramp loaders, stairways on truck-beds, move up to "Super jet's" doors for passenger on/off loading.

Scene at Orly Field, serving Paris, France, shows Pan American World Airways' "Super jet" in process of loading, surrounded by various types of new ground equipment. Size of 747, in particular its height above the ground, necessitated many changes in terminal loading arms, docking facilities and parking areas.

(Photo courtesy Ciche Aeroport De Paris, Jean J. Moreau)

Inside the world's largest building, The Boeing Company's Everett, Washington facility, the No. 1 "Super jet" (top) nears stage of completion.

A majestic thing of beauty, the No. 1 Boeing "Super jet" towers high above milling crowds that turned out for her September 30, 1968 debut.

Flying majestically in the skies of her Great Northwest, the first 747 is a shining symbol of progress, a high heritage Bill Boeing left for all.

Airlines vary as to crew complement for 747s. Here is typical TWA Flight Crew: Captain, First Officer, Flight Engineer, Steward and ten Hostesses.

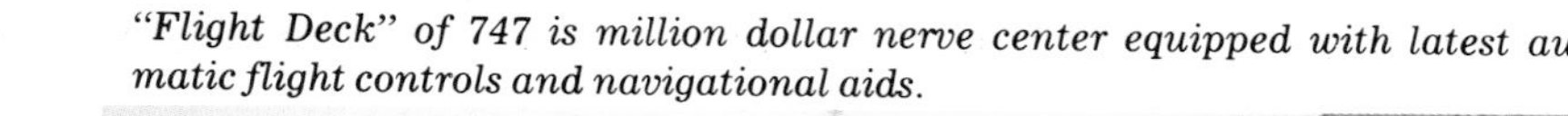

"Flight Deck" of 747 is million dollar nerve center equipped with latest automatic flight controls and navigational aids.

From this angle, the giant engines and their fairings show smooth lines of "Super jet." TWA was first airline to put 747s into domestic service.

ABOVE: *Walking up the famous "spiral staircase," passengers emerge into the spacious and luxuriously appointed "First Class" lounge.*

TOP RIGHT: *"First Class" section features wider, two abreast seats, forward lounge and spiral staircase to upper deck.*

BOTTOM RIGHT: *"Economy Class" section shows nine abreast seating, wide, double-aisles, overhead carry-on luggage bins and high ceiling.*

A Cross Section of the Great Airlines of the World

BOAC

JAL
JAPAN AIR LINES
JA8102

AIR FRANCE

Alitalia
I-DEMA

Resplendent in the colors of the great airlines which first ordered 747, these production models await acceptance on flight line at Paine Field.

CHAPTER SEVENTEEN

Flight To Remember

Pan Am's "Clipper Red Jacket," five hours and 55 minutes after leaving London's Heathrow Airport, touches down at New York's Kennedy International, and is directed into new 747 docking facilities.

THE rays of a brilliant noon-day sun bounced off the glistening metallic wings of the Pan American World Airways 747 making its final approach into Kennedy International Airport. It was a beautiful day in April, New York in the Spring, the year of Our Lord, 1970. The plane, *"Clipper Red Jacket,"* listed as Flight 101, westbound, in the time-table, had left London's Heathrow Airport at 11:00 A.M. (London Time) racing the sun across the Atlantic. Now, it was 12:30 P.M. (New York Time) five minutes ahead of schedule, as the plane touched down at Kennedy, completing Pan Am's 90th crossing of the world's second largest ocean with 747 service. And it was less than 90 days since Pan Am had inaugurated daily 747 service, linking together the world's two largest English-speaking Capital Cities, and introducing the Spacious Age aloft for everybody.

"Clipper Red Jacket," named after one of the trim sailing clippers of yesteryear – once the fastest means of communication between Europe and America – was virtually brand, spanking new as aircraft go. It was two-and-a-half months before, that she had been delivered to Pan American, the thirteenth 747 off the assembly line at Everett. She had flown about 210,000 miles, approximately 300 hours in the air.

After a landing that used up less than half the long runway, the plane taxied up to the International Arrivals Building at JFK where 38 First-Class passengers and 161 Economy-Class passengers disembarked, and some 38,000 pounds of mail, express and freight in those specially-designed containers were off-loaded by an "army" of ground personnel. Then, one of those flat-top, Unit Rig 747 tow tractors hitched on, and towed her, ever so slowly,

After passengers and cargo have been off-loaded, the big plane is towed by special 747 tractor tug to Hangar 17 to be made ready for return flight to London. Sometimes, she taxies under her own power.

to Pan Am's Hangar 17 where we are going to join her.

II

OUTSIDE Hangar 17 on the ramp, and inside the big structure itself, another "army" attacks *"Clipper Red Jacket"* to make her ready for the return trip to London, which we are making tonight. Scheduled departure time – 7:00 P.M. For the next five hours a lot of things will happen to the plane, involving hundreds of people, each performing a multitude of specifically delegated tasks.

During her five-hour-and-fifty-five-minute flight from London along the Atlantic skyway, she had picked up some skin film from the salt air, and some residue from her own engines' exhaust stream. Understandably, she needs a bath. And so, a Cleaning Crew goes to work. They wash her on the outside using special cleaning fluids and equipment.

Inside, they vacuum and shampoo the carpeting, clean all the seats and ashtrays. They clean all the windows on the inside, too, and check all the hundreds of individual lights. They check the closets and all the blankets and pillows, replacing those that have been used. They clean and disinfect and sweet-spray the big plane's twelve lavatories, four in the First-Class Section including one upstairs in the First-Class Lounge, eight in the Economy-Class Section.

It is the same with the Clipper's six galleys. When the "Clean-up Gang" is finished, they are as spic and span as a new bride's kitchen.

Now, all bright and shiny once more, and ready to accept her 362-guests – if there are that many on the manifest tonight, a full complement – *"Clipper Red Jacket"* is turned over to another crew for a rigid inspection routine.

First, they will give her a thorough check-up. Licensed aircraft mechanics, electronics technicians, jet power plant specialists, all of whom have gone through months of 747 training, will examine her skin with X-ray eyes. With delicate and sensitive instruments, they will test each and all of her various hydraulic, electronic and mechanical systems. If they find the slightest thing wrong; they will fix it.

During inspection in Hangar 17, "Clipper Red Jacket" undergoes a tire change. It takes matter of only minutes with special equipment developed for 747 maintenance. Many parts are interchangeable with 707.

Preventive maintenance, they call it. The plane must be in *perfect* condition before it will be released for flight.

"Every twenty-four hours, the plane gets a thorough inspection like this," explains Ray (Pete) Pietrasinski, Maintenance Shift Foreman, the Crew Chief in charge of *"Clipper Red Jacket"* this particular day. "Those who perform these duties are guided by volumes of Tech Orders and Maintenance Forms, and they must go down a check list of hundreds of items."

"The Maintenance Manual for the 747," he adds, "is about 12,000 pages long, three feet thick, and it covers about 1500 dif-

Pre-flight maintenance inspection is very thorough. Here, mechanic checks landing gear hydraulic lines.

Out on ramp, ground crews inspect the big jet's engines. Note height of nacelle off the ground.

Swarming all over the JT9D turbine and nacelle, mechanics use special electronic devices for checks.

Special maintenance stand that can reach 747's towering tail, helps to expedite inspection procedures.

ferent pieces of hardware."

Like the Training Manuals which we mentioned in the last chapter, these data have been fed into computers, and through a Master Control Center, information on any system or part of the 747 is virtually at a mechanic's finger-tips. It is the same way with the Parts Catalog, about the same size, which lists some 120,000 items that Pan Am must stock to keep its 747 fleet in the air.

Because of its thousands of parts and multiplicity of systems, it would seem that the 747 would be a maintenance man's "nightmare." But this is not true; the great size of the plane, itself, in many areas, makes its systems more readily accessible to the maintenance crews. This ease of access, combined with such things as easier installation of replacement components, single-point hydraulic service, and location of connections for all ground service items on the lower fuselage, have cut-down on service-time requirements.

When the "turn-around" inspection was completed, any minor adjustments made, or needed parts replaced to the Crew Chief's satisfaction, *"Clipper Red Jacket"* was parked out on the ramp in front of Hangar 17. There, another crew of specialists took over the task of fueling her, and provisioning her for the long journey.

We would not see her again, until she was in docking position at the terminal and ready for boarding.

Her name wouldn't change. But she would become *Flight Two*, Pan American's *eastbound* trip, New York to London.

III

WHILE all of this was going on in and around Hangar 17, hundreds of other people were "working" *Flight Two*. Pan Am Flight Dispatch was closely monitoring the changing weather pattern over the Atlantic, and with the help of computers, they were beginning to plot "Clipper Red Jacket's" course for the night's run. In Payload Control, others were piecing together the minute-by-minute changing manifest, the number of passengers she would carry, the pounds of mail and cargo. There were

While "Clipper Red Jacket" is on ramp outside Hangar 17, ground crews get aboard, turn on internal power and work flaps and other systems to make sure everything is OK before turning plane over to Flight Dispatch.

Because of the size of the aircraft, compartments housing electronics components are easily accessible.

thousands of questions that had to be answered. All of the answers, as fast as they came in, would go to Flight Dispatch, responsible for the over-all, on-the-ground, "Make-ready" preparations.

The Flight Dispatcher, it has been said, is the "ground captain" of any scheduled airliner. In the last analysis, he and the Clipper's Captain, make the final decision if the flight is "Go!" On this particular day, Pan Am Flight Dispatcher, Frank Clune, was handling *"Clipper Red Jacket."*

He described his job in these general terms — "We work closely with our Meteorology Section and the U.S. Weather Bureau National Meteorology Center in Southland, Maryland, to come up with what we call *'minimum track time'* which translated into layman's terms, means calculating the most advantageous operating conditions for the flight; taking advantage of favorable jetstreams (tail-winds) aloft, to save on fuel, and setting up the most economical cruise speeds for the aircraft, the most efficient altitude at which it will fly . . We must work with the proper 'weights and balances' formula for the aircraft, based on known data coming in relative to the ultimate payload; coordinate and confirm these dictates and restrictions in the loading of the aircraft . . . We determine the right amount of fuel to be put on board, with enough reserve to meet possible changing emergencies at the destination . . . We must put all of this information together — with a hundred-and-one-other details — to be presented to the Captain at a pre-flight briefing."

Clune points out, that all the flight plan information is contained in IBM computers located in the Pan Am Building, downtown Manhattan where up to the very last minute, the computer will refigure and update the Flight Plan in seconds. He emphasizes: "The human element in Flight Dispatch, the best-trained personnel in the world, are supplying data to the computer. A robot is not dictating *Flight Two's* destiny . . .

"But the computer does eliminate a lot of chances for human error, and it gives Flight Planners more information than ever before to insure the safest possible journey."

"If one man took all the data about your flight tonight that will be stored in the computer, or fed into it before departure, and started to figure out the Flight Plan," he adds, throwing up his hands, "God, it would take him a hundred years to complete it!"

The preliminary Flight Plan that Dispatcher Clune and the computer had worked up for *Flight Two* this day, went something like this: On the basis of weather data, *"Clipper Red Jacket"* would fly a Great Circle route that would take her northward over Halifax, Nova Scotia, then over Gander, Newfoundland, out across 1100 miles of open Atlantic with a landfall at Belfast, Ireland, thence, on a straight line southeast to London, a total distance of about 3,540 miles. The best cruising altitude was 33,000 feet, where about 600 miles out from Gander, she could pick up a 140-mile-an-hour Jet Stream.

Clune's computerized data said *"Clipper Red Jacket"* for this trip would weigh out at about 690,000 pounds gross. Up to 124,000 pounds of this weight would be payload — passengers, baggage and cargo. The remaining 566,000 pounds would be the aircraft itself, fuel, water and oil. *Flight Two* would require about 28,800 gallons of fuel for her journey. That would give her plenty of reserve. Estimated flying time — 5 hours, 48 minutes!

They had been working in Flight Dispatch since *"Clipper Red Jacket's"* arrival to gather together this information. It would be presented to the Clipper's Captain and Flight Crew when they reported in, about two hours before departure time. There probably could be some last minute changes, but these would be worked out to the satisfaction of the Captain and Flight Dispatcher within the general framework of the above plan.

All this while, other things were happening to expedite *Flight Two* on her way, at locations far from the aircraft itself. In the main Pan Am terminal and at satellite locations, ticket counter personnel had been "checking-in" passengers for *Flight Two,* helping them to get their passports in order; helping them with seat selection; weighing in their baggage. In many cases, peculiar to the 747, baggage was already loaded in the containers, put on special buses to the airport, and made-ready at cargo loading locations, awaiting the plane itself to be moved into position. To relieve congestion at the airport — a "bugaboo" the big jets were supposed to bring with them — as much pre-processing as possible is done at the time a passenger purchases his ticket. Certainly, at time of "check-in" wherever that location may be.

To describe each operation involved, would require a volume as large as the 747's Parts Manual, but one other pre-flight requisite — because it is different with the 747 — seems appropriate to look at more closely. That is, Pan Am's Flight Kitchen at Kennedy International Airport. Preparing meals for 362 people coming to dinner, can be a king-sized job.

"It takes a lot of planning," says Jay Treadwell, Pan American's Manager of Food & Beverage Service at Kennedy International. "We have to plan meals right to the exact number of passengers booked, give or take a few. And we have to know

About an hour before departure, Captain and First Officer check in at Flight Dispatch, and get with Briefing Officer to check latest weather charts and last minute changes in computerized Flight Plan.

about how many steaks or how many lobsters (if that's the fare) to prepare in advance, or we could *'filet mignon'* or *'lobster'* ourselves right out of business. That's why you may be asked at check-in which entree you prefer.

"We know, too, that all our passengers want the very best of everything, and in this area, we are well aware that the competition is oven-hot. It's a known fact, that many air travelers pick their airline because of the food and service . . . like they pick their favorite restaurants. Many of Pan Am's dishes are prepared from recipes gleaned from world famous chefs, like Maxim's in Paris . . ."

The menu for *Flight Two*, which we saw in advance, included: roast tenderloin of beef with truffle sauce, Maine lobster thermidor, curried lamb, mango chutney, breast of chicken in champagne sauce, for entrees; buttered garden vegetables, potato fondantes and saffron rice; hearts of palm salad; a selection of cheeses, puff pastry and cream, Bavarian cake in rum sauce, coffee with cointreau.

"The main dishes," Treadwell explains, "are prepared many hours in advance, then frozen, put aboard the aircraft in special galley containers, and cooked to order, hot and savory on board at serving time."

All of this is not really new, the same

Pan Am Reservations Clerk, Lois Moran, using Panamac, a computerized world-wide reservations system, checks latest manual for carriage of live animals. Clippers carry thousands of pets and other animals.

food preparation routine applies to other aircraft in Pan Am's world-wide fleet. But for the 747, they have created a new kind of mobile, plug-in galley. (There are six on board) "Each of these units is completely stocked in our Flight Kitchen," according to Treadwell. "Like say, filling up a king-sized refrigerator and freezer with everything you need. Then, the complete package is installed in the 747 about three or four hours before flight time. When a flight terminates, the galleys are removed – complete with dirty dishes – to be replaced by a new unit for the next trip. The whole operation takes about 20 minutes!"

IV

THE *canapes*, the *Hors D'Oeuvres*, the *entrees*, the *salade*, the *fromages*, from *caviar* to *cointreau;* the chinaware and trays and, would you believe, a total of 3,230 knives, forks and spoons already were on board *"Clipper Red Jacket,"* when the Flight Crew and Cabin Attendants, reported in for duty. All during the day, Crew Scheduling had been checking the seniority and number of hours aloft for each crew member, and alerting the individuals, to confirm the roster. A Flight Crew of three, *Captain, First Officer* and *Flight Engineer*, would take *Flight Two* to London tonight. There would be fourteen cabin attendants – A *Flight Director* in over-all charge, four pursers, each in charge of a section and ten stewardesses.

At your service in the cabin for this trip would be: *Flight Director*, Jay Koran;

Chief Purser, Joseph Zaski; *Chief Purser,* Nicholas Mueller; *Senior Stewardesses,* Carola Vasquez, Pamela Eng, Catherine Mellquist and Karen Westlin; *Stewardesses,* Kirsten Chase, Christel Yvonne Olofson, Marie Confalonieri, Elyse Renaud, Chrystal Thurston, Linda Parades, Meredith Bixley and Christine Reindl. Their nationalities made the roster read like the United Nations; seven different countries represented – Germany, Finland, Sweden, Puerto Rico, Italy, Haiti and the United States.

On the Flight Deck, *"Clipper Red Jacket"* would be in command of: *Captain* Robert M. Weeks (He flew the Innaugural Flight, remember?) who started flying with Pan American on the Pacific-Alaska Division in 1942, a four-striper since 1944. *First Officer,* (co-pilot) Captain John T. Nolan, native New Yorker, who earned his wings as a Navy flying instructor and joined Pan American in 1936, based in Miami, Florida. *Flight Engineer,* August G. McKinney, of Denville, New Jersey, who also joined Pan-Am in 1936, served as a flight mechanic at the airline's Brownsville, Texas installation, was raised to F.E. rating in 1940, and has been flying ever since.

Indeed, an aggregate of 96 years experience "flying the line" will be *up front* tonight, plus three auto-pilots, and over a million dollars worth of electronic "flight partners" and navigational aids. It is reassuring to know. And, like the man says – *that's what makes the going great!*

For this "know-how" the Flight Crew is paid a total in annual base salaries of more than $115,000 (*Captain,* $59,000; *First Officer,* $32,000, *Flight Engineer,* $30,000) plus expenses away from home,

As flight time approaches, "Clipper Red Jacket" is towed back to passenger terminal dock for last minute preparations, further inspections, cargo & food service loading, before passengers board.

and many other fringe benefits. Stewardesses get a starting base of $460.00 a month and up to $655; a purser starts at about $612.00 per month. The maximum time flight personnel can fly each month is 65 to 80 hours, set by Federal Air Regulations. *Flight Two's* payroll for its Flight Personnel on the five-and-a-half hour trip to London will run roughly $2600. It varies for night flying, over-time, ground time and other factors.

One 747 Captain we talked with about his pay scale put it this way – "When the door slams shut, I'm President, general manager, public relations man, and chauffeur for a $22,000,000 corporation. A lot of folks only see us sitting there, smoking a cigarette, and being served steak by a pretty stewardess. But we don't get paid for the whip cream; we get paid for the sour milk."

After Captain Bob Weeks checked-in with Crew Scheduling, he went directly to Pan Am's Terminal Building and got into a huddle with the men on duty in Crew Briefing.

On Pre-Flight Line, there is final ground check of Clipper's nose gear and hydraulic control system.

Postal clerk at last minute "closes-out" mail that will go aboard the Clipper. Mail sacks are put inside the specially-designed 747 cargo and luggage containers. Loading containers goes on all day as mail arrives.

Just before engine start, late cargo goes into the aft bin. Containers move on rollers and elevator lift, and are shaped to conform to fuselage cross-section. Weight & balance of aircraft is all computerized.

"How's the IBM doing?" Weeks asked.

"On the Stock Market, or the Flight Planning computer?" jibed his Briefing Officer.

"Cute joke," Weeks retorted. "Let's get to work . . . "

There were really two pre-flight briefings; one for the entire group of "flight service personnel" who would be in charge of *"Clipper Red Jacket";* the other, for just the Flight Deck officers. The latter, when it was finished required both Weeks and Clune to sign an FAA form saying that they had agreed to the Flight Plan. By this time, it was getting to be less than 45 minutes until scheduled departure.

While Weeks, his crew and the others had been going through the "briefings," the plane itself with two mechanics in the cockpit, had been taxied from Hangar 17 into docking position at one of the 747 gates in the new still unfinished $70,000,000 Pan-Am Terminal complex. In about a half hour passengers would start boarding. Except for some last minute details *"Clipper Red Jacket"* was ready to accept them. There was a lot of activity going on around the aircraft.

One unusual point of interest: Some cargo handlers were walking a pair of Afghan hounds, before putting them in their special cages in the bulk cargo hold. An Angora cat named *"Tam-O'Shanter,"* the name on its aluminum traveling case, several other cats and dogs and a baby leopard belonging to some movie starlet, were also going to make the flight. One never knows what's riding below deck. The Clipper, sometimes, is a virtual "Noah's Ark" with wings.

The first official crew member to go out to the aircraft was Flight Engineer "Gus" McKinney. There, he started to run down

Just before passengers board, there is all kinds of activity around the departing "Clipper." This is typical scene as one of 747's glistens in the flood lights at New York's John F. Kennedy Airport. (Photo by Ezra Stoller)

a list of what had been done to the aircraft during the day. Then, McKinney made his own inspection of the aircraft, inside and out. After that he went up on the Flight Deck and took his position at the Flight Engineer's Console, checking all systems.

About the same time he went out to the plane, the pursers and stewardesses also boarded, and began a routine inspection of the cabin, galleys and lavatories. *Was everything on board that should be there?* It would be embarrassing to explain to a thirsty passenger after they got "upstairs," that there wasn't any Scotch, or Vodka, or olives for a martini. The disposable head-rests on the backs of the seats; they should all be straight and neat.

More important, they double-checked all the emergency equipment; escape chutes, life-rafts and all their auxiliary items, flash-lights, walkie-talkies, first-aid kits – in case of ditching. And don't forget to make up the basinets. There would be, according to the manifest, twelve infants on board; three in First-Class and the others in the Economy Sections. Were there bottles and nipples and diapers, just in case mothers had forgotten?

Last to come aboard before the passengers began to stream in was Captain Weeks.

He entered the airplane, and took his position in the Left-Hand seat, the Captain's chair.

Captain Nolan, who, incidentally, is also a fully rated 747 command pilot was already in the co-pilot's chair. Together, they went down a pre-flight check list of about fifty items.

This included one thing very new with the 747, feeding the computerized Flight Plan inputs into the Inertial Navigation System. The 747 was the first commercial airliner to use the INS, a "black box" linked to the auto-pilots, a commercial version of the flight control "magic" aboard our Spacecraft like "Apollo," which made *"Clipper Red Jacket"* virtually an automatic airplane.

In flight, the INS would give Captain Weeks the vital navigation data he needs, instantaneously, including the aircraft's exact position at all times, directional heading, pitch and roll attitude, wind direction and speed, and the distance and time to go to the next way point or final destination. At the same time, the system would feed steering commands through the autopilots to operate the 350-ton 747's control surfaces.

By pushing a series of buttons (like dialing with those push-button phones) Weeks can set up *Flight Two's* entire journey, the plotted course, altitude, cruising speed, and the INS will tell the autopilots what to do, and do it. He can, however, take over manually at any time. And, if conditions change rapidly, he can "punch out" the original plan and put in the new factors that will compensate for the changes.

Welcome Aboard! The minute you step aboard, there is beauty and spaciousness. Note Spiral Staircase.

About the only things the INS won't do, pilots will tell you, is say "Coffee, Tea or Milk?"

Thank God, INS can't talk. The words sound much better coming from a pretty stewardess.

One of whom, in her chic new Pan Am spring ensemble – galaxie gold jacket, skirt and white blouse – completewith the latest English "derby-style" hat, is standing just inside the wide door leading into the First-Class section of *"Clipper Red Jacket"* to welcome us on board.

Flight Two will have 312 passengers on board tonight. It is filling up fast. There isn't time to look around as we go to our seat; cabin attendants want to get everybody seated as quickly as possible. They move about checking individual boarding passes, taking top coats to hang in closets, and helping stow small flight bags, tote bags, hat boxes, and other carry-on articles in the hinged, enclosed overhead racks. Already you like the 747. No more stuffing things under the seat.

Fasten your seat belt!

It is 6:58 p.m. by your watch, and you hear them closing the door. We're going to leave right on time.

Well, almost. The door opens again. There are voices, a short exchange of words, some last minute detail, and then, it slams shut a second time.

Sometimes, you wonder, if they don't do this on purpose. It's nice to know every-

On board "Clipper Red Jacket" there were 312 passengers, with the Economy Class sections almost filled. Here, stewardesses, in the two aisles of the wide-bodied jet are making guests comfortable.

In forward First-Class Section, passengers relax waiting for upstairs lounge seats to be available.

thing isn't computerized. *"Clipper Red Jacket"* is also very *humanized.*

Minutes later, the big plane starts moving slowly away from its docking position.

Our trip to London, the airborne portion, is about to begin. Interestingly, there is still some daylight in the sky in the direction of the setting sun. But in London, it is just past midnight – about thirteen hours since the plane had left Heathrow Airport.

We'll catch that sun again in about six hours, when Old Sol peeks up over the horizon and casts its morning rays on the green hills of Ireland.

V

TAXIING out to the end of the runway to get into take-off position, we get a glimpse of a United Airlines' "stretched" DC-8 jetliner coming in on another taxiway. The DC-8 is the biggest of the *first generation* commercial jetliners. But it looks so small from our window view. Actually, although we are taxiing parallel, momentarily, the height of *"Clipper Red Jacket"* above the ground, makes it seem as though the DC-8 is below us. And we are riding on the 747's main deck, in a window seat in the very front row of the First-Class section. There is an "upstairs" First-Class Lounge above us. It is a different sensation of the size of the 747, than we have ever experienced before.

Riding up here, this far forward in the nose is another feeling one could never experience in previous jetliners. The 747's nose section is tapered so that our window angle flush left with the fuselage, permits a good degree of forward vision. You can actually see where you're going, which is why we chose this seat in the first place. You feel almost as if you were "flying" the aircraft.

Your fellow passenger, next to you in the aisle seat, a London businessman, who made the trip over two days ago *(Flight 101)* makes the remark: "If you've never experienced this *'forward look,'* you'll get a kick out of it, when the nose goes down for the landing . . . the runway comes up terribly fast . . . "

The voice of one of the Flight Attendants over the loudspeaker system interrupts, with the usual explanation of the plane's egress features for emergency evacuation; the location of life-vests, and the pop-out oxygen masks in case of decompression. There is the usual demonstration of how to use the oxygen mask.

When this required "safety" briefing is finished, the plane is in position and starting her take-off run.

You're glad you picked this seat . . . the *forward look* is truly, an exhilerating experience.

As a passenger, flying was never like this before.

The tremendous surge of power that you had expected from the 747's great engines was not there at all. The plane, weighing now about 688,000 pounds (she had burned 2,000 pounds of fuel in warm up and taxiing) lifted off gracefully, seemingly effortlessly, with a quietness that was almost eerie. Whoever it was that called this plane, "The Big, Quiet One," knew what he was talking about.

When the FASTEN SEAT BELT sign goes off, you get up and take a walk around.

Flight Director Jay Koran is your guide on a tour of *"Clipper Red Jacket,"* and he points out features that you probably never would have noticed.

The interior color scheme, for example, makes the cabin seem even larger than all the statistical measurements can describe it. The decor also has been worked out with passenger psychological reactions in mind. The carpeting, mottled dark and intermediate browns throughout the whole cabin, has a "mod" look, but there is a feeling of solid underfooting. The almost vertical walls, a beige color, and the creamy high ceilings, make for a bright and cheerful atmosphere. And the seat upholstering color combinations – stone beige and dark blue in the two forward First-Class Sections; the stone beige side seats with the red, yellow and orange center seats in the three Economy Class sections – tend to break up the whole interior into "little theaters." There is, a feeling of not being inside an aircraft's fuselage at all.

"Passengers tell us this is what really makes flying in the 747 different," Koran explains. "They confess that at first they are apprehensive about its size, especially the first-timers. How can such a huge thing get off the ground? But once we are airborne, and they look around and walk around a bit, invariably, they say – *why, it's like not flying at all; more like being in a small hotel lobby."*

"Of course," he adds with a grin. "There are those veteran air travelers, who say – *'The Hell with it! You've taken all the fun out of flying.'* Maybe, that's a compliment, too."

It takes us about ten minutes to walk slowly down the wide aisle from our seat in Row One in First-Class to Row 56 in the rear Economy Section, and then back again, up the second wide aisle on the other side of the cabin to our seat.

You are impressed in another way of the size of the plane.

So big, that the wide aisles make it possible for the stewardesses to wheel small carts, each with as many as three dozen dinners on trays, through the cabin to expedite serving the greater number of passengers. Much different from the service on the 707, where stewardesses had to carry back individual trays to the seats. "If we had to do it the old way," Koran says, "we'd be in London before everybody got his dinner."

Back in our seat again, Koran excuses himself, and says for us to enjoy our own dinner. He'll be back later and take us "upstairs" in the First-Class lounge, and for a peek into the Flight Deck and a word, perhaps, with Captain Weeks.

While you are enjoying the champagne, cocktails and caviar (from the Caspian Sea with iced Vodka), the *Filet deBoeuf roti, sauce Perigourdine* (that's the roast tenderloin of beef and truffle sauce, from the menu you saw earlier) and all the other goodies, *"Clipper Red Jacket"* also has been eating up the miles. The city, whose lights you see far below, is Halifax, Nova Scotia. Time and distance seem almost

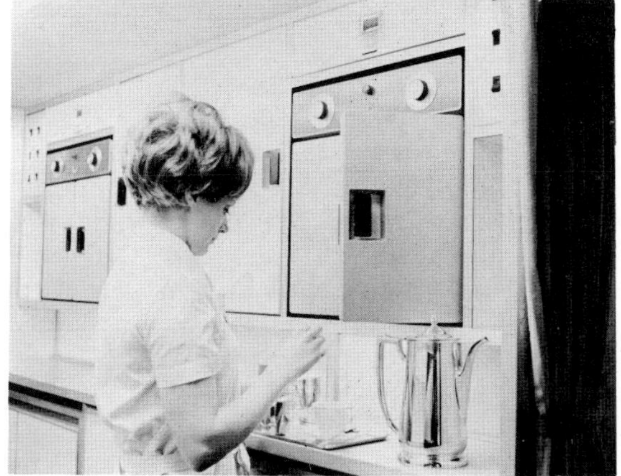

At one of plane's six galleys, stewardess prepares coffee and apertif. Service is gold-plated and real china.

Meals cooked on board, served from cart which can carry 32 full-course dinners, speeds up service.

meaningless in this spacious environment.

Perhaps, the delicious meal and the way it is being served has a lot to do with it. The crystal glasses, the distinctive china, the gold-plated utensils; dining aloft in the 747 is an epicurean experience you won't soon forget. Admittedly, it has always seemed thus on previous crossings in the 707 or the Douglas DC-8 jetliners. But the 747 is different in several ways.

Your "table," for instance, pops up out of the arm-rest on the seat and unfolds like a note-book. Moreover, you can see the food come right out of the galley. Psychologically, you know because of the additional space, the means of in-flight food preparation is better. In fact, the galley is much larger than your own kitchen at home. There are other built-in "creature comforts" to make dining more pleasurable: The wider seats no bumping elbows, fork-lifting a piece of savory beef. The push-button controls on the armrest, that allow you to select from several channels, classical music, pop music, or listen to the news, through individual earphones. The soft-lighting, and the "Cathedral" windows that add to the effect of roominess.

Over the *Cafe au Cointreau* (coffee with brandy) you reflect a moment about the first flight you made over this ocean, New York to Paris in a four-engined, 49-passenger Lockheed *Constellation twenty years ago!* Oh, it was luxurious, then, and you thought air travel had reached its ultimate.

But there was a lot of vibration, the constant drone of the engines, and occasional bumpiness at the lower altitudes. Even the walk back to the lavatories in the rear of the plane, along the narrow aisle, and the tube-like contour of the cabin, despite its decor, gave a sense of confinement. There was always that feeling that you were in an airplane, a piece of machinery, high above the deep, dark waters of the Atlantic. There is *not* that feeling now, in the room-like cabin of the 747. and it is so quiet, and seemingly, a motionless platform, riding the currents of the air ocean.

Flight Director Koran is back, interrupt-

In the "front office" this is typical scene as Flight Crew takes a coffee break. First Officer, right front, is at the controls. The push-button console in center is part of Inertial Navigation System.

ing your reminiscing, to say that Captain Weeks has agreed to let us visit the Flight Deck.

We go up the winding stairs, walk through the First-Class Lounge to the door that leads into the Crew Compartment. The door is locked. But Koran identifies himself, and we are permitted to enter. He locks the door behind us.

Surprisingly, the Flight Deck is not much larger than that on the 707, the cockpit itself, that is. The plane's Captain, First Officer and Flight Engineer are quite close together, amid a maze of instrument panels and controls. It is not really bright up here. There is indirect lighting of a special kind to make it easier on the eyes, and giving special emphasis to the galaxie of instrument dials, gauges, control buttons and switches. But the windows seem huge, and the night sky with its own galaxie of stars, comes in, as a backdrop of black curtains, all around.

"The INS and the autopilots are flying the airplane," Captain Weeks explains. "But we are getting some updated weather reports that may make us want to go upstairs to catch some better winds."

He tells us that the IBM computer back in the Pan Am Building in Manhattan (some 1000 nautical miles behind us now) indicates a change of altitude would put us in the fast-moving jetstream a little ahead of schedule.

"As soon as we get the confirmation," he says, "we'll execute the maneuver."

As a point of interest, he identifies the lights below which are coming up dead ahead: "That's Gander, Newfoundland . . . When the first of our landplanes (The DC-4s, DC-6s and *Constellations)* started flying this run, Gander was a *must* for refuelling before heading out over the ocean . . ."

He interrupts himself to say, "They've confirmed the Flight Plan change. Now, watch how simple it is . . ."

He pushes several buttons on the INS control panel.

There is a little whirring sound, and the "black box" at his fingertips seems to emit its own language . . . *click* . . . *click* . . . *click* . . .

"We're still on automatic," Weeks points out. "The INS is telling the autopilot what to do . . ."

You don't need to be told what's happening. Almost instantaneously, the big plane's nose tilts upwards, and you know it is climbing.

Weeks points to one of the dials on the instrument panel in front of him. The Altimeter. And you can see the greenish-yellow needle swinging clockwise until it quivers and stops at 350 . . . the numbers are in 100-foot readings. At the same time, a digital reading, like the mileage indicator on the speedometer of your car, clicks off to read — 35,000 feet.

"Clipper Red Jacket" levels off.

Another dial on the instrument panel which Weeks is pointing to, the Air Speed Indicator, gives another reading. Registering in Knots Per Hour, its needle is also swinging around . . . and its numerical indicator is adding up like an abacus. It steadies at 678.4 . . . "We're riding the Jetstream now," Weeks says. "And we're flying at almost the speed of sound!"

He lets us put on a set of earphones and we can hear numerous voices in the Atlantic sky . . . A KLM DC-8 that is talking with Montreal for landing instructions. It is 300 miles behind us at 24,000 feet . . . An *Air France* 707, Paris-bound, about a hundred miles behind us, at 31,000 feet, encountering some turbulence, and requesting an altitude change . . . *Nan Charlie,* the radar ship about 400 miles off the Irish Coast, giving the weather to a BOAC (British Overseas Airways Corp.) jetliner heading out over the ocean for landfall at Gander . . .

As we take off the headset, Weeks with a grin, seems to be reading our thoughts. "We're the only 747 in the sky tonight," he says proudly.

When we take leave of this fascinating world "Up Front" in *"Clipper Red Jacket,"* Captain Weeks informs us — "We should be on the ground at Heathrow in about three hours and 11 minutes. Have a pleasant trip. We'll try and keep it smooth."

We stop for a night-cap in the First-Class lounge which is like being in a small cocktail lounge of an exclusive hotel. There is a small bar in one corner, but drinks are served at tables. Over a Cream de Menthe

Directly behind the "Flight Deck," on second floor, is the First Class Lounge. Here, businessmen can have semi-privacy for conferences. There is also a small bar and galley. Seats in lounge are not for sale.

on the rocks, the events of the past half hour, spent on the Flight Deck, keep reappearing in our mind. It is nice to know what is going on "Up Front."

There are many people, and many sophisticated machines to guide and steer this leviathan of the skies safely and surely on its way.

Back "downstairs" again, with the wide and comfortable seat in full reclining position, these reassuring thoughts blank out the final scenes of the Sophia Loren movie on the wide-screen, and sleep takes over . . .

"Clipper Red Jacket" swooshes on through the night sky.

IV

YOU have flown more than 1,200,000 miles in your lifetime on the scheduled airlines, riding in everything from the rattling old, cumbersome, Ford trimotors to the sleek, silent wings of the jetliners, but always — even with the advent of the pressurized cabin — when the plane starts to descend you can feel it in your ears. Maybe, it doesn't effect everybody that way. But it does you, and that feeling right now awakens you. *"Clipper Red Jacket"* is starting its descent. You stretch, take a deep breath, yawn and swallow hard to relieve the pressure in your ears, and sit up straight. The seat back, automatically snaps upright to conform with your body position, a new feature in the 747. You glance at your watch, and take a look out the window.

The watch says it is 12:10 A.M., just after midnight, New York Time. You never change it, because you like to know what time it is at home. (It is 7:10 A.M. London Time.) You should be about 300 miles out from Heathrow Airport. And there should be the morning sun's rays streaming through the window. But there is no sun; just a solid grey mass of nothingness. The weather must have changed suddenly over this part of the world from what the forecast had predicted. And you wonder what's happening up on the Flight Deck now, as the *Clipper* mushes down through the overcast.

The voice of Captain Weeks over the loudspeaker system answers part of that question: "Good morning, Ladies and

Gentlemen, as you can see, the weather turned a little sour on us. It is like this, the rest of the way. At Heathrow, we are advised the ceiling is below 1,000 feet and dropping. There is a slight drizzle. We have been cleared for final approach, however, and should be on the ground almost right on schedule. Thank you."

You know now what's happening; *"Clipper Red Jacket"* will be making a "blind" approach using all the facilities of the Instrument Landing System on the ground and its own on-board automatic flight capabilities. Because it is the first commercial jetliner to be designed around the INS and other new and more sophisticated electronic flight aids, the 747 will probably make a fully automatic landing. The system can bring the big jet down to the runway at some airports.

Here's how it works in layman's terms: The INS, linked to the autopilots, guides the plane through various stages of descent and directional change until it can link onto the Heathrow ILS, an invisible electronic beam or glide path slanting right down to the center of the runway. When it "hooks on," the plane, like "Tinker Bell" at Disneyland sliding down the cable from atop Mt. Everest, rides the beam to touchdown.

Captain Weeks can take over manually at any instant. But he doesn't have to. The INS and the ILS and the autopilots will find and lock onto the "invisible beam" slanting up from the ILS ground station; the aircraft will automatically throttle back for normal descent; the flaps will adjust also compensating automatically for the plane's changing attitude, and smoothing out the bumps; the massive landing gear will drop down and lock into place, and the autopilot will steer the big plane on target down the center line of the glide path to touchdown.

Descent is steeper now. You have to "pop" your ears again. Pressurization isn't as sophisticated as the automation.

Huge as it is, you can feel the plane changing its attitude; nose down, a little more, level off again, nose down again; banking a little, turning, to the left, then to the right; "braking," the pressure on your seat belt tells you so, the flaps extending; a slight vibration, the dual nose-wheel locking into place . . .

The NO SMOKING sign flashes on, and you know you are in final approach.

Out the window, the grey stuff seems to be thicker.

She is "staggering" a little in her blindness, searching for that invisible guide path, the "magic clothesline" . . .

Down . . . down . . . down . . . you can feel the back of the seat pressing you forward.

There are tiny raindrops on the window now. Then, suddenly, out of nowhere, lights appear, and dead ahead, is the runway. Boy! It *is* coming up fast!

The Englishman beside you, nudges with his elbow – "You, see, it is rather sensational. Rather, don't you think?"

You don't need to be reminded. It's like the big dip on your first roller-coaster ride. The caviar is swimming in the iced Vodka.

The nose comes up. And there is a *thump* as the nose-wheel, almost directly below, touches the runway sending up a spray from the wet surface.

The reverse thrusters take hold, almost throwing you forward, straining the seat belt. By the time you straighten up, the plane has almost rolled to a stop.

And as *"Clipper Red Jacket"* moves slowly, nose first into the Heathrow docking facility, similar to the one at JFK, there's something else you can't help thinking – *in this seat, you're going to get there ahead of the pilot!*

It takes only about fifteen minutes to deplane all of the Clipper's passengers, all 312 of us. The only real delay is at the door; everybody wants to say "good-bye and thanks" to the pretty Stewardesses.

Perhaps, a solution, is to get ugly gals.

Heaven forbid! And one remembers that 40 years ago Boeing Air Transport was first airline to introduce stewardesses on board.

Later, after a quick run through customs, in the Heathrow lounge over a cup of coffee, you are looking out the window at *"Clipper Red Jacket"* being towed slowly away to another Pan Am hangar, where they will repeat the "turn-around" procedures for her return trip to New York.

She looks so big, compared to the other planes around her. You can't help wondering . . .

How big will they get?

In the early thirties, Pan American World Airways, on some of its South American routes was flying the old Ford Trimotors. Here, a refurbished "Tin Goose" – as pilots affectionately called the all-metal Fords – rests in the shadow of the giant 747 Clipper's tail. The "old" and the "new" represents forty years of aviation progress.

CHAPTER EIGHTEEN

Beyond Tomorrow

Nose hinges up, and giant 40-foot long (small box car length) cargo containers are moved aboard cargo system mock-up of the Boeing 747C (convertible) and 747F (jet freighter) during evaluation of design.

SOON after the first 747 was rolled out of the hangar at Everett, The Boeing Company announced that it was building four different versions of the biggest commercial jetliner in the world. These would be the standard 747, an all-passenger plane with a 710,000-pound maximum takeoff weight; the 747B, an all-passenger configuration with a 775,000-pound maximum takeoff weight; the 747C, a convertible model which can carry either passengers or cargo; and the 747F, a jet freighter which can carry nearly 260,000 pounds of net payload (all cargo), the latter two planes both in the 775,000-pound category. Interestingly, all four aircraft, even the heavier airplanes, have the same external dimensions. But the higher gross weights allow the airplane to carry more payload for greater distances.

M. Lynn Olason, Director of Product

Development for the Commercial Airplane Group at Boeing in his paper – *"The Performance and Economic Design Aspects of the 747 Family of Airplanes"* – gives us a good picture of what happened to bring into being the heavier versions of the 747 *"Super jet."*

"One of the fundamental performance improvements considered for the 747 is an extension of the payload-range capability," Olason says. "Trans-Pacific and trans-polar routes require longer range capability than is available in the basic 747. Extended service on these routes could be expected about two years after the basic 747 enters airline service. Initially, the 747 is expected to serve high-density routes, such as the *domestic transcontinental* and the *international North Atlantic.*"

Although he did not spell it out, the fact is, the wide-bodied 747 offered a great improvement over the 707 long-range jetliner because of its size ("The plane with all the room in the world") and a slight increase in speed (about 30 mph), but it *could not* fly the long non-stop distances with comparable payload/size performance capabilities. This was the challenge Boeing accepted – *to increase the payload/range capability of the 747, without compromising takeoff field length or initial cruise altitude performance.*

To achieve these objectives Boeing instigated an all-out weight-reducing program for the basic 747. According to Olason – "Over 55 per cent of the design engineers assigned to the 747 submitted ideas . . . and thousands of pounds of net weight have been trimmed from the empty weight (of the airplane) . . . This weight reduction took place in all design areas and ranged from one through several hundred pounds for hundreds of changes . . . These changes did not compromise structural integrity, reliability, or any aspect of safety of the airplane . . ."

At the same time, engine growth paralleled the weight reduction program. According to H. S. Crim of Pratt & Whitney Aircraft – "The JT9D (747 high-by-pass ratio engine) has advanced from its initial design thrust of 42,000 pounds to 43,500 pounds to 45,000 pounds the JT9D-7 en-

The 747F (jet freighter) version can carry nearly 260,000 pounds of net payload in cargo. Here, engineers inspect loading technique for large cargo containers on main deck. Smaller containers go below in belly.

gine to be certified in June of 1971 . . . and an increase to 48,000 pounds has been offered to be certified in July of 1972 . . . And this can be achieved without altering the configuration of the engine or the installation in the aircraft in any major degree."

Such things resulted in the planned increased takeoff gross weight to 775,000 pounds for the 747B, 747C and 747F models within the same geometry as the basic 747 airplane.

These growth versions, however, incorporate such changes as: enlarged wheels, tires and brakes to accommodate the higher gross weights on existing runways and taxiways modified leading-edge flaps to improve takeoff performance without adversely affecting the landing performance.

"The net result of these changes," says Olason in his paper, "increases payload-range performance substantially . . . The trans-Pacific and trans-polar flights could be conducted with full passengers and baggage plus moderate amounts of cargo.

"Operating with the new JT9D-7 engine ratings, the 747B will compete favorably, from an operational standpoint, with the 707-320B or any other airplane likely to be available in the early 1970s."

He concludes: "These early growth versions appear to be only the beginning of what we fully expect to become a large family of 747s."

At this writing, the 747B has not yet flown, but 29 are on order by foreign carriers which fly the long-range trans-ocean and trans-polar routes. (i.e. Lufthansa, Japan, KLM, Air India, Qantas, Swissair, SAS and El Al airlines) The same flight status is true of the flight status of the 747C (five on order by World Airlines and Universal Airlines) and the 747F (Freighter) one of which has been ordered by Lufthansa. The heavier-gross weight airplanes, however, are expected to be flying late in 1970 or early in 1971.

Meanwhile, there are other growth versions of the 747 which are being "thought about" in view of previous trends which saw extended versions of the 707 and the 727 appear quite suddenly – as traffic demands increased and the planes' performances demonstrated growth potential.

Boeing President, T. A. Wilson believes today's largest jetliner (747) will be small by comparison with growth versions ahead.

Boeing President T. A. Wilson sums it up thusly – *"We feel that in a new program such as this, the aircraft should be sized to fit its particular market about one-third of the way through a 10 to 12-year period of normal production: that means it will be slightly over-sized at first, and then become too small for its intended route segments late in the production run."*

Indirectly, he is saying that in the mid-seventies the 747, today's largest jetliner, could become *small* by comparison with growth versions of tomorrow . . .

II

"THE short-range, high-density air traffic market can absorb much larger aircraft than is generally recognized," says John E. Steiner, now Vice-President, Requirements and Marketing for The Boeing Company, Commercial Airplane Group. "Jack" Steiner, whom we met earlier as the credited designer of the fabulous 727 trijet (Chapter Ten) has further stated that he believes, "over the next 10 years the new, large *"Superjet"* types will play an increasing role in short range (200-500 miles) operation just as they will in 1970, set the new standard on long-range services."

With an eye to the future, Steiner notes – "The basic tooling involved in the Boeing 747 production program allows body extensions which will afford over 500 passengers in two-class (first and economy) operation, and perhaps, *700 or more passengers in high density, short-range operation.*"

"The present 747 now in large scale production in the Boeing Everett, Washington factory," Steiner explains, "can carry as many as 508 passengers in the short-range one-class configuration – a practical load – as early as 1972 in some markets."

"Body extensions of up to 40 feet are feasible within the next ten years," he adds. "And such an advanced type 747 could carry 575 passengers in two-class arrangements as compared to the 360-370 passengers of the 747s now in production. Up to 750 passengers *could be* accommodated in advanced 747s when used in one-class, short-range services."

Roy A. Strandberg, Chief of Airport Studies at Boeing with whom we talked, had some other ideas about a bigger 747. He says – "All Boeing jetliners, including the 747, are continually studied for possible size changes that might be required to fulfill future airline needs. History has proven that airplanes of a given model can be built smaller as well as larger in order to accommodate the changing needs of the industry.

"Should the need develop, possible growth versions of the 747 might include linear dimension changes up to approximately 20 per cent on the present basic 747 structure. This *could* stretch the body by 50 feet, wing span by 35 feet, and tail height by 10 to 15 feet which *could* result in an airplane with a total ramp weight in the vicinity of 800,000 pounds!"

Projecting the 747 fifteen years into the future, Strandberg points out, "a *possible* requirement is foreseen for an airplane of this size, say, an 800 passenger-carrying capability, by the 1980 time period . . .

"For an intermediate range airplane (1,000 to 2,000 miles) an 800-passenger airplane *might* weigh approximately 400 tons! . . . An airplane with comparable passenger-carrying capability for long range routes of 4,000 to 5,000 miles *could possibly* weigh a *million-and-a-quarter to a million-and-a-half pounds.*

"Optimum utilization of the interior volume of an 800-passenger airplane *could mean* carrying passengers on more than one deck. It is *conceivable,* an upper deck could be added, or the belly space fore and aft of the wing box *could be* utilized to accommodate passengers. This leads to the *possibility* that some future airplane might combine these approaches with an end product having three passenger decks."

He concluded: "I want to emphasize that these (sizes) are what *could be* designed, not what *are* being designed."

Strandberg, who has made extensive studies of the major large airports throughout the world, also declared that he believes programs for progress have "taken into consideration" the potential growth in size of planes like the 747.

At the same time, P&WA's Crim believes that more powerful engines will be available for such huge aircraft. He says: "We have studied an engine in the 75,000-pound thrust class over several years time as the JT9D engine design evolved, and it is clear that the concept employed in the JT9D can be extended easily to engines well above the 75,000-pound thrust size. Such engines (would) offer the same benefits of efficiency, low noise and long life which are the characteristics of the (747s) engines."

Thus, we can see, that the men who gave us the 747, today's "*Super jet*" certainly are not standing still in their "thinking" about even larger planes for the future.

The basic design of the 747, undoubtedly, will play a major role in the size and shape of wings to come.

Beyond that, however, comes a "*Third Generation*" jetliner, the Boeing Model 2707-300 Supersonic Transport. The Boeing SST will be in about the same weight category as the 747B, a little larger in linear dimensions – wing span and fuselage length – and with an entirely different configuration. It will not carry as many passengers – about two-thirds as many – but it will be able to fly *three times* as fast.

Prompting Boeing President T. A. Wilson

to remark – "The next big step will not be by virtue of *size* but *speed!*"

Let's take a quick look at where we are going in that direction. Where do we stand in the SST race?

III

ON the last day of 1968 and on March 2, 1969, the Russian supersonic transport (TU-144) and the Anglo-French supersonic transport (the *Concorde)* made their first flights. No longer could there be any doubt that air transportation's "*Supersonic Age*" had arrived! But where was the U.S. entry?

Anyone interested knows that the United States does not have an SST flying. It is interesting to point out, however, that The Boeing Company started some serious "thinking" about a supersonic transport about the time that the first 707 jetliner went into service, as far back as 1958. The company has gleaned considerable experience in the area of supersonic flight with its all-purpose fighter design entry in the now famous, or infamous TFX, Army/Navy joint competition. When Boeing lost that competition, a similar situation to that which occurred with the C-5A heavy logistics transport, there was considerable thought given to a commercial version on a much larger scale – probably the true beginning of initial design studies for the potential SST.

In the middle of all of this, spurred on by reports that Britain and France and Russia were developing SST designs, the U.S. Government (some men with vision, at least) initiated preliminary programs for financing an american SST development with a resultant design competition. Ultimately, the competition narrowed down to designs submitted by Boeing and Lock-

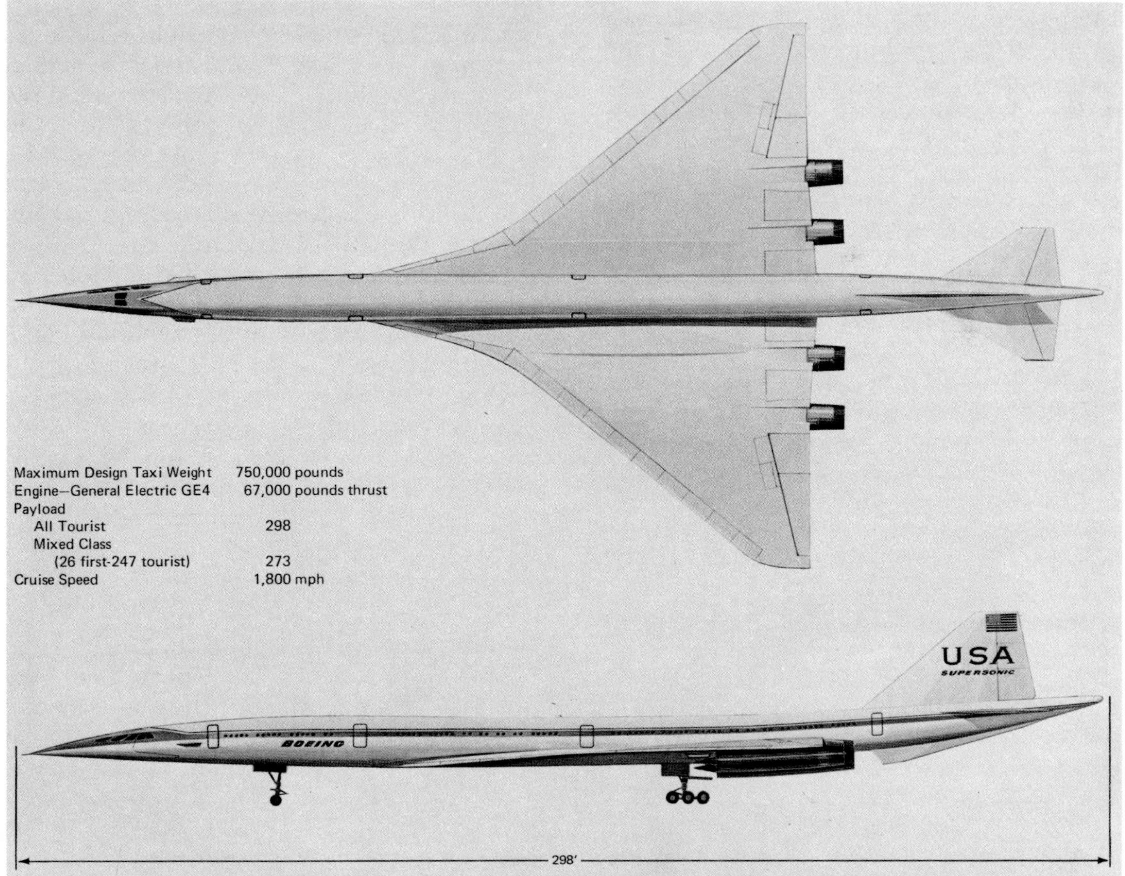

Artist's concept of Boeing supersonic transport design, Model 2707, showing plane's delta-type wing, long, slender fuselage. SST will have more powerful engines than 747, and will cruise three times as fast.

heed. But there, the whole program mired itself in an aura of "politics, dollar-signs and indecision" until the *reports* from abroad became *realities*, and there loomed the prospect of the U.S. one day losing its world-wide leadership in the commercial airplane field.

It was not until December of 1966, after approximately eight years of research and analysis, that the Boeing design was selected; not until December, three years later, that President Nixon gave the final stamp of approval to the U.S. supersonic transport development program, and funds were made available for the start of construction of two SST prototypes.

And there it stands at this writing: The prototypes will be built by Boeing and General Electric in a government-industry program administered by the Federal Aviation Administration. Boeing will build the airframes and General Electric the engines. Parts and major sections of the two airplanes will be provided by a nationwide team of subcontractors and suppliers.

Money for the prototype program is being advanced by the Federal Government, the customer airlines, and the manufacturers. The program, it is estimated, will cost approximately *one and a half BILLION DOLLARS.* Of this the Government is advancing 90 per cent, minus some $60,000,000 risk money from the airlines who have ordered to date 122 U.S.-built SSTs, plus 10 percent contributed by the aircraft manufacturing community involved and millions of dollars in commercial and capital expenditures not covered by the government contracts. On a minimum sale of 500 of the SSTs, the government will be repaid all money invested, plus a return of over $1-BILLION.

Front view of Boeing SST, Model 2707, showing wing and engine arrangement. It will be built mostly of titanium.

Admittedly, all of this sounds complicated and, perhaps, that it doesn't belong here. It *is* complicated, but it *does* belong here. Probably, working out this financial arrangement — an unprecedented industry/government program for a commercial airplane development — is the main reason the American SST isn't flying.

Suffice it to say, in the long run, it may pay big dividends. Certainly, the cost of developing future aircraft with the sophisticated materials and equipment involved, would be prohibitive for any single manufacturer or airline. Just as it would be prohibitive for a single manufacturer to send a man to the moon.

Meanwhile, at Boeing, the SST Division is working on a schedule to roll out the first prototype in the late summer of 1972, with the first flight before the end of that year. Actual "hardware" construction for the prototypes was begun in the spring of 1970 with peak prototype activity scheduled for early 1971.

What will the SST, designated Boeing Model 2707-300, be like?

IV

IT is a long, sleek, aerodynamically clean airplane with a slender fuselage, swept delta wing, and conventional tail. Power is supplied by four General Electric GE4 turbojet engines mounted in individual pods at the trailing edge of the wing. It will be built entirely of titanium, a metal stronger per pound than most stainless steels, and fully capable of the heat generated by flight at almost three times the speed of sound.

This is the BIG difference between the American SST and the Russian and British/French supersonics. The foreign designs are built of aluminum with respective speeds of 1500 and 1400 mph. The Boeing 2707-300 will fly at 1800 mph!

Flying in the U.S. SST will be as safe as traveling in today's subsonic commerical jet planes. Test data gained from experience with military supersonic aircraft such as the B-70, F-111 and others are being used in the 2707.

Perhaps, the best way to describe the 2707, latest in the family of Boeing jet-

Fuselage and wing mock-up for Boeing Model 2707 Supersonic Transport nearing completion. Mockup of forward section (at right) shows how nose drops to permit better visibility. Note small round windows.

Close-up of aft section and tail cone of SST. The fuselage, nose-to-tail is two feet shorter than football field, goal-line-to-goal-line. Boeing has "go ahead" on two prototypes of U.S. supersonic transport.

liners, is an imaginary trip from Washington to London. Excerpts from a Boeing brochure put you on board:

"The wheels begin to turn – 750,000 pounds of engineering and scientific achievement are in motion. There are 298 passengers aboard the aircraft, which is approximately 300 feet long (the length of a football field) with a wing span of nearly 145 feet. The fuselage is longer than the 747, but it is not as wide in cross-section.

"The sleek bird will come racing down the runway with the four GE engines producing a total of 268,000 pounds of thrust, the equivalent of 600,000 horse-power – enough to propel three aircraft carriers. as it clears the runway, flight management computers take over and point the nose toward an electronic highway in the sky – 12 miles above the Atlantic.

"The plane accelerates and begins to outdistance its own sound, Mach 1 speed . . .

"Minutes later the voice of the Captain says – 'Welcome aboard the first scheduled flight of the United States Supersonic Transport . . . Our altitude is 60,000 feet, speed 1800 miles per hour. We have clear weather all the way to London. Relax and enjoy your flight.'

"In the cabin there is no illusion of speed. It is quiet and pleasant, and you have your choice of color movies with refreshing beverages and food. The fully adjustable seats are comfortable and roomy.

"The air is thin at 60,000 feet, but, even so, at 1800 mph aerodynamic (friction) heating raises the temperature of the plane's surfaces to almost 500-degrees F. But insulation and an effective air conditioning system keep the inside cool and comfortably pressurized. (You're glad the plane is made of titanium; aluminum could not stand such temperatures).

"A look into the Flight Deck shows the sophisticated flight management systems. Equipment is constantly computing the flight path, monitoring the engines, reading temperatures and pressures. It is all designed to be fail-safe; if one system should fail another takes over. Key elements are installed in tandem . . .

"The interior of the passenger cabin is bright and colorful. There is a long center aisle running the whole length which is divided into First Class, SST Class and Tourist Class sections. There are pairs of seats on each side of the aisle in First Class; two abreast and three abreast seating arrangements in the SST Class; three abreast seating on each side of the aisle in Tourist Class. Although the fuselage appears from the outside to be a long tube, the inside has been designed with a high-flat ceiling to provide a spacious environment. Windows are round and small (like the old DC-4) because of the extreme pressures at such high altitudes.

Another report from the Captain interrupts this description – "Our Flight Computers have calculated a total flight time from Washington to London of 2 hours and 45 minutes . . . We are exactly on course with 35 minutes remaining, and will begin descending soon for a straight-in approach to land . . ."

"The 2707 has a "droop snoot," the nose tilts downward to compensate for the high-angle of the wing during landing. In a sense, the entire wing area serves as a braking effect.

"You sense this, by the floor angle, during final descent and touchdown . . .

The brochure also puts it another way: *"The visored nose is down to give the pilot better vision. Touchdown is made on the same runways used by today's subsonic aircraft."*

The landing is fully automatic. And arrival is right on schedule. In the "Supersonic Age" you have flown the Atlantic from Washington to London in 165 minutes!

It will be like that when the Boeing 2707 goes into service which Boeing President T. A. Wilson has said "our calculations show to be about 1978."

When that day comes, President Nixon, in announcing his "go ahead" decision for the SST program reminded us – "We are going to be able to bring the world closer together in a true physical and time sense. Tokyo will be as close to Washington, D.C., as far as hours are concerned, as London is today."

By mid-seventies, U.S. plans to have prototype of Supersonic Transport flying. This is artist's concept of proposed Model 2707 design. The Boeing Company is prime contractor. SST is multi-billion dollar gamble.

Perhaps, that is what Bill Boeing had in mind when he started The Boeing Airplane Company back in 1916. It is said that he often confessed to friends – "At first I thought flying was a great sport. Then, I saw in the airplane a swift means of transport to bring peoples everywhere closer together."

In the Boeing family of airplanes, from the first B&W to the sleek Delta wing SST, Model 2707, he has left his country a High Heritage.

★★ end ★★

Index

A

B

C

D

E

F

G

H

I

J

K

L

Mc

M

N

O

P

Q

R

S

T

U

V

W

X

Y

Z

BRANIFF

SOUTH AFRICAN

NORDAIR

JAPAN

PACIFIC SOUTHWEST

ALOHA

PAKISTAN

BRITANNIA

CALEDONIAN

MALAYSIA-SINGAPORE

SAUDI ARABIAN

EASTERN

ETHIOPIAN

ALITALIA

BRAATHENS

OLYMPIC

AMERICAN FLYERS

TRANS CARIBBEA

TRANS-AUSTRALIA

DELTA

ARIANA

LUFTHANSA

CP AIR

TRANS WORLD

LAN-CHILE

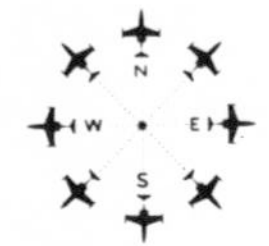

EXECUTIVE JET

AMERICAN

NORTHWEST

TRANS INTERNATIONAL

GERMAN GOVT.

SOUTHERN AIR

WIEN CONSOLIDATED

NATIONAL

SABENA

TRANSAIR LTD.

ROYAL AIR MARO

VARIG

TAP

NORTHEAST

CONTINENTAL

PACIFIC WESTERN

ALL NIPPON